A History of the Circle
of Concerned African Women Theologians

Copyright 2017 Rachel NyaGondwe Fiedler

All rights reserved. No part of this publication may be reproduced, stored in a retrieval system, or transmitted in any form or by any means, electronic, mechanical, photocopying, recording or otherwise, without prior permission from the publishers.

Published by
Mzuni Press
P/Bag 201
Luwinga, Mzuzu 2. Malawi

ISBN 978-99960-45-22-6
eISBN 978-99960-45-23-3

Mzuni Press is represented outside Malawi by:
African Books Collective Oxford (also for e-books)
(orders@africanbookscollective.com)

www.mzunipress.blogspot.com
www.africanbookscollective.com

Index: Jan Stapperfenne
Cover: Josephine Kawejere

Printed in Malawi by Baptist Publications, P.O. Box 444, Lilongwe

A History of the Circle of Concerned African Women Theologians (1989-2007)

Rachel NyaGondwe Fiedler

MZUNI PRESS

A Mzuni Monograph

2017

Contents

Introduction 7

Chapter 1: Mercy Amba Oduyoye as Mother and Leader of the Circle (1989 - 1996) 10

Chapter 2: Growth of the Circle under Consecutive Continental Leaders (1989-2007) 41

Chapter 3: Local Chapters and the Growth of the Circle (1989 – 2017) ... 55

Chapter 4: Birth and Growth of the Circle in Malawi (1993 – 2017) 82

Chapter 5: The Role of Zones, Regions and Study Commissions in the Growth of the Circle 116

Chapter 6: Contributions of the Circle to Theological Education 132

Chapter 7: The Circle, Women and Development 149

Chapter 8: Celebrating Maturity: 28 Years of the Circle of Concerned African Women Theologians (1989 – 2017) 164

Bibliography 175

Abbreviations

AACC	All Africa Council of Churches
BACOMA	Baptist Convention of Malawi
CCAP	Church of Central Africa Presbyterian
DRCM	Dutch Reformed Church Mission
EATWOT	Ecumenical Association of Third World Theologians
EBCOM	Evangelical Bible College of Malawi
EDICESA	Educational Information and Documentation Centre for Eastern and Southern Africa
IFES	International Fellowship of Evangelical Students
IPC	International Planning Committee
LWF	Lutheran World Federation
NEGST	Nairobi Evangelical Graduate School of Theology
NIST	Nairobi International School of Theology
PACAnet	Pan African Christian AIDS Interfaith Network
PCEA	Presbyterian Church of East Africa
PROCMURA	Programme for Christian – Muslim Relations in Africa
PTE	Programme for Theological Education
SCOM	Students Christian Organization of Malawi
TRS	Department of Theology and Religious Studies
VVF	Vesico Vagina Fistula
WCC	World Council of Churches
YWCA	Young Women's Christian Association
ZAWO	Zambezi Women's Organization
ZEC	Zambezi Evangelical Church

Introduction

The first major work on the Circle had a systematic approach, and it was written from a Western perspective.[1] I write a history of the Circle bearing in mind that I offer a Malawian woman's perspective who has joined the Circle only in 2001, twelve years after the genesis of the Circle. This means that I was not there when the Circle was conceived and birthed into the world. But certainly, I was there when the Circle became a teenager and saw how it has developed even into a mature woman reaching this adult stage. I also feel confident to write this story because I have met and interacted with many of the key personalities that have woven the story of the Circle. I even have visited the mother of the Circle, Mercy Amba Oduyoye in Accra, Ghana and I am very much aware of her passion not only in building elitist theologians but grassroots theologians who may not even speak our foreign languages. This was clear when I visited her in Ghana and was even hosted by her at the Institute of Religion and Culture.

When my visit came to an end, I even boarded the same plane with Mercy Amba Oduyoye as she was going to America to visit Letty Russel. I dropped off in Kenya to familiarize myself with the Circle in Kenya, the hub of the Circle in the East African region. For Circle women in Southern Africa, I have mingled with them at the Universities as a researcher especially with Circle members in KwaZulu Natal (Pietermaritzburg), Cape Town, UNISA in Pretoria, and the University of Stellenbosch where I met the likes of Sarojini Nadar, Devakarsham Betty Govinden, Christina Landman. Thus, I have met many key Circle women even outside official Circle conferences. So, I think I qualify to write the history as an insider not only because of the fact that my name has appeared in the directory of the Circle, but that I have interacted with Circle members. After all I am a disciple of Isabel Apawo Phiri, who has always been there as a mentor in my postgraduate studies before I joined the Circle. In the Circle, I have my main contributions in the area of writing histories of women. Infact it was through one of the contributions I made at a workshop on Biographies of Women of Faith in Johannesburg where Musimbi Kanyoro must have noticed that I could ably write a history of the Circle. She is the

---

[1] Carrie Pemberton, *Circle Thinking: African Women Theologians in Dialogue with the West*, Leiden: Brill, 2003.

one who organized a part scholarship for me from the World Council of Churches to research and write on a history of the Circle. In the bibliographical section, you will meet some of my contributions. So, I can easily say that I write as an insider because I am one of the beads that are woven into this story.

I have followed the standard approaches in writing church history in this story of the Circle. A history of the Circle is a story of the Church. Histories of the church often include elements of other religions, this is also part and parcel of the Circle story. It includes African women theologians of other faiths and after all the Circle is a movement that includes women of other faiths. In the earlier centuries histories of the church were often about men and their work. The presence of women in these stories was limited. Often their names were not even recorded, and often women that had negative contributions were made visible. The story of the Circle makes contributions of women in church and society more visible. Thus, I prefer to call this book Her-Stories of the Circle.

Characteristic of this her-story is that it uses a mixed approach, different from histories that were written from the perspective of the leaders. This her story applies both a top-bottom approach and a bottom-up approach. As such, it is a story of the mother of the Circle, Mercy Amba Oduyoye and her collaborators as well as a story of grassroot members of the Circle at Regional, Zonal and Country level. Because of the language barrier, the story has excluded much of French speaking and Portuguese speaking Africa.

This book traces the Circle history from 1989 to 2007, based on the cutoff point of my PhD research on the Circle.[2] Thus, some of the present tense verbs refer to the status of the Circle in 2007. However, I also include a sketch history of the Circle from 2007 to 2017, to highlight some of the developments in the later period. However, the history of the Circle from 2007 to 2017 is mainly based on email correspondences and internet sources, thus it is less balanced compared to the story of the Circle between 1989 to 2007.

---

[2] Rachel NyaGondwe Fiedler, "The Circle of Concerned African Women Theologians (1989-2007): History and Theology," PhD, University of the Free State, 2011.

It is my hope that this monograph will energize upcoming historians to fill the gaps and improve on biases in this story. More critical is that a comprehensive and fair treatment of the Portuguese and French speaking Circles is weaved in academia. I have written this book as a historical theologian belonging to the Evangelical tradition, and my hope is that it will highlight a wide scope of African women theologians and their place in the promotion of God's image for both men and women in the world.

Chapter 1: Mercy Amba Oduyoye as Mother and Leader of the Circle (1989 - 1996)

The Circle of Concerned African Women Theologians is an African Baby, born in an ecumenical surrounding. There were other movements addressing the issue of gender inequalities in church and society before the Circle was born. The mother of the Circle and those that launched the Circle were in one way or the other in touch with earlier voices of women's liberation. These early women's liberation movements coloured the theology of the Circle. However, Circle theologies are distinct from other women's liberation movements in that they are theologies formed in the context of African culture and religion.

The Circle is an African, firstly, because it is widely accepted that the Circle is a movement born by Mercy Amba Oduyoye, a Ghanaian married to a Nigerian, Modupe Oduyoye. Secondly, the birth attendants who became the first organizing team of the Circle were African. They were called the International Planning Committee (IPC) and came from different nations of Africa. Some of them were African women in the Diaspora. The IPC organized the first Africa wide Circle Conference, held in 1989, in Ghana. Further, the Circle was formed to deal with the liberation of African women.

Because the Circle was born in Africa and for African women, Circle theologies are also called either African feminist theologies or "African women's theologies."[3] The latter is a commonly used definition by the Circle. They are distinct from other feminist theologies developed elsewhere, but also belong to a wider family of feminist theology, which can be further categorized as one of the liberation theologies.[4] They are African feminist theologies written by African women with the aim of empowering African women.[5]

---

[3] A quote from Isabel Apawo Phiri, "HIV/AIDS: An African Theological Response in Mission," *The Ecumenical Review*, vol. 56, no. 4, 2004.

[4] See Isabel Apawo Phiri, "African Women's Theologies in the New Millennium," *Agenda* 61, 2004, p. 16.

[5] See Rachel NyaGondwe Fiedler, Johannes W. Hofmeyr, Klaus Fiedler, *African Feminist Hermeneutics. An Evangelical Reflection*, Mzuzu: Mzuni Press, 2016, p. 314ff.

Even though these theologies are written by African women, it is not all women in Africa that are concerned with women's issues in church and society. Circle theologians, by definition, are concerned with women's issues. This does not imply that African women theologians outside the Circle are not concerned with women's issues.

Circle theologies are also much differentiated because of differences in religious and cultural contexts. These African women come from different countries of Africa. However, African cultures are grouped into two major categories: matrilineal and patrilineal cultures. Thus, there is a way in which African culture can be classified as one. This is why there is much similarity within the theologies of Circle women. The major element of differentiation in Circle theology is how women reinterpret culture and religion to empower women.[6]

Mercy Amba Oduyoye as an African

There are two kinds of Africans, those that are born from African parents that live abroad and those that are born and raised up in Africa. Mercy Amba Oduyoye belongs to the latter. African women that belong to the former group are Africans by name because they are socialized in a non-African cultural environment. Mercy Amba Oduyoye was not just born to an African family, but she was raised up in an African cultural environment. She also received her early theological training in Africa.[7]

For Africans, growth of an individual is linked to an extended family. In the life of Mercy Amba Oduyoye, it is the roles of her mother, father, grandfather, siblings and husband that were crucial in her growth and development.

Mercy Amba Oduyoye was born in 1934 to an African mother, Mercy Dakwaa Yamoah.[8] She was educated by her uncle. However, her grandfather also played a major role in her mother's life. The grandfather of Mercy Amba

---

[6] Ibid.

[7] For more information on her see: Carolyn Roncolaro, "Meet the Mother of African Feminist Theology," https://sojo.net/articles/sheroes-faith/meet-mother-african-feminist-theology, accessed 12.3.2017.

[8] Yolanda Smith, "Mercy Amba Oduyoye" (www.talbot.edu/cezo/educators/protestant/mercy-oduyoye/, accessed 12.3.2017). She was named "Atriba" bcause she was the first-born.

Oduyoye was J.E. Turkson of Asamankese. He is the one who took care of her mother since her father died at an early age.[9] Mercy Dakwaa Yamoah's father died after an accident that occurred at a time he was helping his friend to build a house in Abease, Ghana. A branch from a tree fell on him and hurt him badly. Since the accident, he became sickly and eventually died.[10] Mama Mercy's uncle sent her to school early. She was put in a Wesleyan kindergarten at a very tender age and was looked after by Wesleyan deaconesses (sisters).[11] After kindergarten, she went to WeGeHe (The Wesleyan Girls High School), which was well recognized for its academic excellence, hence Mercy Amba Oduyoye's mother had a long Methodist heritage.

To appreciate the role of her mother in shaping her Africanness and her spirituality, Mercy remembered her mother after her death in a special way. At the opening ceremony of the Institute of Religion and Culture held in the premises of Trinity Theological Seminary in Ghana, in 2005, Mercy organized a special unveiling ceremony of an inscription about her mother, Mercy Dakwaa Yamoah: This was a practical step by Mercy Amba Oduyoye to honour her mother as someone important in her life. Apart from this inscription, for a period of time, she set up, in one of the rooms, photos depicting some memorable moments in her mother's life. The inscription clearly shows that her mother was not just relegated to domestic roles; she was an activist in her Methodist church who worked hard towards liberation of women in her church. The inscription reads like this:

> The Hearth
> To continue the ministry
> of Mercy Dakwaa Yamoah
> 1912-2005
> Spouse of Charles Kwa Yamoah
> And mother to many
> Unveiled by Mrs Sophia Duker

This inscription has been placed in the house that has been a home for the Institute of Religion and Culture for some time. At a conference held in South

---

[9] Nana Adwao Atta-Konadu, The Helper's Ministry, 2002, p. 1.
[10] Ibid.
[11] Nana Adwao Atta-Konadu, The Helper's Ministry, 2002, p. 6.

Africa at Kempton Park, Mercy reported that Circle activities in Ghana are really those that are organized by the Institute. The placement of this inscription at the Institute speaks volumes concerning the role of Mercy Dakwaa Yamoah in the establishment of the Circle. The Circle in a way is "to continue the [her] ministry."[12]

The inscription is but a partial summary of what the mother was as a model to Mercy Amba Oduyoye and beyond. It gives a glimpse of the reasons why Circle women should not wonder at how Mercy was able to create the Circle that has impacted many lives. When one looks at the history of the Circle, it is clear that no person other than a self-starter would be able to accomplish this task. According to Mercy, the Circle has only been possible because of God. It is logical to say that God also used her mother to model Mercy into such a challenging position. Her mother was in many ways a self-starter in doing women's ministry in her church.

The role of Mercy Dakwaa Yamoah was not only visible in the church but also in her dedication to her family. In the document signed by Mercy A. Oduyoye, Kojo Ewudzi, Essie T. Blay, Essie J. Cobbina, and Joseph A. Yamoah on Saturday, June 4th, 2005 titled "Resolution", one of the statements about Mercy Dakwaa Amoah was that she was a dedicated mother to her family.

> 2 Corinthians 5:1: And whereas Mama was a dedicated mother to her children and her family—and whereas; she kept her family close to her heart.
>
> Not only did she extend love to her own children but she also extended her motherhood to others that were not her biological children.

This is also testified in the Resolution:

> and her love and compassion was to all humanity; and whereas, she became mother to many successful young men and women whom she raised like her own.

Mercy Dakwaa Yamoah also contributed positively to women taking up leadership in society by helping her children to take up such leadership positions. This is also testified in the Resolution, where it is clear that her children occupied key positions in society as is visible from the record of Mercy's siblings.

---

[12] These words are in the inscription above.

Mrs Mercy Dakwaa Yamoah had eight other children apart from Mercy Amba Oduyoye. Interestingly, all her children grew up into key positions in church and society. This is a testimony of how she and her husband were efficient in raising up children as is visible from the record of their profile below.

> Kojo Ewudzi Yamoah served in the Police Force of Ghana, providing security to the people of Ghana. Her brother Dr Eggie Harris became a doctor and served in the United States of America. Johnny B. Yamoah had a blossoming career as Captain with Ghana Airways. Mrs Essie F. Bobbina served on the Board of Ghana Cocoa Industry. One of her children became Professor of Agriculture in the University of Ghana, Prof (Mrs) Essie T. Blay. Sister Essie Ewusiwa Yamoah served in Tema General Hospital in Ghana. Sister Martha Yamoah served in the University of Ghana Hospital.

From the employment profile outlined, it is clear that Mercy Dakwaa Yamoah was a woman of gender equality. It was not only her sons that attained high profile in church and society, but her daughters too. Her feminism was not to rob boy children of their talents.

The profile of her children shows that she influenced her children to be partakers in the liberation of social, economic, political and religious lives of the people of Africa. She was not like those stereotyped missionaries that moved with the Bible under their armpits everywhere and had no regard for issues of justice in society. She oriented her children towards issues of justice. Mercy's leadership in the Circle is therefore not an anomaly in the context of her family.[13]

Mercy Dakwaa Amoah also had grandchildren. These are Lillian, Norman, Charlotte, Ofosu, Abena, Ntsifoa, Yamoah, Kingsley Yamoah (Dorik), Mrs Nana Adwoa Asiam, Mrs Essie Saint-Claire Ebow Yamoah, Mrs Joyce Ewuradwoa Boham, Faustina Yamoah, Caroline Yamoah, Mercy D. Yamoah II, Charles K, Yamoah II, Dr Kofi Kweenu Yamoah, Kojo Ewudzi Yamoah II, Kojo Dodom Yamoah, Nenya Blay, Johnny Blay, Mokoa Blay, Kweku Cobinna (Coma), Osa Kojo Cobinna, Dr Ekua Cobinna, Mrs Catherine Allo, Dr Josephine Amoah, Mercy Amba Yamoah II, Essie Y. Yamoah, Aba S. Yamoah, Kobbie John Yamoah, Jeremia Nana Kofi Yamoah, Dzifa Sena Kpodza and Afefa-Delali Kpodza.

---

[13] Details extracted from poster, Celebration of Life, 4.6.2005.

There is no doubt that even these grandchildren are well positioned in church and society.

The role of the mother of Mercy Amba Oduyoye in establishing her children in leadership positions is also stipulated in the Resolution document:

> and whereas she held a position of valour to defend her children and to safely situate them in lives dedicated to goodness and service to their communities.

Indeed, what Mercy Dakwaa Amoah did and was to church and society deserves such a statement stipulated in the Resolution:

> And whereas; she was a lady of great character and a woman of high holy standards; and whereas, she was a woman of deep spiritual ambitions; and whereas, her message was universal ... in the loving memory of Mercy D. Yamoah. Blessed are the Dead which die in the Lord from henceforth; yea, saith the Spirit, that they may rest from their labours, and their works do follow them. (Revelations 14:13.) For we know that if our earthly treasure house of this Tabernacle dissolves, we have a building of God, a house not made with hands, eternal in heavens.

Mercy Dakwaa Yamoah provides an example of how independence in a marriage relationship can be a source of transformation of gender inequalities in church and society. She was able to achieve progress of her own and that of her own children without sabotaging her family. She went beyond the traditional roles of just being a wife and was active in church and society as can be viewed from this statement in the Resolution:

> And whereas, she held her responsibilities as a leader and the spouse of the President of the Methodist Church of Ghana in highest esteem, she immersed herself during the era of "Mass education."

However, she carved out her own space in life and that was acknowledged. Some of the areas where she created her own space are as follows:

> In the effort to spread literacy in the Gold Coast; her ground work resulted in the establishment of the "Women's Training Centre" at Kwadaso. She exhibited undying love for the women's fellowship of the Methodist Church of Ghana, being the founder of many. Be it therefore resolved, we accept death as the permissive will of Almighty God. And commend our family and friends to the loving care of Jesus Christ through His servants, the people of God.

Part of the reward for creating her own distinct role is the record of her name and extracts of her achievements kept in the archives of the church as evidenced from this quote from the Resolution:

> and let it further be resolved that the copy of this resolution be entered into Mama's memorial and submitted for entry into the permanent records at the Methodist Church of Ghana. Done by the order of: The Children of the Rev Charles Kingsley and Mrs Mercy Dakwaa Yamoah.[14]

Mercy Dakwaa Yamoah was a committed pastor's wife. In 1940, when her husband was posted to his first ministerial station in Achinacrom near Ejiso in Ghana, she found no women's fellowship there, and was the first to start it in nearby places such as Aslaninpon, Kwaso, Berposo and others.[15] Again, when Mercy Amba Oduyoye's parents moved to Trinity College in Kumasi, she also started a women's fellowship in places such as Suame Pankromo and other villages.[16]

But of all the work that her mother did, Mercy Amba Oduyoye considers the founding of Kwadaso Women's Training Centre as the most significant one. She started this work in a bungalow at Affiduase, where a missionary, Miss White, lived. The target for the school was the wives of ministers and women leaders of the church. This school was a distance from Affiduase; however, Mama Mercy was able to commute to the place to teach when it was her time.[17]

Just as Mercy was modelled by her mother in some aspects, she was also modelled by her father in other aspects. Rev Charles Kwa Yamoah was a successful minister and theologian as evidenced from the comment extracted from his tribute.

---

[14] Details from the "Resolution," 4 June 2005.

[15] Nana Adwao Atta-Konadu, The Helper's Ministry. A letter to my Grand Children, Circle meeting 17-21 January 2002, p. 9.

[16] Ibid., p. 10.

[17] Ibid.

And by his lectures and sermons, he won deep affection, admiration and respect of many students who became preachers of the gospel and teachers on our nation's educational system.[18]

These remarks are in the context of his career as tutor at Trinity Theological College and Principal of Akropong Trinity College (Ashanti). During these years he influenced the minds of many towards a better understanding of God's work. He also lived his teachings by maintaining an outstanding ministry, which even saw him becoming the president of the Methodist Church in Ghana. Evangelizing, pastoral work and teaching characterized his ministry. Apart from these, he was an expert organizer and wise administrator. Above all, he was a man of God and of choice Christian character.

> As a person, he had much charm. He was good and generous to friends and colleagues. He had love for his master Jesus Christ. In one of his conversations, he had this to say: "In my funeral service the less said about me; and the more about my saviour, the better."[19]

In all this, the mother of Mercy is seen as playing an important role. This is well summarized in this quote:

> Mrs Mercy Yamoah a product of Wesley High School has been most helpful to the husband and during his years of Trinity [Theological College] and travelling, always humble as a dove giving as much help as any husband could ask for.[20]

Mercy's commitment to the work of her husband and of the Lord was unswerving. An example is given in this quote:

> Mercy had to undergo a minor operation. Before she regained consciousness, she started reciting certain passages from the prophet Ezekiel which the

---

[18] Tribute to the Very Rev Charles K. Yamoah B.D. by the Very Rev T Wallace Koomson, G.M. K.C.B.

[19] Tribute to the Very Rev Charles K. Yamoah, Friday, January 23, 1987.

[20] Ibid.

husband was at that time teaching. Her mind was with her husband as he taught in the classroom as trainer of ministers and school teachers.[21]

It is clear that Mercy's ability to lead and inspire the Circle is influenced by this rich heritage from her father as well. Rev Charles Kwa Yamoah was born on 1st June 1905 and died on 12th January 1987. He was the third President of the "Conference" of the Methodist Church, Ghana, from 1973 to 1977.

The funeral ceremony was mostly in the hands of the church because he was a high-ranking church leader in the Methodist Church. The Rev Dr Jacobs A. Stephens, Bachelors, MA (London) STM, MSC, who was president at the time of his death, was among the officiating clergy.

The past president, the very Rev T. Wallace Koomson K.G.B. also took part in the service. He was the secretary of the Conference then. The Rev Dr H.E. Brew-Riverson, Bachelors, MA (London) was also present. The Rev Emmanuel A. Ashley, the chairman of Accra District, the Rev Kodjo Hazel BD, (London), chairman of Winneba District and Rev Justice K.A. Dadson, BA (Hons) (Legon) MTh (Princeton), who was at the time the Assistant Secretary of the Conference were also present.

Rev Charles Kwa Yamoah was not only respected in his church tradition but also beyond, as was visible at his home calling service. Representatives from former students of WESCO organizations for example were also present.

After completing her teaching course at Kumasi in 1952, Mercy Amba Oduyoye taught at a Methodist Girls Middle School in Kumasi from 1955 to 1959. Then she enrolled in the Department of Religious Studies at the University of Ghana in Legon in 1959. This experience in theological progress would probably not have happened without Noel Q. King, who inspired her to study theology. He was at that time one of the professors in the Department.[22]

Her decision to study theology was supported by her mother and father. It is amazing that, although her mother had wanted to study theology, she never told her about this. However, Mercy Amba Oduyoye's mother admits that

---

[21] Tribute to the Very Rev Charles K. Yamoah in a Brief Biography of the Very Rev Charles Kwa Yamoah BD (London) in Souvenir Programme for the Home Call of the Very Rev Charles Kwa Yamoah B.D. (London).

[22] Int Prof Noel Q. King, Ndangopuma, Zomba, November 2002.

she may somehow have transferred, unknowingly to her, her vision to study theology.[23] The other two lecturers that taught Mercy Amba Oduyoye were Professor Christian G. Baëta,[24] a Ghanaian and Kwesi A. Dickson,[25] also an ordained Ghanaian Methodist minister. Even with the background of ordained ministers as her early mentors, she has remained unordained. Kwesi A. Dickson is among those that pioneered African theology.[26]

The Circle with Mixed Parenting

The Circle has a mixed background because its theologies are cooked by women from an ecumenical surrounding. Even though Mercy Amba Oduyoye did her undergraduate theological training in Africa, her postgraduate studies were done abroad. She has for many years worked and served in ecumenical surroundings which exposed her to the wider feminist movements. Apart from such an exposure, her husband was also exposed to ecumenical surroundings.

Mercy Amba Oduyoye's ecumenical background has also been seasoned by her husband of many years, Modupe Dube. In relation to the development of the Circle, Modupe played a role as someone also involved in ecumenical institutions that had a relationship to the bodies Mercy Amba Oduyoye worked in. He worked with the All Africa Council of Churches and the World Christian Students Federation for example, which had contact with the World Council of Churches where Mercy worked at the dawn of the Circle.[27]

Mercy met Modupe in the context of both of them being actively involved in the Lord's work in their respective countries: Modupe Dube in Nigeria and Mercy Amba Oduyoye in Ghana.

Both of them occupied key leadership positions in a Christian youth organization known as Student Christian Federation. Mercy Amba Oduyoye was the treasurer of the Student Christian Federation of Ghana while Modupe Dube

---

[23] Nana Adwao Atta-Konadu, The Helper's Ministry, 2002, p. 10.

[24] 1908-1994. He was a leading Presbyterian. Easy information on Wikipedia.

[25] 1929-2005. He was a pastor in the Methodist Church of Ghana, and became in 1989 its seventh President.

[26] Kenneth R. Ross, "The Theology of Hope," in Kenneth R. Ross, *Gospel Ferment in Malawi: Theological Essays*, Gweru: Mambo-Kachere, 1995, pp. 65-80.

[27] Modupe's full name is Adedoyia Modupe Oduyoye.

was the General Secretary of the Student Christian Movement in Nigeria. This was in 1966. Mercy and Modupe met each other first at the West African Student and Youth Christian Leadership Conference in Accra. Their second meeting was in Nigeria in the following month, September 1966.

Another encouragement to Mercy from Modupe in establishing the Circle is in the area of his proficiency in writing and publishing, the main focus of the Circle. His talent was a positive motivation in her publishing work. Modupe's key training is as a linguist. He is a master of many languages including Arabic. This has enabled him to be a seasoned author and publisher, a talent that is very much needed to fulfil the Circle objectives, which Mercy Amba Oduyoye is passionate about.

This does not imply that Modupe published Mercy Amba Oduyoye's books or that without Modupe Mercy Amba Oduyoye would not have published as Carrie Pemberton argues.[28]

Apart from his skills in publishing, he has attended many ecumenical events: The All Africa Christian Council (AACC) assemblies in August 1969 in Abuja; August 1974 in Lusaka and the 6th Assembly in Addis Ababa in September 1977. He also attended many conferences such as that of the World Christian Students Federation in Argentina in August 1964, way before he met Mercy. He attended the Quadrennial Conference of the World Student Christian Federation in Ohala, USA in December 1963. In 1960, he attended a conference on missionary evangelism in Strasbourg in France, and in the same year he also attended a World Christian Students Federation General Committee meeting.

Modupe Dube is also experienced in issues of Inculturation. While in Nigeria he spent one month doing an African Bible Translators' Course in 1967, when

---

[28] Carrie Pemberton, *Circle Thinking: African Women Theologians in Dialogue with the West*, Leiden: Brill, 2003, p. 64. – In fact, Circle books took priority as opposed to publishing her own. Carrie Pemberton undermines the capability that Mercy Amba Oduyoye has in publishing. A glance at books and articles written by Mercy and widely acknowledged on the globe is a proof for the lack of credence of such remarks. Her remarks indirectly undermine all women who have achieved well in professions, which are similar to their husbands.' To such women Pemberton suggests that it is actually their husbands who did the real work. It could also be said about her that the book she wrote was written with much help from her husband and that is why there are flaws in the text.

Mercy took up employment with the World Council of Churches in Geneva. Probably this too could easily be interpreted to mean that the focus on culture and religion was inspired by Modupe Dube. This is contrary to the facts. Coincidences do exist in life. It is clear that Mercy Amba Oduyoye and Modupe Dube are good partners in that they both had a wide experience of the Ecumenical world way before Mercy got employed by the WCC.

Apart from his profound role in the AACC and World Christian Students Committee, he has been active in many other organizations. Between 1981 and 1984, he was a member of the UNESCO Committee for the "Access by Third World Countries to Foreign Copy Right Works."[29]

In the period between 2001 and 2005, he was in the standing committee of the WCC/Vatican study committee, "The Contribution of Africa and her Peoples to the Religious Heritage of the World." All such exposure to ecumenical contacts was useful to Mercy in her endeavour to establish the Circle.

Mercy Amba Oduyoye's exposure to ecumenical surroundings also happened during her further training in Theology abroad. Her studies at the University of Legon concluded in 1963, and the same year she proceeded with her postgraduate studies in Dogmatics at Cambridge University in Britain.[30] This was yet another place to develop non-traditional forms of theology. It was also around this time when there was a rise in liberation theologies in Europe.[31] Van den Bosch states some of them:

> In the struggle for liberation and freedom from patriarchy, hierarchy, sexism, racism and economic exploitation; the ecumenical movement named men

---

[29] This information is based on a personal interview with Modupe Dube, Sept 2005.

[30] Written Interview by Mercy Amba Oduyoye, Circle meeting, Kempton Park, Johannesburg 13.10.2003.

[31] Mercy Amba Oduyoye came from a privileged family because she was not the only member of her family that went abroad for further studies, a rare opportunity at that time. Her father also had gone to study for three years in England, ten years earlier than her in 1953. Her father studied for his further theological studies at Richmond College in London, where he received the Degree of Bachelor of Divinity. Mercy's father also took her mother with him to London, at the time of the study. Her father's theological career may also have encouraged Mercy to do theology (Nana Adwao Atta-Konadu, The Helper's Ministry. A Letter to my Grand Children, Circle Meeting 17-21.1.2002, pp. 7 and 15).

and women equally as constituent members of the Church as the body of Christ and allowed women's issues a place in the ecumenical and theological agenda; the liberation movement helped expose the damage done by cultural, political and religious imperialism.[32]

However, even though there were such movements at this time, Mercy Amba Oduyoye saw that they did not tackle the root issue of marginalization of women. Thus, she organized the Circle to act as a forum where to articulate a theology of women's liberation.[33]

The other root of exposure to global feminist theologies was through Letty Russell. Mercy Amba Oduyoye learnt a lot from Letty Russel whom she had closely related to for years. Letty Russel worked with the World Council of Churches on the study of "The Community of Women and Men in the Church."[34] She was Professor of Theology, had taught at Pacific School of Religion and at Yale Divinity School. Mercy Amba Oduyoye is not the only person that has benefited from Letty Russel; many Circle women were in touch with Letty at Yale Divinity College during the student exchange visits that Circle women were engaged in. Others met Letty Russell at Circle or other ecumenical conferences and workshops. She died in 2007 while her husband, Hans Hoekendijk, had died in 1975.[35]

The IPC and Mercy Amba Oduyoye were an international group. Among them were African women based in the West. This meant that from the beginning the Circle was exposed to other feminist movements. This exposure inevitably influenced them in the processes of constructing Circle theologies.

The international composition of the Circle from the beginnings has continued into the later years, both at continental and national levels. National Circles are also often international because they are usually linked to academic institutions, which often have international students or staff. At such academic institutions, students are exposed to feminist theologies from the West. This situation and the international composition of the student body are a reason that Circle theologies are flavoured with Western feminist

---

[32] H.M. van den Bosch, "African Theology: Is it Relevant for Global Christianity?" *NGTT*, 2009, pp. 530-537 [537].

[33] Ibid.

[34] Letty M. Russell, *The Future of Partnership*, Philadelphia: Westminster, 1979, p. 13.

[35] Ibid., p. 14.

theologies. In addition, Mercy Amba Oduyoye and the International Planning Committee members were in touch with other feminist theologies in the world as they all were members of ecumenical bodies. As mothers, they set the pace of Circle theology with that background. Such background makes Circle theology hybrid because it borrowed some aspects from worldwide feminist theologies in constructing Circle theologies. However, since Circle women are African, Circle theologies have an African slant. In addition, Circle theologies emphasize the importance of the Bible and African culture in developing theologies. The emphasis of the Bible is lacking in some of the other feminist theological movements. Thus, Circle theologies are distinct from such feminist theologies.

Brigalia Bam is the first member of the IPC that had a significant influence on the birth of the Circle. She, a South African, and Mercy Amba Oduyoye conceived the idea of the Circle while they both worked with the World Council of Churches. Brigalia Bam was also a member of the International Planning Committee. A crucial time in the realization of the Circle was when Mercy Amba Oduyoye met Brigalia Bam for the first time in 1967 when Brigalia was also working with the WCC. During this time, the World Council of Churches was also working on women's issues in different religious groups.[36] Brigalia Bam met Mercy Amba Oduyoye at this time because Mercy had come there on a programme on cooperation between men and women in the church. Mercy, at this time, did not feel the need to look at women specifically. She was working in the Youth Department of WCC. Brigalia Bam, however, encouraged her to take the issue of women seriously and that, with time, she would realize that although men and women belong to the same churches, women are faced with challenges that need special attention.

In the 1980s, Brigalia Bam was on a Board that coordinated the project of women writing feminist theologies. This oriented her to feminist theologies globally. To her dismay women from Africa were not participating in the programmes. There were women from Latin America and Asia in addition to those from the West, but there were no participants from the African Continent.[37] This made Brigalia Bam and her colleagues invite Mercy Amba

---

[36] Jeanne Becher (ed), *Women, Religion and Sexuality. Studies on the Impact of Religious Teachings on Women,* Geneva: WCC, 1991, p. ix.

[37] Oral presentation, Mercy Amba Oduyoye and Brigalia Bam, Pan African Conference, Institute of Women in Religion and Culture, Accra, Trinity College, 12.9.2005.

Oduyoye to Harvard to be involved in this research. At this invitation, Mercy Amba Oduyoye agreed to be involved in writing African women's theologies. According to Brigalia Bam, although there were many feminist theologies at that time, Mercy maintained her identity as an African Theologian and wrote a distinctly African theology. She made it clear in her writings and public persuasions that African Women's Theologies cannot be understood unless they are looked at from the perspective of both Culture and Religion. This stand was new in the theological thinking then where many women wrote from the perspective of Western Feminism. This was in the 1980s when feminist women such as Elisabeth Schüssler-Fiorenza and Rosemary Radford Ruether wrote theologies. Letty Russell was also influential in the study of Women Theologies at that time. Thus, Mercy was the first African Woman Theologian to create African Feminist Theologies. Brigalia Bam was the first African woman who supported her in this vision.[38] This also testifies to the fact that Mercy Amba Oduyoye is the mother of the Circle. This is because the model of writing Circle theologies in the realm of religion and culture has been the pillar of the Circle. Before establishing the Circle in 1989, Mercy Amba Oduyoye was already active in writing African Feminist Theology. In 1985, for example, she wrote an article on "Women Theologians and the Early Church,"[39] where she states the problem of how church history excluded the experiences of women. At this time Mercy Amba Oduyoye already had read works by feminist theologians such as Elisabeth Schüssler Fiorenza. She quotes her in the above article.[40] Thus the Circle is not the only mouth piece that has contributed to the liberation of women in church and society. The struggle for women's liberation is earlier than the Circle. The earlier paragraphs only mention a few: WCC and First World Feminist Movements.

The Role of the UN Decade for Women

It should also be noted that the Circle was only born after the UN Decade for Women in the 1970s. This movement also had an imprint on the life of Mercy Amba Oduyoye and might have contributed to her passion to found the

---

[38] Ibid.

[39] Mercy Amba Oduyoye, "Women Theologians and the Early Church. An Examination of Historiography, " *Voices from the Third World Women*, Colombo: EATWOT, vol viii 3, pp. 70f.

[40] Ibid., p. 70.

Circle. Thus, it makes sense that the beginning of the Circle was a fulfilment of what Mercy Amba Oduyoye and Brigalia Bam had had in mind many years before the institution of the Circle. Although the 1970s were a period when much focus was put on women's voices through the UN Decade for Women, Mercy was, by that time, already clear that she needed to do something for Africa, in appreciation for the good things that God had given her. She believed that all the good things she enjoyed in life came from God. Brigalia Bam also thought about what one could do to show appreciation to God. Whereas Mercy Amba Oduyoye was focused on starting something that would reach all Africa and involve women in theology, Brigalia Bam wanted to establish an Institute.[41] It is interesting that Mercy Amba Oduyoye is currently the founder and Director of the Institute on Religion and Culture. Brigalia Bam has been involved in training upcoming parliamentarians and her main involvement is in the area of politics.

The other drive that led Mercy Amba Oduyoye to start the Circle was that she was aware that she was "one lone" woman in the theological field and found herself among men! "She decided to have a community of women in theology and this was the embryonic stage of the Circle."[42] The Circle in its embryonic vision was already aimed at transforming gender inequalities. This was complementing the efforts by other gender activist movements in the world. One of the areas where Mercy Amba Oduyoye sought to bring equality was in the area of equal representation of women theologians over against male theologians in Africa. The Circle has further developed this passion to include the promotion of the engagement of African women theologians in paid employment.

The Role of Theological Institutions

Theological institutions have remained key to the development of the Circle since the beginnings. Theological institutions that offer training to women which is the same as that offered to men are crucial in this development.[43]

---

[41] Written Interview by Mercy Amba Oduyoye, Circle meeting, Kempton Park, Johannesburg 13.10.2003.

[42] Mercy Amba Oduyoye, *Ecumenical Review*, pp. 1-4.

[43] Not all theological institutions in Africa offer equal training to men and women. Some institutions offer "wives' courses" which do not adequately equip women on equal terms with

Mercy Amba Oduyoye and members of the IPC were able to produce the vision of the Circle because they had some theological orientation. Those that did not have such a background were at least enlightened in issues of culture and religion. The fact that these women had theological training equal to that accessed by men, made them acquire paid employment in key organizations. At this time, such training was possible mostly through secular universities, though a few churches based seminaries also offered such training.

Mercy's vision to begin the Circle was only realized in the 1980s, after a long and independent effort of making friendships with other African women, some of whom were not theologians, as seen in the group of founding members of the Circle.[44] However, even though the initiative to find other women between 1980 and 1987 was Mercy's own project,[45] it had to take her collaborative spirit with others to establish the Circle.

Mercy was convinced that she needed others to achieve this goal, and this inspiration was typically Akan, the ethnic group she comes from, but also African in general. An Akan proverb says that it is not good to be a lone star. She, therefore, from the start organized the Circle in collaboration with others. The first collaborative effort was finding others to join the Circle. Mercy felt that she was the only African woman who wrote African Feminist Theology at that time, and was such for many years.[46] This put her in a dilemma as an Akan woman and she wanted to change the situation. She knew that the only way to change the situation was to find more African women to write feminist theologies, as African theology was dominated by men. Women were inadequately represented in print. This period is referred to by the Circle as a period of the 'dearth of African women theologies.'[47]

---

male theologians. See Rachel Fiedler, "Theological Education for Women in Malawi", *Studia Historiae Ecclesiasticae*, vol. 35, 2009, Supplement, pp. 119-134.

[44] Musimbi Kanyoro, "Revisiting the History of the Circle," 2002, p. 1.

[45] Written Interview by Mercy Amba Oduyoye, Circle meeting, Kempton Park, Johannesburg 13.10.2003.

[46] Mercy Amba Oduyoye, *Ecumenical Review*, pp. 1-4.

[47] Musimbi Kanyoro, "Revisiting the History of the Circle," paper presented at a conference on Biographies of Women, Kempton Park, 2003.

Mercy wanted to work with other African women theologians to correct this situation.

According to an Akan wisdom saying, a person that is unable to co-opt others on the road to the goal is seen as a fool. Mercy refused to be a fool by working hard to find other women to write theologies with her. In this she has not only become wise as an Akan woman but also as an African woman, because in Africa we believe in this proverbial saying "I am because we are."[48] In other African contexts, such as Malawi, indeed, a person that is a 'loner' is even considered to be a witch or a wizard. Mercy worked hard to find other women theologians by searching through theological colleges, seminaries and Departments of Religious Studies in Africa. The instrument used in finding others was through speaking to women about the Circle at conferences where such women were found. Further, letters were written to colleges, universities, and churches for lists of women that could become part of this network.

The Role of the Institute of Church and Society

One of the first meetings where she started getting connected to other African women theologians took place in Ibadan, Nigeria and another one in Port Harcourt in the same country. At these meetings Mercy was able to make ties with other African women theologians.[49] Through casual conversations at such meetings she also came to know African woman abroad.[50]

In 1980, Mercy was able to organize the first meeting of African women theologians at the Institute of Church and Society in Ibadan.[51] Mercy was assisted in organizing this meeting by Isabel Johnson who was on the AACC women's desk and Daisy Obi, who was with the Christian Council of Nigeria as a director of the Institute of Church and Society.[52] This meeting was an

---

[48] Written Interview by Mercy Amba Oduyoye, Circle meeting, Kempton Park, Johannesburg 13.10.2003.

[49] Ibid.

[50] Mercy Amba Oduyoye, *Ecumenical Review*, pp. 1-4.

[51] Written Interview by Mercy Amba Oduyoye, Circle meeting, Kempton Park, Johannesburg 13.10.2003. Also, Mercy Amba Oduyoye, *Ecumenical Review*, pp. 1-4.

[52] Mercy Amba Oduyoye, *Ecumenical Review*, pp. 1-4.

independent effort by Mercy. Dr Constance Parvey of the WCC, however, took advantage of the meeting. This happened because she was looking for a venue to hold an All African Regional Conference of WCC, concerning the study on "The Community of Men and Women in the Church," which was proposed at the fifth Assembly of the WCC.[53] At this Conference, there were no papers to publish.[54]

Although Mercy's meeting was an independent effort to that of Dr Constance Parvey, together the meeting was well animated as WCC's effort.[55] After the African Regional Conference of WCC was finished, Mercy Amba Oduyoye with the help of Daisy Obi, a Nigerian, and Isabella Johnstone, a Sierra Leonean, held their women theologians' meeting.[56] But even then, the idea of the Circle was not hinted at.

The Role of the Programme for Theological Education (PTE)

The first formal discussion of a possibility of an Africa wide Circle of women theologians took place at a PTE meeting in Accra, Ghana, organized by John Pobee. It was at this meeting that Mercy Amba Oduyoye called the women together outside the conference programme and shared with them her vision to start the Circle. At that conference there were more than ten women interested in joining EATWOT, but it was not possible for all because EATWOT had restrictive quotas. Mercy took this opportunity to challenge the women as to why starting a Circle, which would be their own women's forum, was necessary. This would allow many more African women theologians to join and associate with other women theologians. The women received Mercy's challenge with much enthusiasm.[57]

In 1987, after Mercy completed her teaching contract at the University of Ibadan in Nigeria, she became a Deputy General Secretary of the WCC. The vision of the Circle at that time was alive and was widespread. Her

---

[53] Musimbi Kanyoro, "Revisiting the History of the Circle," 2002.

[54] Mercy Amba Oduyoye, *Ecumenical Review*, pp. 1-4.

[55] Written Interview by Mercy Amba Oduyoye, Circle meeting, Kempton Park, Johannesburg 13.10.2003; Mercy Amba Oduyoye, *Ecumenical Review*, pp. 1-4. – The Women of the World Council of Churches also focussed on gender issues.

[56] Mercy Amba Oduyoye, *Ecumenical Review*, pp. 1-4.

[57] Int Mercy Amba Oduyoye, Kempton Park, 14.10.2003.

appointment was to work in the Programme Unit on Education and Renewal. Mercy was able to lobby for support to establish the Circle even in some of the departments of the WCC.[58] At that time Brigalia Bam was still in Geneva. Mercy started searching for funds in 1988 to hold the first Circle meeting. She was able to call together the first group of African Women Theologians that became the birth attendants of the Circle that was born in 1989. These were the International Planning Committee.

In August 1988, the first members of the Circle, who are considered to be the founders of the Circle, met in Geneva upon invitation by Mercy Amba Oduyoye. These formed the IPC. Mercy was at that time living in Geneva and working with WCC. All the invited women were members of EATWOT with a high dose of academicians teaching in a University. Being part of EATWOT oriented them to feminist theologies in the Third World, but also to First World theologies. They were oriented to feminist theologies of the First World through their theological education. This advantaged them to lead the movement of African feminism in Africa. Mercy Amba Oduyoye refers to Circle theology as an "irruption within an irruption,"[59] because at the time she established the Circle she belonged to EATWOT,[60] also involved in developing theologies of Africa. In fact, she was elected as President of EATWOT in 1997.[61]

Mercy had joined EATWOT in 1976, the first African woman to do so. During this time, she was not working with WCC but as a lecturer in the Department of Religious Studies at the University of Ibadan, Nigeria. In the same year Brigalia Bam held a conference of women seminarians, and Mercy also had this list of women seminarians.

---

[58] Musimbi Kanyoro, "Revisiting the History of the Circle," 2002 and Int Mercy Amba Oduyoye, Kempton Park, 14.10.2003.

[59] See Virginia Fabella and Sergio Torres (eds), *Irruption of the Third World. Challenge to Theology*, Maryknoll: Orbis, 1983.

[60] Ecumenical Association of Third World Theologians, founded 1976 in Dar es Salaam.

[61] Carrie Pemberton mistakes this position to be that of General Secretary (Carrie Pemberton, *Circle Thinking: African Women Theologians in Dialogue with the West*, Leiden: Brill, 2003, p. 61).

The Role of EATWOT

EATWOT was the organ that produced the first Circle members. Its agenda was "to develop new models of theology which interpret the gospel in a more meaningful way to the peoples of the Third World and to promote their struggles for the fullness of humanity."[62] All members of the IPC were members of EATWOT. These women were mostly in the Diaspora. This means they learned to write feminist theologies as members of EATWOT through the Women's Commission.[63] Through this forum members of IPC were oriented to First World Feminist Theologies as well as other Third World Theologies. Thus, they had enough experience required for the planning of the launching of the Convocation of the Circle in September 1989, in Accra, Ghana.[64] Even in later years key Circle women like Philomena Njeri Mwaura and Mary Getui were members of EATWOT.

Apart from being members of EATWOT, the members of IPC were also members of other organizations or academic institutions that promoted the cause of liberation for women in church and society. Brigalia Bam was at that time working as the General Secretary of the South African Council of Churches. Brigalia had to travel all the way from South Africa to attend this meeting. Betty Ekeya was a lecturer at Egerton University in Kenya. She is a devout Catholic and an ex-nun.[65] However, she has not retained ties with the Circle since her return to the USA. Sr Bernadette Mbuy-Beya was serving in her community of Sisters in Lubumbashi in Zaire.[66] The other Catholic women

---

[62] "Report of the EATWOT Women's Commission Conference, St. Lucia Park, Harare, Zimbabwe, 21st – 25th June 1999", in Philomena N. Mwaura and Lilian D. Chirairo, *Theology in the Context of Globalization. African Women's Response*, Nairobi: EATWOT Women's Commission, 2005, pp. 96-106 [102-103].

[63] Even in later years key women of the Circle were members of EATWOT.

[64] See Isabel Apawo Phiri, "African Women of Faith Speak out in an HIV/AIDS Era," in Isabel Apawo Phiri, Beverly Haddad, Madipoane Masenya (ng'wana Mphahlele), *African Women, HIV/AIDS and Faith Communities*, Pietermaritzburg: Cluster, 2003, p. 5.

[65] Int Sr Annie Nasimiyu, 14.7.2005, Kempton Park.

[66] Sr Bernadette Mbuy Beya. She later becomes the Regional Research Coordinator of Francophone Africa in 1996. She is an Ursuline Sister. At this time, she was Mother Superior of a small community of five in Lubumbashi. She was working as the Director of the Institut Superior des Sciences Religieuses. She did post graduate studies at Lumen Vitae, the Institut des Sciences Religieuses in Brussels. She was at this time working as an urban community

were Sr Rosemary Edet, who was teaching in the Department of Religious Studies at the University of Calabar in Nigeria,[67] and Sr Teresa Okure. Sr Rosemary Edet died in 1993. At the 1996 conference a moment of silence was observed to mark her death.[68] Sr Rosemary Edet was instrumental in the organization of the Nigerian conference in 1990.[69] She was also among the founding members of EATWOT. She was Vicar General of the Congregation of the Handmaids of the Holy Child Jesus[70] and had a PhD in Religion and Culture from the Catholic University of America, Washington, DC.[71]

The number of Catholic women as pioneers of African Feminism at this time was high, because, although the Catholic Church does not ordain women to the ministry of the Priesthood, Catholic Sisters from some congregations are given chances to advance their education for women. In 1988, she organized an International Planning Committee (IPC) to strategize on the launch of the Circle. One of the members was her close friend Brigalia Bam, whose contribution to the Circle has been shown in earlier paragraphs. Other members were Catholic Sisters. Since Feminism originated in the Liberation movement, Roman Catholic women had to be in the majority because the wind of liberation touched the Roman Catholic Church earlier than the Protestant churches.[72] Carrie Pemberton lists four Sisters as leading members of the Circle: Sr Teresa Okure, Sr Rosemary Edet, Sr Bernadette Mbuy-Beya and Sr Annie Nasimiyu-Wasike. All the Sisters were faithful

---

health coordinator (Carrie Pemberton, *Circle Thinking: African Women Theologians in Dialogue with the West*, Leiden: Brill, 2003, p. 99).

[67] Musimbi Kanyoro, "Beads and Strands: Threading More Beads in the Story of the Circle," in Isabel Apawo Phiri, Devakarsham Betty Govinden, and Sarojini Nadar (eds), *Her-stories: Hidden Histories of Women of Faith in Africa*, Pietermaritzburg: Cluster 2002, pp. 15-38 [22].

[68] This is in many cases done in Africa. Hence this observance of her death had nothing to do with Carrie Pemberton's claim that Africa faces challenges of lack of communication, as such, people heard of her death only at such an occasion (See Carrie Pemberton, *Circle Thinking: African Women Theologians in Dialogue with the West*, Leiden: Brill, 2003, p. 114.)

[69] Carrie Pemberton, *Circle Thinking*, p. 93. All Sisters occupy or have occupied senior positions in their religious communities (p. 92).

[70] Her order was started in 1923 in Nigeria by an Irish missionary, see www.hhcjsisters.org.

[71] Carrie Pemberton, *Circle Thinking*, p. 114.

[72] Gustavo Gutierrez, "The Meaning of the Term *Liberation*," in Deane William Fern, *Third World Liberation Theologies. A Reader*, New York: Orbis, 1986.

members of their Catholic Church at the time when the Circle was being established.

> They are convinced of the importance of making the Catholic religion relate to the hearts, minds, cultures and societies of modern Africa. They all use the documents of the Second Vatican Council and the papers generated by the African Synod of 1994.[73]

In addition to these there was Sr Betty Ekeya. This advancement of education for these Catholic Sisters was not only in the area of theological training; as such some of the Sisters in this group had further training in Biology and Philosophy among others.[74] Some have been given opportunity to major in theology like Sr Annie Nasimiyu-Wasike who joined the Circle later. Although she was not in the pioneer group, she has become one of the leading religious in the Circle.[75] Sr Annie Nasimiyu-Wasike was the Mother Superior of the Congregation of the Little Sisters of St Francis (LSSF) in Kampala.[76] Her order was started by Mother Kenna, an Irish woman, in 1923. It was one of the earliest African congregations. In 1952 the order became independent and became a Pontifical Congregation. Sr Annie Nasimiyu-Wasike was Senior Lecturer at Kenyatta University.[77] The fact that these Sisters had postgraduate training enabled them to make a considerable contribution to the Circle. Their major contribution was in the area of mentoring other women to research, write and publish on women's issues. The other advantage Sisters had in becoming members of the Circle is that their church was at the point of renewal instigated by Vatican II.[78]

Apart from Roman Catholic Sisters, there were other women in the IPC. Rose Zoë Obianga was a linguist. Her theology was that of practice as she was very

---

[73] See Carrie Pemberton, *Circle Thinking: African Women Theologians in Dialogue with the West*, Leiden: Brill, 2003, p. 92.
[74] Int Sr Annie Nasimiyu, 14.7.2005, Kempton Park.
[75] See Carrie Pemberton, *Circle Thinking*, p. 92.
[76] www.lsosf-org/about_LSOST.html.
[77] See Carrie Pemberton, *Circle Thinking*, p. 116.
[78] See Carrie Pemberton, *Circle Thinking*, p. 99.

much involved with her church in Cameroon.[79] There were also Grace Ereme and Elizabeth Amoah. At that time, Elizabeth Amoah was teaching at the University of Ghana in Legon.

Musimbi Kanyoro was a linguist but she also was very much involved in church work. She had worked in Bible translation with the United Bible Societies in Africa, and at this time she was working on the Women's Desk of the Lutheran World Federation (LWF). The Women's Desk was commissioned to work on women in church and society.[80] The LWF is one of the ecumenical bodies that have a history of promoting women's liberation. Musimbi Kanyoro was advantaged by this. She is an international speaker. She was involved in the Vienna World Conference on Human Rights in 1993 and in the Beijing Conference in 1994.[81]

Musimbi Kanyoro had not been invited to the meeting. She learnt of the meeting when she met Mercy.[82] However, she became Mercy's chief collaborator. She writes; "There are facts about the Circle which can only be told by Mercy Amba Oduyoye or myself."[83]

When these founding members met, they became the International Planning Committee that organized the official launch of the Circle in 1989.[84] This is the beginning of collaborative teamwork in promoting a theology of transforming gender inequality in church and society.

The Ecumenical Association of Third World Theologians had a Catholic beginning with a prior aim of strengthening churches in the Global South ("Third World"). Both women and men constructed theology together, but later there was a provision of the Women's Commission. EATWOT is a forum that was developed within Liberation Theologies, spearheaded by Fr Sergio

---

[79] Musimbi Kanyoro, "Beads and Strands: Threading More Beads in the Story of the Circle," in Isabel Apawo Phiri, Devakarsham Betty Govinden, and Sarojini Nadar (eds), *Her-stories: Hidden Histories of Women of Faith in Africa*, Pietermaritzburg: Cluster 2002, pp. 15-38 [23].

[80] Ibid. "Revisiting the History of the Circle."

[81] Carrie Pemberton, *Circle Thinking: African Women Theologians in Dialogue with the West*, Leiden: Brill, 2003, p. 129.

[82] Int Mercy Amba Oduyoye, Kempton Park, 13.10.2003.

[83] Musimbi Kanyoro, "Revisiting the History of the Circle," 2002, p. 1.

[84] Ibid. "Revisiting the History of the Circle,"

Torres, a priest from Chile.[85] Some refer to this theology as the Theology from the Underside of History.[86] EATWOT was launched in 1976 in Dar es Salaam in Tanzania. According to the schedule of meetings, the first EATWOT continental conference was to be held in Africa. In the year 1977, it was indeed held in Accra, Ghana. The next meeting was planned to take place in Asia, and in 1979, the EATWOT conference indeed took place in Sri Lanka at Wennappuwa. [87] By this time, women were more developed in their thinking.[88]

From 1976 to 1986, African Women Theologians had cooperated in doing theology together with men within this forum of EATWOT. However, in 1986, at the regional Conference of EATWOT, which took place in Mexico, women expressed their discontent over theologies that sidelined women. This expression from women came as a surprise to the men present then.[89] Pemberton expresses this incident in this way:

> During the opening prayers at New Delhi, African American Women were amongst the delegates, including Jacquelyn Grant. She called on a Mother God as "Our Creator, God our Sustainer, God our Liberator."[90]

Male participants objected, calling her audacity un-theological and unbiblical. Grant's illicit use of the maternal in relation to God was followed by Marianne Katoppo, an Indonesian theologian, who appealed for a fresh regard for inclusive language in "Our language about God and before God."[91]

According to Bishop Kalilombe, the incident at Oaxtepec, Mexico, in 1986 was a significant move in the establishment of the Circle. He also recollects that the African Women Theologians in EATWOT were also encouraged by women, especially those from Latin America, who were also developing their

---

[85] See Carrie Pemberton, *Circle Thinking*, p. 41.

[86] Int Bishop Kalilombe, Postgraduate Colloquium 2003, Department of Theology and Religious Studies, University of Malawi.

[87] Virginia Fabella (ed), *Asia's Struggle for Full Humanity,* Maryknoll: Orbis, 1980.

[88] Int Bishop Kalilombe, Postgraduate Colloquium 2003, Department of Theology and Religious Studies, University of Malawi.

[89] Ibid.

[90] Carrie Pemberton, *Circle Thinking: African Women Theologians in Dialogue with the West*, Leiden: Brill, 2003.

[91] See Carrie Pemberton, *Circle Thinking*, p. 50.

own Mujerista theology. [92] Mujerista theologians are women who are concerned about the justice for Latin American Women and participate in the Liberation struggle for these women.

Latin American women come from diverse cultures, races and languages.[93] Besides Latin American women, Asian women were also getting organized in doing their own women theologies. It was therefore only African women who were not yet organized in any way.[94] Apart from Mujerista Theology, the black minority in America also had their own theology. Black Feminist Theology is commonly called Womanist Theology. The women that adhere to this theology consider themselves to be responsible, outrageous, audacious and courageous to fight for the liberation of Black women's culture and history.[95]

African Women Theologians became an "irruption within an irruption" because they felt, while their male African counterparts were doing well as regards challenging the First World theologies, they had not contended with the deeper issue, that of women.[96] In their struggle for independence, social and economic justice, and against racial discrimination, women felt that at the base of all these injustices the female gender was at stake. Since men were failing to address this, women felt they needed their own forum where they could do theology. However, tracing the origins of the Circle from EATWOT would be simplistic. We should also be aware that EATWOT had already made a provision for women to meet separately before the general EATWOT conference takes place.

---

[92] See Ketie Geneva Cannon, "The Emergence of Black Feminist Consciousness," in Letty Russel (ed), "Feminist Interpretations of the Bible," in Letty M. Russel, *Feminist Interpretations of the Bible*, London/New York: Basil Blackwell, 1985. Mujerista is derived from the Spanish word mujer – woman.

[93] See Susan Frank Parsons (ed), *The Cambridge Companion to Feminist Theology*, Cambridge University Press, 2002, p. 27.

[94] Int Bishop Kalilombe, Postgraduate Colloquium 2003, Department of Theology and Religious Studies, University of Malawi.

[95] See Alice Walker, *In Search of Our Mothers' Gardens. Womanist Prose*, New York: Harcourt, Brace, Jovanovich, 1983, pp. xi-xii.

[96] Int Bishop Kalilombe, Postgraduate Colloquium 2003, Department of Theology and Religious Studies, University of Malawi.

The EATWOT Women's Commission was established at Oaxtepec at the same time when the women voiced their concern. However, the Circle was timely because the women's commission was restrictive due to the fact that it followed a quota system. In this setup, not all women concerned with women's issues could join EATWOT. Thus, emerged Mercy Amba Oduyoye to begin the Circle in 1989.

Mercy Amba Oduyoye as Continental Leader of the Circle (1989 – 1996)

The delegates appointed Mercy Amba Oduyoye to lead the Circle at this first Convocation. It is clear that Mama Mercy, mother of the Circle, had made unique contributions to the Circle even way before she became the continental leader. Her achievements and contributions to the Circle have been described in both the previous and upcoming chapters. After attaining her role as the continental leader and in the years that followed, she continued to make admirable contributions as will be observed in this book.

Mercy Amba Oduyoye propelled the vision of the Circle forward through many approaches. Pivotal to all approaches was the opening of local chapters in many African countries. In addition, she encouraged African women in the diaspora to be involved in the Circle. Details of her work cannot be adequately covered under this section but are described in the later chapters in the context of describing the history of the Circle. In this section, I only point out some of the highlights under her leadership.

Firstly, she established an Institute of Religion and Culture in the premises of Trinity Theological College where women in Ghana as well as from Nigeria (at the zonal level) come to read papers. This seems not to have any parallel in local chapters outside Ghana. Did Mercy Amba Oduyoye envisage such a development to take place in other Zonal areas or regions?[97]

Secondly, Mercy led the Circle through collaboration since its inception. It is a strategy that continues to be emulated by the consecutive Continental Circle leaders.

---

[97] The story of the establishment of the Institute of Religion and Culture is documented elsewhere in the dissertation.

Thirdly, she had a good mastery in the art of delegation. Mercy Amba Oduyoye employed this art, for example, at the time the second Convocation was being organized. She worked with a coordinating committee that had representatives from the IPC and from different Zones and regions. Mercy Amba Oduyoye also co-opted Joyce Boham, to coordinate communication that took place in the organization of the 1996 Convocation together with other Circle women. She did this through Planning Committee meetings specifically organized for the conference.

Forthly, she held meetings with Circle women in the Diaspora to plan for the same 1996 Convocation. The planning group consisted of Musimbi Kanyoro, Nyambura Njoroge, Rose Zoë Obianga, and Sr Justine Kahungu (Lubumbashi), Mary Getui and Mercy Amba Oduyoye. The meetings were also graced with the presence of one man, John Pobee, who was at that time still with the WCC.[98]

The meeting of Circle women in the Diaspora took place in 1995. The consultation was for 15 women to help them prepare for their contributions to the 1996 Conference. It is another example of a collaborative effort that the Circle enjoyed through the efforts of WCC. The collaboration was very natural because the WCC, through the Ecumenical Theological Education Desk, was also interested in theological training for African women. The Circle was in turn strengthened in that theological training was important for enabling the women to write theological papers. This was a consultation conference for African women theologians who were studying or teaching theology outside Africa.

For Mercy Amba Oduyoye the 1996 Continental Conference was to be the conclusion of the gestation period of seven years and the beginning of what she prayed would become a biennial event.[99] The spirit of cooperation by the Circle and Mercy in particular was seen in how she was able to agree on a proposed programme by PROCMURA[100] to hold a joint workshop in Nairobi, Kenya. Using women's wisdom, Mercy Amba Oduyoye consulted with Musimbi Kanyoro and Nyambura Njoroge about the programme. They finally

---

[98] Mercy Amba Oduyoye - Rev Janice Nessiboo, Women's Coordinator, PROCMURA, 14.7.1994.

[99] Ibid.

[100] Programme for Christian – Muslim Relations in Africa.

agreed that the joint meeting should take place preceding the Continental meeting.[101]

This joint project of Christian/Muslim relations in Africa attracted ten participants, five Muslim women and five Circle women. This was the time when Mercy Amba Oduyoye was Deputy General Secretary of WCC. She was able to take advantage of her position to facilitate such meetings as such projects fit into what her office stood for.

Again, in preparation for the Continental Conference of 1996, there was need to do more advocacy work. To sum up the activities that were done in the advocacy programme a quote will suffice:

> In preparation for the 1996 Institute, a survey will be undertaken to ascertain the progress made by theological institutions in Africa in the recruitment and admission of women to the faculty and the student body. We need to know the curriculum changes that have taken place to indicate inclusion of women in religion and culture. The visit is also aimed at strengthening the networks especially in Sierra Leone, Gambia, Benin, Togo, Uganda, Tanzania, Zimbabwe and Kenya where the 1996 Institute will be held.[102]

Such an exercise was made possible through personal visitation, but also through sending invitations to various institutions. Some of these letters came from John Pobee's office, and others came from Mercy Amba Oduyoye and Nyambura Njoroge.

At the 1989 Convocation it had been agreed that continental conferences were to be held after every seven years. In this case, after the 1989 Convocation, it was high time for the 1996 continental conference.

The Genesis of the Circle

The genesis of the Circle is often linked to three viewpoints. The first one is that it was started by EATWOT and WCC. The second theory is that it was born through the activities of the general movement of Women's Liberation, which began in Europe in the 1960s. The last theory, which is defended in

---

[101] Mercy Amba Oduyoye - Rev Janice Nessiboo, Women's Coordinator, PROCMURA, 14.7.1994.

[102] Report on the 1996 Institute of Women in Religion and Culture, no date, no author, accessed 14.9.2005.

this book is that it was born by an African woman though in an Ecumenical environment.

The historical development shown in this chapter clearly answers these claims. In fact, discussions on these arguments go further and show that there was much collaboration as women consolidated themselves through ecumenical movements (in this case EATWOT and WCC). However, this collaboration does not deny the fact that Mercy Amba Oduyoye is the mother of the Circle. The arguments for this have been already spelt out in the above discussions. In summary, she is the one who conceived the idea and even the parameters within which African Women Theologies should be done. It was also her plan to involve others, as such she engaged an International Planning Committee. And further it cannot be denied that the earlier contacts were achieved mainly through Mercy Amba Oduyoye. Further, while there was the possibility of copying theologies of other Third World countries, Mercy created her own slant of theologizing where Religion and Culture would be the only parameters. This theme was conceived by her during the Harvard days and was put forward at the International Planning Meeting.

Circle theologies have a different agenda and dialogues within a context that is African. The Circle is further concerned about issues of Religion and Culture (a two-winged theology) in Africa. This is different from some feminist concerns of Europe and other Third World countries.[103] Secondly, the Circle is concerned about researching and writing from a faith point of view. Theologians in the Circle have a religion. Christians and Muslims believe in God. Traditionalists also believe in God in other ways. These are not dialogues with atheism as is the case with some feminist writing in Europe.

Issues that are of paramount importance, such as those articulated at EATWOT about the gender of God, are not of central concern in Circle scholarship. The major task was to address inequalities that lay in the suppression of the African specifity in constructing women's theologies.

At funerals or weddings, where African theologies are also expressed, the space is open to African people from all religious backgrounds. One does not go to the funeral because the deceased belonged to one's particular religion.

---

[103] Rachel NyaGondwe Fiedler, Johannes W. Hofmeyr, Klaus Fiedler, *African Feminist Hermeneutics. An Evangelical Reflection*, Mzuzu: Mzuni Press, 2016, p. 20.

Even if she/he did that, there will be many people at the funeral that do not belong to that particular religion. The same goes with ecumenism at initiation ceremonies. Those giving instructions and the initiates in a traditional initiation come from a variety of religions.

However, from the story of the Circle it is clear that the Circle developed within an ecumenical setting: The role of EATWOT was strong. Mercy Amba Oduyoye married Modupe in 1968, who has a vast interaction with Ecumenical bodies such as the All Africa Council of Churches and World Student Federation that for years have associated with the World Council of Churches. Her parents belong to a church that is a member of WCC, and it is within this background that Mercy Amba Oduyoye has been nurtured.

Immediate to the formation of the Circle is her own involvement in the ecumenical activities for a long time. This is mainly through the World Christian Students Federation, the World Council of Churches and EATWOT. Whatever position one has on the birth of the Circle, it is clear that the Circle is growing and maturing. And this is the task for the following chapters.

Chapter 2: Growth of the Circle under Consecutive Continental Leaders (1989-2007)

This chapter documents and assesses the growth of the Circle from 1989 to 2007. The humble beginnings of the Circle that culminated in the 1989 Convocation have led to an impressive movement in Africa. The Circle has attained growth in geographical coverage, leadership as well as administrative development. After the first Convocation in 1989, Circle women from Africa and beyond gathered at the second Convocation in 1996.[1] This second Convocation was followed by a third Convocation in 2002.[2] The fourth Convocation was held in 2007. Each Convocation elected a new continental leader: Mercy Amba Oduyoye, Musimbi Kanyoro, Isabel Apawo Phiri and Fulata Lusungu Moyo in that order from the first to the fourth. This chapter provides an interpretative historical and theological account of the developments that occurred during the first three convocations from 1989 to 2007. Even though the fourth convocation took place in 2007, it is the same year when Isabel Apawo Phiri concluded her term as continental leader. Even though the book ends with the reign of Isabel Apawo Phiri, I have also added limited historical developments between 2007 and 2017.

The move of the Circle to choose a woman other than the founder of the Circle marks a real growth towards the independence of the network. It marked an assertion that the Circle is a movement that is for all Circle women and that its life was beyond the boundaries of the life span and ethnicity of a

---

[1] Isabel Apawo Phiri, "African Women of Faith Speak out on an HIV/AIDS Era" in Isabel Apawo Phiri, Beverly Haddad and Madipoane Masenya (ng'wana Mphahlele) (eds), *African Women, HIV/AIDS and Faith Communities,* Pietermaritzburg: Cluster 2003, p. 6.

[2] The 2002 Circle Convocation took place in Addis Ababa, Ethiopia, where 140 Circle members drawn from 25 countries met. The conference was opened on 5th August 2002, in the Africa Hall of the Economic Commission for Africa (ECA). The President of Ethiopia and the chairman of the HIV/AIDS council, His Excellency Girma Wolde Giorgis, officially opened the meeting. Apart from the Circle participants, there were influential church leaders in attendance at the opening ceremony. Among these were: His Holiness Abba Paulos, Patriarch of Ethiopia, Archbishop of Axum and Echeque of the See of St Tekle Haimanot, Ethiopian Orthodox Tewhdo Church, Rev Iteffa Gobena, President of the Ethiopian Evangelical Church Mekane Yesu, and Pastor Seyeum, the General Secretary of the Ethiopian Evangelical Church Fellowship.

founder. Further, it is a testimony of selfless life as well as a lack of selfishness by the founder that was useful in the advancement of the network.

The Circle under Musimbi Kanyoro (1996 – 2002)

At the second Continental Circle Conference held in Nairobi in 1996, Mercy Amba Oduyoye was replaced by Musimbi Kanyoro, a Kenyan. In the year 2002, Musimbi Kanyoro was replaced by a Malawian, Isabel Apawo Phiri. At these three convocations, the Circle really rotated the leadership. However, at the fourth convocation in 2007, the unexpected happened when another Malawian was elected to be the continental leader of the Circle. There was much hope that the leadership of the Circle would leave the hands of Anglophone and go to either Francophone or Lusophone Africa. Again, even though Anglophone leadership continued, it was indeed unexpected that this leadership role went to Malawi for the second time. One of the reasons was that the Circle still wanted to capitalize on the support of the World Council of Churches and since Fulata Lusungu Moyo was at that time (and still is) coordinator for the Women's Desk at WCC, she was the right person to provide the needed link to WCC.

Musimbi Kanyoro's family background is that of a typical African family in her times. She comes from a family of seven girls and three boys.[3] Her father died in July 1994 and was buried in Bwase, his village. Even though Musimbi Kanyoro hailed from a large family and was a girl, her opportunities for education were not negatively affected. She completed her early education and studied at the University of Nairobi. The University of Nairobi was a college of the University of East Africa before it became a separate institution. At this college, she completed her undergraduate studies in 1976. After this she was privileged to go to the USA for postgraduate studies, from where she returned in 1982. This road to education had prepared her for a senior post. Indeed, it is not surprising that in 1988 she took up an international position in Geneva, Switzerland. At the time, she was being elected as Continental Coordinator of the Circle, she was still based in Geneva.

From the conception period in the early 1980s to 1995, leadership of the Circle had been in the hands of Mercy Amba Oduyoye, so a change in

---

[3] Isabel Apawo Phiri, "African Women of Faith Speak out in an HIV/AIDS Era," pp. vii – viii.

leadership at the 1996 Convocation was bound to have some effects. One effect was that Musimbi Kanyoro's leadership was received with mixed reactions in some quarters. This, however, was not from Mercy Amba Oduyoye, who herself had foreseen this transition and even planned for it.

It is clear from earlier discussions that Mercy Amba Oduyoye saw Musimbi Kanyoro as a strong candidate to take over her role. She had met Musimbi in Geneva and knew that she would be an able leader of the Circle given the chance. Musimbi Kanyoro had several plusses to her being a leader. She came from another part of the continent, East Africa, while Mercy Amba Oduyoye is from West Africa. It was natural for other women to receive such leadership from another part of the continent.

Secondly, Musimbi Kanyoro came from Kenya, where prominence of Circle women in ecumenical organizations at international level was second only to that of women in West Africa. There was Musimbi Kanyoro with the YWCA and Nyambura Njoroge with the World Council of Churches at that time.

For the progress of the Circle, a leader with an ecumenical and international environment was needed to link the Circle to sources of funding. That Musimbi Kanyoro was working for YWCA, an ecumenical body, was an advantage. It was also helpful to be able to organize Circle activities taking advantage of the Ecumenical environment and support base, just as Mercy Amba Oduyoye had done.

Such advantages were in addition to the fact that Musimbi Kanyoro had moved with Mercy since the International Planning Meeting to this stage. On the grassroots level, however, some Circle women expected that Mercy would continue to coordinate the Circle. This is shown in that, even though Mercy was in tune with Musimbi Kanyoro's succession to leadership at the 1996 conference, the election of the new coordinator was done in her absence.

Others envisaged that Nyambura Njoroge would lead because she was at that time taking up an appointment with the WCC to work in the PTE (Programme for Theological Education) Department which earlier in the life of the Circle had supported Circle work. Some even thought that the Circle had been started by this office. To them it was automatic that the coordinator of that office should coordinate the Circle as well.

Further, there are two possible reasons that made Circle women vote in the absence of Mercy Amba Oduyoye. Firstly, they might have thought that Mercy Amba Oduyoye would block a move to replace her. Secondly, they might have thought that she might influence others to vote for a candidate of her choice. In fact, the discussion to vote in her absence was unnecessary as all the three candidates would have made able leaders of the Circle at that time. And the three continued to work together in the promotion of the Circle regardless of who was picked as a leader. It must be recognized that each of the three had advantages in promoting the cause of the Circle. Nyambura Njoroge from her vantage point of working with the WCC was key in sourcing funding for women to advance in their theological education. Mercy Amba Oduyoye knew avenues of funding that might be necessary to keep the Circle running. Musimbi Kanyoro's advantages have already been articulated.

Mercy Amba Oduyoye wasn't astonished that it was Musimbi Kanyoro who was chosen. Some of the reasons for choosing Musimbi Kanyoro were: She was a close friend to Mary Getui, who was chair of the local organizing committee. While Nyambura Njoroge would have likely scooped more votes from the grassroots because of her linkage to Circle women at Limuru, the presence of Limuru women in the organizing committee was not prominent. The experiences of 1996 are still remembered by those that were close to the issue, but for the majority of the Circle members it is not an issue any more.

Leadership development in the Circle often occurs in the context of modelling. This kind of modelling is mainly by assigning roles to women which would bring them into noticeable visibility among fellow Circle women. Even before Musimbi Kanyoro was elected, it was very much envisaged by some members of the Circle that she would become the leader. Musimbi had been the right-hand woman of Mercy Amba Oduyoye and she knew things about the Circle and Mercy that others did not know.[4] Musimbi's presence at the IPC also gave her some advantage over Nyambura Nyoroge. These factors show that she was better positioned to take up leadership. However, those that were key at the 1996 Continental Conference also ended up in positions

---

[4] Remark by Musimbi Kanyoro, Biographies of Women of Faith Conference, Johannesburg, 2001.

of one kind or another. However, Nyambura Nyoroge continued to make significant contributions to theological formation, including Circle members.

The Circle under Isabel Apawo Phiri (2002 – 2007)

At the 2002 Convocation Isabel Apawo Phiri was elected as continental coordinator for the Circle for the period of 2002 to 2007. She was then director of the School of Theology at the University of KwaZulu Natal, Pietermaritzburg.[5] Since 1989, Isabel Apawo Phiri had exhibited leadership abilities to such an extent that it was not surprising that she became Circle coordinator. She had successfully facilitated the establishment of Circle chapters not only in her home country Malawi but also in the Southern Africa region. Namibia and Durban Circles are examples of chapters that she had organized. Isabel also had become director for the Centre for Constructive Theology in 1997. Her leadership position broke new ground in South African universities where it was not customary at that time to have a woman of colour serve in such a position.[6] Her experience with the Centre for Constructive Theology gave her contact with grass roots people. She was part of the academic community as well as member of the community where being infected with and affected by HIV/AIDS was most pronounced. This experience has been an invaluable resource to construct theologies of transforming gender inequalities in the era of HIV and AIDS.

Isabel Apawo Phiri became the first continental coordinator who did not reside in Geneva at the time of her appointment. Mercy Amba Oduyoye had been coordinator when she was working in the WCC office in Geneva, and Musimbi Kanyoro was also working in the YWCA office in Geneva at the time of her appointment.

The advantages of Mercy Amba Oduyoye and Musimbi Kanyoro were that they were able to use their workplace to advance the cause of the Circle. This was possible because the Circle was not seen as a different thing in the context of their work. It could also be done in the context of them doing their duties as employees of their ecumenical bodies. Most importantly, they

---

[5] Provisional Addis Ababa Circle Report, p. 3, accessed 6.3.2006.

[6] Isabel Apawo Phiri, "Transformation in South African Universities: The Case of Female Academics in Leadership Positions in Theological Institutions," in Roswith Gerloff (ed), *Mission is Crossing Frontiers*, Pietermaritzburg: Cluster, 2003, p. 414.

enjoyed their links with persons of power in the Ecumenical world as is shown by Musimbi Kanyoro. From the department of PTE, John Pobee and Ofelia Ortega had offered Mercy much support in her Circle work.[7]

> The Africa Desk of the WCC was another partner recruited by Mercy Amba Oduyoye. The Circle's accounts were managed by the staff of the Africa Desk. The two executives, Lal Swai and Richard Murigande, initially gave their support and thereby began an important tradition ... Another very prominent supporter of the Circle was the WCC Sub-unit on Women. Mercy had established this link way back in the 1980s, when the Circle was just a concept.[8]

Other people that assisted the Circle from Geneva were: Annah Karin Hammer,[9] Aruna Gnanadason,[10] Evelyn Appia[11] and Janet Thomson, who worked with the Africa Desk and assisted Mercy Amba Oduyoye with Circle work.[12] Others that worked with Mercy were: Annelies Hoppe, Brigitte Constant, Diana Chabloz, Doris Appel and William Temu.[13]

The other advantage of working in Geneva was that the finances of the Circle were kept in Geneva using WCC office resources. The fact that Isabel Apawo Phiri became coordinator of the Circle and yet was not in Geneva, posed questions regarding where the funds would be kept and also how far earlier connections would be available to her. There were different views concerning how Circle funds should be kept. Some members had the opinion that Geneva should keep the funds.

On the other hand, some found no problem for Isabel to keep the funds in South Africa, also using the structures available to her through her

---

[7]   Isabel Apawo Phiri and Sarojini Nadar (eds), *African Women, Religion, and Health: Essays in Honour of Mercy Amba Ewudziwa Oduyoye*, Pietermaritzburg: Cluster 2006, p. 29.

[8]   Ibid.

[9]   Ibid., p. 29. She started the Ecumenical Decade of the Churches in Solidarity with Women.

[10]   Ibid., p. 29. She is a member of EATWOT, and member of the Association of Asian Women Theologians. See Aruna Gnanadason, *No Longer Silent: The Church and Violence against Women*, Geneva: WCC, 1993.

[11]   Ibid., p. 29. She worked with the Ecumenical Decade of the Churches in Solidarity with Women in Geneva.

[12]   Ibid., p. 29.

[13]   Ibid.

employment. Indeed, the administration of funds moved to South Africa where Isabel was employed as lecturer in the University of KwaZulu Natal in Pietermaritzburg. Earlier on, the Circle had been coordinated from Ghana by Joyce Boham. Isabel Apawo Phiri engaged Lilian Siwila and Bridget Masaiti as her Circle office assistants to help with Circle work.[14] The recruitment of an office administrator had been mandated at the 2002 Continental Conference. Isabel Apawo Phiri was mandated to "find either full time volunteers to support her or several part-time volunteers and possibly outsource or employ someone for the administrative and secretarial tasks of the Circle."[15] This was a necessary step as the feeling that the Circle had grown too large to be effectively managed by a volunteer continental coordinator was ever growing. This feeling had been visible as early as in Musimbi Kanyoro's time. She felt that membership of the Circle "had grown beyond the abilities of a volunteer coordinator."[16]

The election of Isabel Apawo Phiri legitimized further the principle of rotational leadership practiced by the Circle. In fact, it could be predicted that the next continental coordinator of the Circle would come from either Francophone or Lusophone Africa, but more likely so from the Francophone region, which had been more involved in continental and other Circle meetings than the Lusophone one. The art of collaboration and delegation continued even during the period of Isabel Apawo Phiri. Isabel worked with the Circle linguistic coordinators as follows: Hélène Yinda, research coordinator for the Francophone Region; at this time she was working with the YWCA and was based in Geneva; Dorcas Olubanke Akintunde, at this time teaching at the University of Ibadan, Nigeria, was the research coordinator for the Anglophone Region. The coordinator for Lusophone Africa was Felicidade Cherinda, who was working with the Igreja Presbiteriana de Moçambique in Maputo.[17] These leaders were elected to assist Isabel Apawo Phiri in the work of the Circle. In addition, she was much assisted by Sarojini Nadar, Fulata Moyo and Lilian Siwila, who were at the University of KwaZulu Natal where Isabel Apawo Phiri was professor at that time.

---

[14] Ibid., p. 36.

[15] Provisional Addis Ababa Circle Report, p. 12, accessed 6.3.2006.

[16] See Isabel Apawo Phiri and Sarojini Nadar (eds), *African Women, Religion, and Health: Essays in Honour of Mercy Amba Ewudziwa Oduyoye,* Pietermaritzburg: Cluster, 2006, p. 36.

[17] See Provisional Addis Ababa Circle Report, p. 41, accessed 6.3.2006.

The 2002 Convocation would have taken place in 2003. This would be the time when the seven-year period after the 1996 conference would have elapsed.[18] The next Continental Convocation (after 1996), on the contrary, was held in 2002 from 4th to 9th August. The announcement was in December 2001, which meant that there were only eight months to prepare for the conference.[19]

It is not just the shift in the date that was peculiar to this meeting. The venue and focus of the meeting also changed. Firstly, the normal focus for the meeting would have been to evaluate the effectiveness of the Study Commissions instituted in the earlier period. However, this was only attended to briefly, "one day prior to the conference." The reason for this was to allow as much time as possible for deliberations on HIV/AIDS.[20] Secondly, the venue for this conference was originally to be Yaoundé, Cameroon but was shifted to Addis Ababa in Ethiopia.

The Circle under Fulata Lusungu Moyo (2007 – 2013)

The Continental Coordinator for the Circle during the period 2007 to 2013 was Fulata Moyo, a Presbyterian and Ngoni of Mzimba in Northern Malawi. There was less focus on opening new chapters and holding Circle workshops, Zonal meetings as well as Regional meetings during her time. There were also no meetings by the Study Commissions. Thus, there have been few Circle publications during this period. The fact that Fulata Moyo was discharging her responsibility as a Circle coordinator from Geneva, is not a reason for this shift from earlier approaches. Mercy Amba Oduyoye and Musimbi Kanyoro had also discharged their duties as Circle Coordinators while they were working in Geneva at the time of their office. The reason seems to lie in other factors.

One of the key factors is that there was an appreciation of Circle Theologies in global movements. This meant that key Circle women that were strategic to promoting the Circle in their countries and regions were employed by some of the movements. Isabel Apawo Phiri who was key in opening up new chapters in Southern Africa and promoting Circle publications both as author

---

[18] Institute of Women in Religion and Culture, Ghana - Teresa Hinga, 20.12.2001.

[19] Ibid.

[20] Provisional Addis Ababa Circle Report, p. 7, accessed 6.3.2006.

and editor became the Deputy General Secretary of WCC in Geneva. She is not the only Circle woman in diaspora in similar engagements. These are the likes of Fulata Moyo who is working with WCC, Nyambura Njoroge and Musimbi Kanyoro in different portfolios. Secondly, some key Circle women were engaged in assignments that were intensive and left them with less time to concentrate on strengthening the Circle. Musa Dube for example was involved in HIV curriculum development for some time. Again, there was a reconceptualization of the Circle approaches. Between 1989 and 2007, the Circle concentrated on the Circle as the agent of liberation but the question of engaging with men was less strong. During this period, Fulata Moyo and other Circle women have been involved in Issues of masculinity as an important dimension in liberating women. This seems to have diverted the attention on shaping the Circle as a movement in Africa.

Further, curriculum reforms in theological education also contributed to the slowing down of the Circle. Circle members devised other approaches of promoting Circle Theology by including the teaching of Feminist Theologies at Universities. Rachel NyaGondwe Fiedler, for example has developed African Feminist courses that are now included in the Theology and Religious Studies curriculum at Mzuzu University. While this is a welcome development, she has spent less time in strengthening the Malawi Circle.

The Circle under Helen Adekunbi Labeodan (2013 – 2017ff)

By 2013, the number of country Circle chapters had decreased. Some countries had no chapter, while other countries had a limited number of chapters. In South Africa, for example, three Circle chapters still existed. Countries such as Malawi had no live Circle chapters any more. By 2016, some referred to the Circle as a sleeping giant that needed to be awakened.[21]

As the Circle plans a revival it has to be cognizant of its history and rethink of whether to continue with the modus operandi of the Circle or sketch alternative ways of creating African Feminist Theologies.[22] By this time, the number of active country local chapters had dwindled. In the Southern Africa region for example, there were only three chapters.[23] One of the ways to

---

[21] Nathando Hadebe - Getrude Kapuma, Molly Longwe and Rachel Fiedler, 20.6.2016.
[22] Ibid.
[23] Ibid.

initiate revival was to put a Circle committee in place. The Circle elected the following committee to spur the revival of the Circle. The Continental Coordinator was Dr Helen Labeodan, regional coordinator for West Africa was Rev Sylvia Owusu-Ansah, regional coordinator for Eastern Africa was Prof Hazel Ayanga and Regional coordinator for Francophone was Prof Anastasie Maponda and regional coordinator for Southern Africa was Dr Nontando Hadebe.[24] The other way was to initiate conversations on the Circle with Circle members in the different countries. Another way to initiate revival was to hold national Circle conferences in different countries. A budget was made available for this activity and that the regional coordinators should begin a conversation with different countries to make this happen.[25] In Malawi, the national meeting would have participants from women in theological colleges, leaders in the churches and Non-Governmental Organizations working on women's issues. This one-day conference would re-launch the Circle in Malawi. The third approach was to publish and mentor the next generation.[26] Mzuzu University has been mentoring women through classroom teaching and supervision of undergraduate and postgraduate research on women's issues in religion and culture.

Although Malawi expressed interest to revive the Circle in 2016, the plans did not mature. Other countries in Southern Africa will hold the national Circle meetings in 2017. "I have heard from other sisters that this year may be too soon to plan a Circle meeting in their countries and have rescheduled for next year."[27]

Administrative Development

The need for the consecutive Continental Circle leaders to communicate effectively with the mother of the Circle partly led to the administrative development of the network. There was need for an office that would coordinate such communication. Even though there was change in leadership at the 1996 Convocation, and at 2002, Mercy Amba Oduyoye and the consecutive leaders: Musimbi Kanyoro and Isabel Apawo Phiri needed to

---

[24] Ibid.
[25] Ibid., 20.2.2016.
[26] Ibid., 20.2.2016.
[27] Ibid., 9.6.2016.

continue to share their vision for the Circle. Central to this vision was the understanding that the Circle, though it has a guardian, still had the mother Mercy Amba Oduyoye living in Ghana. For good shepherding of the Circle, it was clear to both Musimbi Kanyoro and Isabel Apawo Phiri that the Circle administration must continue to be near where the real mother was. Mercy Amba Oduyoye knew exactly the birth of the Circle, she knew the ties that her child had and it was wisdom that the Circle should be hosted near her.

Before Mercy Amba Oduyoye retired from the World Council of Churches and returned to Ghana, the administration for the Circle was moved from Geneva to Ghana in 2001. A full-time administrator was recruited to be supervised by Mercy Amba Oduyoye and Elizabeth Amoah, also from Ghana.[28] At this time, Musimbi Kanyoro wrote:

My role as Coordinator now remains to be that of a Board Chair or Board President. I will make sure that the coordinating committee that you elected in Nairobi in 1996 meets for their deliberation and follows-up on the plans agreed upon. I will also support the various coordinators with infrastructure to do their work. Research Reports will be written by the coordinators and compiled in Ghana by the Liaison Officer.[29]

At that time, the Circle "maintained their account with the World Council of Churches and because it is situated here in Geneva, I will be the person who communicates with our donors as well as liaise with the World Council of Churches Africa Desk in matters of custody for our account." [30] The researchers were found at that time through the research coordinators.

> If you need to be associated with Research or get support for publishing your work, correspond either with a specific theme leader or with Mercy Amba Oduyoye as the Research Coordinator.[31]

---

[28] Musimbi Kanyoro to Friends, Circle, c/o World YWCA, 16, Ancienne Route Grand Saconnex, Geneva, Switzerland, 12.4.2001.

[29] Ibid.

[30] Ibid.

[31] Ibid.

The organization of the Circle in 2003 was done by the Ghana Office with the administrative expertise of Joyce Boham.[32] This was not strange because at this time she led the administration of the Circle.[33]

Since 1996, Joyce Boham, a Ghanaian had been developing a data base for Circle contacts. This is what led to the Preliminary Directory.[34] She was also the mastermind of logistics for workshops related to the Circle. Regardless of where the meetings took place, Joyce worked tirelessly in conjunction with the local organizing committee. Some meetings took place in Geneva and some in Ghana as well as in South Africa. Apart from Circle meetings elsewhere, she also helped with the meetings of the Institute of Women in Religion and Culture.[35] One of such meetings, by the International Press Services, took place in Zimbabwe on how to report issues of gender, religion and culture. The objective was to make a manual. Musa Dube represented the Circle in 2000.[36] The manual came to fruition in the year 2001.[37] The IPS had reports from various countries in Africa and these were put together in one publication. After the Zimbabwe meeting, the IPS also asked her to organize a similar workshop to make sure that the delegates were well catered for.[38] She began her work with the Institute in 2000 and with the Circle in 2001.[39] The institute was still viable in 2007.

The Constitution

At the 2002 Continental Conference, views were aired whether the Circle should continue to have informal leadership with a loose network, as it had

---

[32] Email correspondences by Joyce Boham.

[33] See Isabel Apawo Phiri "African Women of Faith Speak out in an HIV/AIDS Era," in Isabel Apawo Phiri, Beverly Haddad and Madipoane Masenya (ng'wana Mphahlele) (eds), in *African Women, HIV/AIDS and Faith Communities*, Pietermaritzburg: Cluster 2003, p. 6.

[34] Int Joyce Boham, 16.9.2005

[35] For more information on the Institute of Women and Culture, read in the upcoming chapter and also see: Isabel Apawo Phiri, *Women, Presbyterianism and Patriarchy: Religious Experiences of Chewa Women in Central Malawi*, Blantyre: CLAIM-Kachere, 2000, p. 17.

[36] Int Joyce Boham, 16.9.2005.

[37] Ibid.

[38] Ibid.

[39] Ibid.

been since 1989. "Since its conception, the Circle has worked with limited resources and only volunteer coordination. A desire for a more permanent structure with paid staff was expressed and the new committee was charged with the responsibility of exploring that possibility."[40]

By then the Circle had already engaged Joyce Boham as "a liaison officer." She thus became the first Circle member of staff to be remunerated.[41] The leadership of the Circle elected at the 2002 Pan African Circle Conference took up the responsibility of working out the first draft Constitution in 2005. The draft was circulated in three languages by the regional Circle coordinators in order to get feedback. The English-speaking Circle studied the draft at the 2005 regional conference.[42] The second draft constitution with corrections on the first was circulated again to Circle members in December 2006. The 2007 continental conference adopted the third revised constitution.[43]

The proponents of formalizing Circle administration were challenged with realities of funding for such a venture. One of the problems was to get a permit of the Circle as a registered entity in countries that opted for formalized administration of the Circle, especially over concerns to where the Circle coordinator would be based. This was one of the challenges and hence institutionalizing the Circle met with mixed reactions. Some members were of the view that registration in certain countries would not be easily attained. The advantages of having a formalized Circle structure are seen in the face of raising funds. If the Circle is legally registered in a particular country, the accessibility to funding for the Circle might improve.

Mercy Amba Oduyoye and her Successors

Whereas it is envisaged that the Circle is committed to a rotational leadership as seen from this history, the question that needs to be addressed is whether it was the right time to have a change in continental leadership or not. This implies the question whether or not Mercy Amba Oduyoye had been given

---

[40] Provisional Addis Abba Circle Report, p. 12, accessed 6.3.2006.

[41] Isabel Apawo Phiri and Sarojini Nadar (eds), *African Women, Religion, and Health: Essays in Honour of Mercy Amba Ewudziwa Oduyoye*, Pietermaritzburg: Cluster 2006, p. 36.

[42] Circle Newsletter no 6, April 2006, p. 2.

[43] Ibid.

enough time to realize her vision concerning the Circle. The answer to this is already unfolding, as the momentum of the Circle in Ghana supersedes other local circles. Is it that Mercy Amba Oduyoye had more concerning where the Circle should be in the future or not?

Under Mercy Amba Oduyoye two things seem to have been central to the Circle: the establishment of local chapters and of zonal institutes, [44] concentrating not only on classroom theology, but also on grassroots theology. The second disadvantage of change in leadership was in the area of funding. Is it possible that Mercy Amba Oduyoye had connections to funding that were prematurely discontinued with the change in leadership? It is very common that financial partners sometimes give funding because of the person who leads the institution. Did this change of leadership cause a loss in funds that would have rendered the Circle more effective?

This also can be assessed fully when relating some of the experiences of the Circle in later years. The 2005 regional conference in Johannesburg nearly got cancelled due to difficulties in raising funds for the air tickets of the delegates. Even in 2006, some of the publication work was slowed down because of lack of funds. Has this anything to do with abrupt change of leadership without much thought?

By 2001, already the chances of holding more Circle conferences were growing dim. Prominent Circle members, who were influential in attracting funding, were questioning the value of whether it was necessary to bring Circle members to a conference/meeting to present papers to each other as was the case before. This questioning culminated in the proposal that for future conferences individual women would no longer present papers but that monographs produced at the local chapter level would be displayed.[45] With the realities of Circle history, where only a few local chapters were well established and had enough mentors, very few local Circles brought a monograph to the 2007 Continental conference. However, this decision was important in measuring the kind of progress in local Circle developments in different regions.

---

[44] Report Circle Study Commissions, Institute of Women in Religion and Culture, Trinity Theological College, Legon, Ghana, 20.-25.3.1998.
[45] Isabel Apawo Phiri, Oral Presentation, Malawi Circle, 13.7.2006.

Chapter 3: Local Chapters and the Growth of the Circle (1989 – 2017)

The analysis of the growth of the Circle in Africa is restricted to the Anglophone region for the reason that I was not able to use sources related to the Francophone and Lusophone Circles because of the language barrier. Further, some Anglophone countries are covered more in depth than others. This is mainly because some countries have more active Circle chapters than others, and those which are more active have more easily found a place in this book. However, this story has also given space to countries where the growth of the Circle is limited. It is clear that penetration of the Circle into other African countries was influenced by many factors and that these factors cannot be generalized to all countries. Thus, this book includes in chapter 4 a detailed analysis of one local chapter, Malawi.

It cannot be denied that the achievements between 1989 and 1996 in the development by the Circle were shaped by "the sustainable effort to discover and cultivate African women doing theology" by Mercy Amba Oduyoye and also through collaborative efforts of some members of the International Planning Committee (IPC) and those that were convened at the Convocation. Some of the members at the IPC became less active in the Circle after the Convocation and delayed the spread of the Circle to countries of their origin. One of such members is Betty Ekeya, who is currently in the USA. She was a former Catholic nun by the time she attended the Convocation.[1]

However, not all women became actively involved in the Circle after the Convocation. This was against the vision of the 1989 Convocation:

> So, for the moment the most important task is to get a couple of people who will make things happen in the countries represented here. There is no need to found a new association at home, but it is important to get a women's caucus of whatever existing Theological Association you belong to. Those who do not belong to any association, but would like to do their theology in community need to seek out our sisters and work together as a Circle of Concerned Women Theologians. Those who find themselves working or

---

[1] Int Sr NN, 15.7.2005.

studying abroad should seek out and assist one another as well as make approaches to women of African descent who are doing theology.[2]

The fact that some women did not go back home to make things happen is seen in the history of the local chapters in different countries represented at the Convocation. However, even though not all women that attended the Convocation started a Circle Chapter in their countries of influence, Mercy, with many other sisters, established local circles in different countries of Africa.[3] This was possible because the Circle is an African network and does not restrict the organization of the Circle chapters within a country to members of the Circle in that country alone. There is room that Circle women open chapters in countries that are not their own.[4] Brigalia Bam was also a member of the International Planning Committee and understandably inspired the early genesis of the Circle in her country of origin. As regards Zaire, Sr Mbuy-Beya, also a member of the IPC, came from Zaire and inspired the genesis of the Circle there.

There are many factors that influenced those that attended the 1989 Convocation to start the Circle. It is interesting that the representation at the Convocation also tallies with the speed at which local chapters were established in different countries. The countries that were more represented started chapters earlier. Indeed, the first countries to set up local chapters after the 1989 Convocation were Nigeria, Ghana, Kenya, South Africa and Zaire.[5] These had been established by the year 1990.[6] The first reason for this was that the particular countries had a reasonable number of women that could start the ball rolling. Another factor was progress in theological education.

---

[2] See Mercy Amba Oduyoye and Musimbi Kanyoro (eds), *Talitha Qumi. Proceedings of the Convocation of African Women Theologians 1989*, Accra-North: Sam Woode, 2001, p. 21.

[3] See Mercy Amba Oduyoye, *Introducing African Women's Theology*, Sheffield Academic Press, 2001, p. 7.

[4] This agrees well with the fact that Isabel Apawo Phiri opened Circle chapters in South Africa though she comes from Malawi. More details in the later chapters.

[5] Document, 1996 Institute of African Women in Religion and Culture History, accessed 14.9.2005.

[6] Ibid.

Ghana

In Ghana, where the first local chapter was established at Accra, soon after the 1989 Convocation, the presence of a good number of educated women played a role in establishing the Circle. The first Coordinator of this Chapter was Rachel Tetteh. The participants at this local chapter were mainly secondary school teachers apart from women from the churches within Ghana who were mainly invited by Rachel Tetteh. The Circle met regularly at the Methodist headquarters in Accra.

Some of the first women that belonged to this chapter were Rabiatu Ammah and Elizabeth Amoah. When Rachel Tetteh passed away, the Accra chapter stopped functioning as a chapter of its own. The members did not meet as regularly as before.[7] However, it is the establishment of the Institute of Women in Religion and Culture that has made a profound contribution to the development of the Circle in Ghana and Nigeria.

Nigeria

By 1996, the Nigeria Chapter continued to blossom. The women were very much ahead in creating theologies of transformation because of the presence of Sr Rosemary Edet, who was also a co-founder of the Circle as a member of the IPC. By 2002, at the close of this period, not only was there an increase in membership of women in the Nigeria Circle, but also an increase in the number of local chapters as well as in the momentum to publish.

The State of Local Chapters in Nigeria

Nigerian women were the first to construct a local chapter after the Convocation. The Circle at this stage was well organized and even had a designed letterhead and a stamp.[8]

---

[7] Ghana chapter is about the activities of the Institute of Religion and Culture at the Trinity Theological Seminary. The Theological Seminary accommodated them till later, when the Institute felt there was need to construct a facility to house the Institute. Comment, Mercy Amba Oduyoye, Malaka-le Theologies, 12.7.2005.

[8] Comment by Mercy Amba Oduyoye, Malaka-le Theologies Conference, 14.7.2005.

Some of the notable women in the Circle in the later years come from Nigeria. Dorcas Akintunde, who became the Anglophone coordinator of the Circle at the 2002 Continental Conference, belongs to this chapter. So, does Margaret Umeagudosu who has led and established other local chapters in Nigeria. Her continued influence is seen in the part she played in Zonal and Circle meetings.

The Ibadan Chapter

The Ibadan Chapter pays tribute to Mercy Amba Oduyoye who revived the chapter when it was losing momentum. Mercy Amba Oduyoye came in 2000 to encourage the women to be involved in the Circle. This meeting took place at the Institute of Church and Society in Ibadan. About 17 women attended. Among them were Shadetaiwo and Kikeedewor, who were very keen about the Circle. Most of the participants were in some kind of ministerial work. Kikeedewor was not a trained theologian but a teacher and a business woman then.[9] These earlier women invited friends such as Ruth Oluwakemi Oke and Helen Labedeodan Adekunbi who joined the chapter in 2000. Her interest in the Circle is to research and write about women's issues. Helen Labedeodan Adekunbi's work has made significant contributions to the discipline of biblical reinterpretation in the Circle.

The Benin and Abuja Chapters

The Benin Chapter came from Ibadan Chapter. Mercy Idumwonyin lead this chapter. The third chapter in Nigeria was the Abuja Chapter in Abuja Federal Capital Territory which was not well developed at that time. Although different leaders lead these Circles, Margaret Umeagudosu is the founder of Abuja, Nsukka and Benin chapters. Margaret Umeagudosu invited women to the Circle through public lectures at church women's meetings organized by different churches.

Kenya

In the beginning Tanzania, Kenya and Uganda formed one chapter. Naturally these countries have much in common. Swahili, though most spoken in Tanzania and Kenya, is also a language known to many of the Ugandans.

---

[9] Ibid.

Notwithstanding the notion that there were not many African women theologians in these countries so as to deserve local country chapters, it was really the feeling of oneness that made them form a joint chapter in the beginning. The woman that led the East African Chapter was Sr Annie Nasimiyu from Kenya. She was also a member of EATWOT at that time.[10] The formation of local country chapters in East Africa was also challenged in the beginning because of factors that are unveiled in the discussion of each East African country below.

The local chapter in Kenya is one of the successful stories of Circle chapters in Africa. This is partly due to Kenya's progress in theological training. Women study theology in Kenya through a variety of openings. Some go to secular universities such as Kenyatta University, while others go to interdenominational theological colleges such as Daystar where denominational policies regarding theological training for women do not play a role. A few go through Church led theological institutions, which are more restrictive. One of the prominent theological colleges led by the church is St Paul's Theological Seminary in Limuru, Kenya.[11] The rise in theological training for women in Kenya as opposed to other countries in East Africa is due to an early rise in literacy levels in this region, much above literacy levels in other countries. These high literacy levels are evidenced even in the fact that more Kenya women have enjoyed privileged positions in the Ecumenical bodies abroad than women from other countries in East Africa. Musimbi Kanyoro and Nyambura Njoroge for example worked in such Ecumenical bodies. It is also not surprising that a Kenyan, Musimbi Kanyoro, became the Coordinator of the Circle after Mercy Amba Oduyoye. Further, because of pronounced theological training for women in Kenya, Kenya is more established than other local chapters in East Africa. This can be seen in its leadership in fulfilling goals of the Circle, number of chapters in Kenya, but also in the presence of Kenya Women Theologians at wider Circle meetings, whether regional or continental meetings since the Convocation in 1989.

The Kenya chapter also benefited from the fact that Musimbi Kanyoro was a close friend of the Coordinator of the Circle, Mercy Amba Oduyoye. Nyambura Njoroge, who has achieved much in promoting women in

---

[10] Int Sr Annie Nasimiyu, Kempton Park, South Africa, 14.7.2005.

[11] It is now called St Paul's University, www.spu.ac.ke.

ministerial formation, comes from Kenya. The Kenya Chapter was not only organized soon after the Convocation, but also had become more established already by 1996. Indicators that back up the argument that the Kenya local Chapter was more established by 1996, can be seen firstly in its leadership in the East Africa Zonal meetings that will be discussed later, secondly in the number of chapters in Kenya by 1996, but also in the presence of Kenyan Women Theologians at the 1996 continental meeting.

It should be recalled that at the 1989 Convocation the number of delegates from Kenya was second to those from the host country Ghana. Apart from other advantages that Kenya had in establishing the Circle as shown earlier, the presence of women belonging to EATWOT also becomes significant. Women that belonged to EATWOT found the agenda of transformation through the Circle not difficult to grasp, because they were already accustomed to doing this kind of theology.

Notable Circle women in Kenya during this initial period 1989-1996 that belonged to EATWOT were the likes of Hannah Kinoti.[12] She is remembered for promoting many Kenyan women to study religion at Kenyatta University, especially encouraging women to research, write and publish on women's issues. "Hannah was a very hard-working person who dedicated her life to helping students to achieve academic excellence."[13] Indeed, those that followed Hannah Kinoti continue to be women that influence others to have a theology of transformation. One of her students was Constance Ambasa Shishanga who also became a lecturer in the same Department of Religions and Culture at Kenyatta University.[14] Hannah Kinoti was a highly motivated Professor in the Department of Religion and Culture at Kenyatta University. Her other contribution to the Circle is that at the time the Circle was organizing local chapters in Kenya, she was the chairperson of the Department of Religion and Culture at Kenyatta University, the home of one

---

[12] She wrote the foreword for Musimbi Kanyoro and Nyambura Njoroge (eds), *Groaning in Faith: African Women in the Household of God*, Nairobi: Acton, 1996.

[13] Constance Ambasa Shisanya, "Professor Hannah Wangeci Kinoti: Your Seeds are Germinating in Kenya," in Isabel Apawo Phiri, Devakarsham Betty Govinden and Sarojini Nadar (eds), *Her–stories: Hidden Stories of Women of Faith in Africa*, Pietermaritzburg: Cluster, 2002, pp. 327-345 [333].

[14] Isabel Apawo Phiri, Devakarsham Betty Govinden, and Sarojini Nadar (eds), *Her-stories: Hidden Histories of Women of Faith in Africa*, Pietermaritzburg: Cluster 2002, p. x.

Kenya chapter. She held this position for 6 years from 1990 to 1996.[15] Hannah Kinoti is one of the few African women theologians that earned their PhDs well before the establishment of the Circle.[16] Hannah Kinoti attained her PhD in 1983.[17]

Theological training is vital in the agenda of research and writing that is the hub of the Circle. Esther Mombo, the master mind behind the Limuru Chapter, which is based at St Paul's Theological Seminary there, also belonged to EATWOT. Mary Getui Nyanchama, who played a major role in organizing the 1996 Continental Convocation, and Philomena Njeri, a prolific researcher,[18] are both members of EATWOT Women's Commission. In this commission Philomena Njeri is not only a member but she has chaired it for five years. The advantage of belonging to this work is that they were already familiar with theologies of liberation, which are in line with theologies of the Circle. Sr Annie Nasimiyu, who led the East Africa Chapter, was also a member of the Kenya Chapter and of EATWOT. The advantage of belonging to EATWOT shared by Kenya women would not have been there if women in Kenya had had limited access to further education. Belonging to EATWOT was advantageous in that these women could easily belong to the Circle since they were already abreast with theological research and writing through their involvement with EATWOT. Contact with other winds of transformation through EATWOT was also clear. These women did theology together with women from other Third World countries that were also in the process of

---

[15] Isabel Apawo Phiri, Devakarsham Betty Govinden and Sarojini Nadar (eds), *Her-stories: Hidden Stories of Women of Faith in Africa,* Pietermaritzburg: Cluster, 2002, p. 335. – Hannah Kinoti was born on 1 August 1941 in Nyeri District in the Central Province of Kenya. She died on 30th April in 2001.

[16] Constance Ambasa Shisanya, "Professor Hannah Wangeci Kinoti: Your Seeds are Germinating in Kenya," in Isabel Apawo Phiri, Devakarsham Betty Govinden and Sarojini Nadar (eds), *Her-stories: Hidden Stories of Women of Faith in Africa:* Pietermaritzburg, Cluster, 2002, pp. 327-347 [333].

[17] Hannah Wangeci Kinoti, "Aspects of Gikuyu Traditional Morality," PhD, University of Nairobi, 1983. Hannah Kinoti earned her BA at Makerere, where Prof Noel Q. King was Professor, having moved there from Legon.

[18] See for example Philomena Njeri Mwaura, "Women's Healing Roles in Traditional Gikuyu Society", in Musimbi Kanyoro and Nyambura Njoroge (eds), *Groaning in Faith: African Women in the Household of God,* Nairobi: Acton, 1996, pp. 253-269.

transforming gender inequalities. Kenya was more represented in EATWOT probably because one of the EATWOT meetings took place in Nairobi.

In Kenya, there are two main local chapters that were established by 1996, Kenyatta University and Limuru. The members of the Circle discussed here are those that come from Kenyatta University. This does not mean that it is the more powerful one, but that I was not privileged to meet members of the Limuru Circle, with the exception of Esther Mombo, who has been mentioned in the earlier paragraphs. One of the notable activities of transformation established through the Limuru chapter is promoting women in theological training and ministerial formation for women. This is where the achievements of Nyambura Njoroge cannot be underestimated. She has established a library to promote women's issues there and has also run seminars for women ministers to empower them further in ministry.

Even though there is a well-established Circle in Kenya, Circle women continue to face the challenge of reaching out to women from the Evangelical interdenominational colleges. These are women who belong to interdenominational colleges such as the Nairobi Evangelical Graduate School of Theology (NEGST),[19] Nairobi International School of Theology (NIST) and Daystar University, who need to be sensitized in other ways of reading their Bible, culture, and Church tradition in such a way that men's theologizing that promotes women's submission and suppression are transformed to liberate these women. This is possible as already a minority from such Evangelical colleges have started trickling into the Circle. Mary Mumo is one of such recent Circle members in Kenya coming from an Evangelical College. She is a lecturer in Old Testament at Nairobi International School of Theology (NIST). Her journey in theological training and ministry is a typical story of women from the Evangelical churches in Kenya.[20]

The Circle also has a task to transform theologies that suppress women in ministerial formation. In the Anglican Church, there was a lag in accepting women to serve in the same capacity as their fellow male students, even if they graduated from the same college in the same class and course. Often the women were ordained to be deacons and not full ministers. This is

---

[19] Now named Africa International University.

[20] Int Mary Mumo, Nairobi International School of Theology, 8.2005.

changing in some dioceses of the Anglican Church after an active promotion of ordination of women to the position of ministers by some bishops.[21]

Histories of some Circle women in the Kenya chapter are interesting. Mary Getui played a major role in organizing the 1996 Continental Conference as a member of the local committee and she also helped in organizing the Southern and East African Zonal meeting in 1994. For the 1996 Continental Conference she was the chairperson of the local committee. It was very handy for her at this time to serve in this role because she was the Head of the Religious Department at Kenyatta University. She had taken over from Hannah Kinoti since headship in this department follows a rotation system where one can only serve for a specific term. Mary Getui's role in the Circle has been broad. Apart from being a seasoned researcher and writer, she was elected as coordinator of the Kenyatta University Circle after Sr Annie Nasimiyu stepped down in 1992.[22] As a Circle member, she has edited books such as *Violence against Women*,[23] which came out in 1996, as well as one on *Conflicts in Africa*.[24]

Mary Getui is another woman from an Evangelical church that joined the Circle during this period. In the beginning of the Circle it has been observed that the majority of women came from mainline/classical churches. Women from Evangelical churches are late arrivals. One of such women is Mary Getui. She joined the Circle soon after the 1989 Convocation. By that time, she was already a member of Kenyatta University. It is clear that Mary Getui was among the first Circle women in Kenya that Nasimiyu recruited in the years 1989 to 1992. This was at the time when Kenya, Uganda and Tanzania belonged to one chapter, as there were too few women theologians in these countries at this time to warrant separate chapters.[25] However, different from Mary Tusuubira, who traces her Evangelicalism from an Ecumenical Evangelical Church (Low Church Anglican), Mary Getui comes from the

---

[21] Int Circle women in ministerial formation, Addis Ababa, 2002.

[22] Int Constance Ambasa Shisanya, Circle meeting, 13.7.2005.

[23] Grace Wamue and Mary Getui (eds), *Violence against Women: Reflection by Kenyan Woman Theologians*, Nairobi: Acton, 1996.

[24] Mary Getui and Hazel Ayanga (eds), *Conflicts in Africa: A Women Response*: Nairobi: Circle of Concerned African Women Theologians, 2002.

[25] Int Sr Annie Nasimiyu, Circle Conference, Kempton Park, 13.7.2005.

Seventh-day Adventist Church which belongs to the denominations that are classified as Evangelical. These are churches that arose from Postclassical Missions and are widely treated as Evangelical.[26] On the other hand Mary Getui is an example of Evangelical Ecumenical women in the Circle. Although she hails from a church that is historically classified as an Evangelical denomination, she shares much with Ecumenical Christianity. Firstly, she joined the Circle at the inspiration by women from the Ecumenical churches: Mercy Amba Oduyoye and also a Catholic Sister, Sr Annie Nasimiyu. Definitely, if she held onto the conservative Evangelical leanings of her denomination, she would have treated the invitation to the Circle by these women as unwelcome. Mary Getui has been a close ally of Mercy for a long time to the extent that they know each others' family members and visit each others' families. Mary Getui has learnt much from Mercy Amba Oduyoye about the Circle. Mary Getui easily identified with Sr Annie Nasimiyu in many ways, as she belonged together with her to EATWOT. Again, they share a common ground as lecturers at Kenyatta University. With this background, Mary was better prepared to structure the Circle from an academic point of view rather than from a religious point of view. Here Mary Getui's Evangelical-Ecumenical leaning is also visible in her involvement with Ecumenical bodies such as WCC and EATWOT. With these organizations, she has been involved in seminars and even published with them.[27]

Kenya is one of the countries that did research and writing at country level. The Kenya Circle did its own project on Women and Culture, which focused on violence against women.[28] In fact, just as Kenya was leader in the East Africa Chapter, it also became the first chapter to publish research papers. Further, the Kenya Chapter became central in the genesis of country chapters in other East African countries.

---

[26] For the sequence of revivals and the consequence on missions see Klaus Fiedler, *The Story of Faith Missions. From Hudson Taylor to Present Day Africa*, Oxford et al: Regnum, ²1995, pp. 11-31. The mainline churches of Africa almost all go back to the earlier revival, the Great Awakening (1734/1792) which produced the classical missions. – For a more recent version of the same concept see: Klaus Fiedler, *Missions as the Theology of the Church. An Argument from Malawi*, Mzuzu: Mzuni Press, 2015, pp. 18-41.

[27] For an example of such publications, see: Mary Getui, "Africa, Church and Theology: Do they Need Each Other?" *Ministerial Formation,* January 1999.

[28] Document, 1996 Institute of African Women in Religion and Culture History.

Tanzania

The Tanzania chapter had a slow start. After being part of the East Africa chapter, it struggled to establish its own chapter. One of the reasons why Tanzania has had a slow start in establishing a chapter is the Evangelicalism factor. The majority of women belonged to the Lutheran Church that held ideas which suppressed women. The other factor is that since the majority of women theologians that came to the Circle meeting were from one church, this took away the steam to meet as a research and writing group. Instead there was a glowing sense of church fellowship, far from the Circle's intentions of building a chapter.

By 2002 this chapter was not active. However, there have been efforts to strengthen the local Circle. In 2002, a research was done by Nyambura Njoroge concerning women in theology. The agenda of the Tanzania Circle for the coming years is to start working with issues that are pertinent to violence against women, HIV/AIDS and counselling. They also are working on having an annotated bibliography of literature by women on women. The project was scheduled to finish in the year 2004. Tanzania women are also working hard on upgrading studies of women in the country so that they can have a stronger Circle. One of the women that have progressed in postgraduate studies is Blandina Sawayael. She has since returned to Tanzania.

Uganda

The situation in Uganda was similar to Tanzania in terms of establishing a local chapter, because the first core group was mainly church ministers from the Anglican Church.[29] This presented a challenge to function as a Circle with objectives beyond just being a "fellowship" of one church. The Circle started with 23 women, but because of the element of fellowship among the dominant group, with time some women began to stay away. If the Circle in Uganda on the other hand had more focussed on the academic objectives of the Circle (research, writing and publishing), such marginalization as the Catholic women faced would not have happened. At the heart of this marginalization was also an aspect of Evangelical conservatism that likely influenced Anglican women in the Circle then. The Anglican Church in Uganda

---

[29] Int Circle woman from Uganda, Kempton Park, 12.7.2005.

has been part of the Anglican Low Church Movement that shares conservative Evangelical leanings. In addition, the Ugandan Anglican women have, most likely, been influenced by the East African Revival, at that time spearheaded by Bishop Festo Kivengere, an Anglican Archbishop himself. This Evangelical tendency seems to have contributed to the slow development of the Circle in Uganda, since the pioneer Circle women had belonged to an ecumenical movement. The Evangelical and Ecumenical movements have a history of contradictions in matters of theological interpretation, the former being conscious of the "liberal" interpretations of the latter.[30] Though the differentiation between Evangelical and Ecumenical is real and important, there is also much cooperation and overlap, and there can be no clear delimitation.

One of the early members of the Circle in Uganda was Grace Nyabaika.[31] She attended the 1989 Convocation with Mabel Katahweire who at the time of the Convocation lived in Mukono. After this conference Mabel Katahweire has remained silent. The Circle dwindled and was only restarted in Kampala in 1996 by Sr Teresa, after she had met Mercy Amba Oduyoye.[32] This was after belonging to the East Africa Circle under Sr. Nasimiyu.[33] Even though Uganda did not start with a big bang in forming the Circle, the IPC invited many women from Uganda to attend the Convocation. In fact, in 1980 the largest list of women theologians came from Makerere University.[34] Soon after the Convocation, the Uganda women who attended the Circle belonged to the East Africa chapter under Sr. Nasimiyu. After the Circle gained its autonomy, Ugandan women coordinated the chapter.

The shying away of non-Anglican women from the Circle in Uganda related more likely to the 'Evangelicalism factor' mentioned above. Churches in Uganda had become more Evangelical in practice including the Roman Catholic Church. In this environment, to belong to the Circle, which was a

---

[30] This dichotomy resulted in the formation of the Association of Evangelicals in Africa as different from the All Africa Conference of Churches, both based in Nairobi.

[31] Int Circle woman from Uganda, Kempton Park, 12.7.2005.

[32] Int Sr Teresa, Kempton Park, 12.7.2005.

[33] Int Sr Annie Nasimiyu, Kempton Park, 12.7.2005.

[34] Int Circle woman from Uganda, Kempton Park, 12.7.2005.

gender group, could not easily be accepted.[35] The position of women was much restricted by policies that were informed by Evangelical enthusiasm. A case in point is the experience of women in the Anglican Church. Mary Tusuubira (neé Mary Barongo) struggled to become a pastor in the Anglican Church. Though she shares an Evangelical leaning, this did not distract her from seeking a transformation of gender inequalities in her church.[36] Because of its Evangelical leanings her church was not open to ordaining women as ministers of the Word and Sacrament. Therefore, her ministerial position was met with many obstacles. Her life depicts the picture of so many African women theologians, especially from an Evangelical background, that remain aflame for God's work but are relegated to the background because of patriarchy engineered by a literalistic and thereby wrong reading of Scripture and culture.

The Uganda Circle grew when Mercy Amba Oduyoye procured scholarships for some Evangelical women to study for higher theological degrees. In the case of Mary Tusuubira's theological training, she was the one that obtained a scholarship for her to do post graduate studies. Increasing opportunities of Evangelical women to do higher theological training was already envisioned by Mercy Amba Oduyoye as a solution to transforming the deep-rooted gender inequalities among Evangelical women. With increased theological training, they would read the Bible with a fresh look. In the undergraduate courses, Evangelical women are mainly exposed to theologies that are deliberately tailored to their church's policies including those that promote women's unequal access to ministry in the church.

By 2002, the Circle in Uganda was not very active. The reason that has contributed to the decline is related to leadership and the composition of the first core group of the Uganda Circle. Due to the fact that women who could lead the Circle had gone abroad to access higher education, the Circle in Uganda had been weakened.

---

[35] Int Ugandan man, Kampala, 28.4.2006.

[36] Though Evangelicalism often objected to women's ordained ministry, since its beginnings it has had branches that promoted the full inclusion of women into ministry. A prominent example here is the Salvation Army which never made distinctions. The first General was a man, the second a woman.

The Circle in Uganda has these goals: to invite women to become members of the Circle; to look into issues of HIV/AIDS; to encourage publication of books on women by women; to network with the Ministry of Gender and women's organizations; to start fund raising for the Circle.[37] By 2005, Uganda had experienced a sudden rise of Circle members as women, who went for further studies, had returned to their countries.

Zambia

The local chapter in Zambia traces its origin to Juliet Matembo, Omega Bula, and Rev Peggy Mulambya Kabonde.[38] They were all members of the United Church of Zambia. Rev Kabonde recalls the time she joined the Circle in 1989, that she was a very young lady. At that time, she had a Diploma in Theology from the United Church of Zambia Theological College. Among them it was Peggy Mulambya Kabonde who presented a paper at the Convocation. Her paper was entitled "Single Women Parents in Africa."[39] In her presentation she demonstrated a good knowledge of how this social problem is being dealt with in the Western World. She refers in her work to Denmark, Norway, Sweden, England and so forth. Her main concept of transformation is that all culture-dictated stereotypes of male/female should be challenged and that everyone including women and all that are at the fringe: children, sinners, the poor should have full dignity as Jesus showed in His ministry and life.

The story of the Circle in Zambia shows that it has struggled in its beginnings for the reason that many of the pioneers of the Circle were not academics. They were mainly involved in the practical life of the church. These positions did not inspire them to research and write. Rev Peggy is an exception to this trend. Although at the time of the Convocation she had just started her work in the church, she was already interested in researching and writing.[40] Being involved in the Circle at this early stage, according to her, shaped her position

---

[37] Focus Group Presentation, 2002 Circle Conference, Johannesburg, South Africa.

[38] Focus Group, Rev Peggy Mulambya Kabonde and Lilian, Malaka-le Theologies, 14.7.2005.

[39] Peggy Mulambya Kabanda, "Single Women Parents in Africa," in Mercy Amba Oduyoye, and Musimbi Kanyoro, *Talitha Qumi, Proceedings of the Convocation of African Women Theologians 1989,* Accra-North: Sam-Woode, 2001, pp. 183-191.

[40] She has an important position in the church. At the time of my interview, she was the minister of a large congregation in Ndola, Zambia. In addition to this role, she is a part time lecturer in Ndola, Copper Belt.

in the church but also helped her to write and publish. Already in the early stages of the Circle in Zambia, she wrote articles in *Groaning in Faith* and *Talitha Qumi*. She also has one in *AMKA*. Another member of the Zambia Circle is Omega Bula. By 2000 she worked with the United Church of Canada on secondment. Before this she worked at Mindolo Ecumenical Foundation. She is a social worker by profession. Rev Juliet Matembo is one of the few women in Zambia who teach theology. She comes from the Southern Province. She is a Tonga and she is now a lecturer at the United Church of Zambia Theological College.

The Zambia local chapter was established in 1990. This first meeting was attended by highly influential women. Among them was Rev Sampa Bredt, the General Secretary of the Christian Council of Zambia.[41] The stability of the local chapter in the beginning was troubled by migration of Circle women to other countries for further studies. However, those that were in the country still kept the Circle alive at individual level. Those that went abroad continued to be committed to the Circle objectives wherever they went.[42]

Though the stability of the local chapter has been troubled by migration of Circle women to other countries for further studies, the local chapter is still alive as Zambia women belonging to the Circle continue to be committed to the Circle objectives wherever they go. A few women in the country decided to call a national meeting in 2007 to look at how to work in the coming years.[43] In the earlier years there was also an attempt to strengthen Malawi and Zambia local chapters through a cooperate project with Malawi, which had also lost its Circle leaders to further studies abroad. Key women leaders of the Malawi chapter who went abroad for further studies included Isabel Phiri and Fulata Moyo.

By 2005, the Zambian Circle had more new members. Lilian Siwila and Kuzipa Nalwamba were among them. The fact that more women were joining the Circle shows that the Zambia Local Chapter had potential to grow. Other women in the Circle included: Mabel Kafwamba, who was a student at the

---

[41] The second Circle meeting took place in Kitwe in 1997 and only four women attended. Focus Group, Rev Peggy Mulambya Kabonde and Lilian Siwila, Malaka-le Theologies, 14.7.2005.

[42] Anecdotal comment, Rev Peggy Mulambya, Malaka-le Conference, 14.7.2005.

[43] Ibid.

United Church of Zambia College, Rev Jane Nyirongo, Mrs Kafwimbi from a Pentecostal church, Bridget Masayiti and Mary Mwiche teaching at an interdenominational Evangelical College. The Circle in Zambia had many members even though they were not all in Zambia at the same time because of going abroad for further studies. Of all the Circle members in Zambia, Rev Peggy Mulambya Kabonde is the most articulate in the theologies of transforming gender inequalities in the era of HIV/AIDS. Related to Zambia is the Circle in neighbouring Malawi, which is treated in detail in Chapter Three.

South Africa

The history of the Circle in Southern Africa begins with Mercy Amba Oduyoye's longtime friend, Brigalia Bam from South Africa, who started the National Circle in 1991 after the Convocation. She was at this time the General Secretary of the South African Christian Council.[44] The participants came from both black and white communities. Brigalia Bam's attempts to develop local chapters were short lived because she concentrated much on empowering women in the secular society as young politicians. This is why, in the later years, she has not been involved in developing local chapters in South Africa. Her work in politics is classic in transforming gender inequalities in South Africa.

After attempts by Brigalia Bam to start local chapters in South Africa in the earlier period, Isabel Apawo Phiri,[45] who was a sojourner in South Africa, continued to develop local chapters there. She started this exercise when she was in the Cape Town Chapter, being a PhD student at the University of Cape Town.[46]

---

[44] Isabel Apawo Phiri, "African Women's Theologies in the New Millennium," *Agenda* 61, 2004, p. 18.

[45] Ibid.

[46] Isabel Apawo Phiri, "Stand up and be Counted. Identity, Spirituality and Theological Education in my Faith Journey," in Denise M. Ackermann et al (eds), *Claiming our Footprints. South African Women Reflect on Context, Identity and Spirituality,* Matieland: EFSA Institute of Theological and Interdisciplinary Research, 2000, p. 152. – Her thesis has been published as Isabel Apawo Phiri, *Women, Presbyterianism and Patriarchy. Religious Experience of Chewa Women in Central Malawi*, Blantyre: CLAIM-Kachere, 2000 (1997).

According to Denise Ackermann, the Cape Town Chapter of the Circle was formed on the 6th March of 1992.[47] The Cape Town Chapter was inter-religious even during this early period. There were Jewish women, Muslim women, Hindu women as well as Christian women.[48] Najma Moosa is a Muslim theologian that became member of this Circle. She had paternal grandparents who hailed from India. Her family comes from the Kanam ethnic group, who speak Gujarati.[49] The watershed to women doing theology in South Africa came way before the establishment of the Circle. This is because South Africa was earlier on influenced by Black Theology. The main concern of Black theology was not to deny the value of the African Independence, but its main concern was with the black people in South Africa, who were denied government - a minority which itself also claims to be Christian. For Black Theology, liberation is not simply a matter of the saving of the soul: rather salvation is the liberation of the whole person from all the forces which oppress and exploit, so that people may be free to be truly human in the way that God intends them to be.[50]

Indeed, a conference on Black Theology was held in 1984 in Cape Town. At this conference, women remarked that women were oppressed in church and society and that Black Theology should also take the liberation of women seriously.[51] The roots of Black Theology in South Africa were in the context of apartheid, the official policy of the South African government from 1947 to 1994.[52]

---

[47] Denise M. Ackermann, "Claiming our Footprints. Introductory Reflections," in Denise M. Ackermann, Eliza Getman et al (eds), *Claiming our Footprints. South African Women Reflect on Context, Identity and Spirituality,* Matieland: EFSA Institute of Theological and Interdisciplinary Research, 2000, pp. 5-15 [6].

[48] Ibid.

[49] Najma Moosa, "The Flying Hadji," in Denise M. Ackermann et al (eds), *Claiming Our Footprints. South African Women Reflect on Context, Identity and Spirituality,* Matieland: EFSA Institute of Theological and Interdisciplinary Research, 2000, p. 98.

[50] John Parratt (ed), *A Reader in Christian Theology,* London: SPCK 1987, p. 7.

[51] Isabel Apawo Phiri, "African Women's Theologies in the New Millennium," *Agenda* 61, 2004, p. 17.

[52] Isabel Apawo Phiri, "Healing from the Traumas of Crime in South Africa: Interaction of African Religion with Christianity as Perceived by African Female Traditional Healers" in *The Lutheran Federation,* 2005, p. 25.

Although Isabel Apawo Phiri does not come from South Africa, she started most of the existing Circle chapters in the South. She started the Namibia Chapter, Pietermaritzburg Chapter, Durban Chapter, as well as the KwaZulu Natal Chapter in addition to the Cape Town chapter she had started in the earlier period.

The Durban Chapter

From Namibia, Isabel Apawo Phiri went to Durban in August 1997.[53] Here she launched the local chapter in 1998. It became a vibrant chapter and at one time 200 women belonged to it. During this time, Isabel Apawo Phiri was professor at the University of Durban-Westville and Director of the Centre for Constructive Theology. Her involvement with the University and the Centre for Constructive Theology gave her the opportunity to write on current experiences of women and girls as will be seen in the following chapters.

Cape Town Chapter

The Cape Town Chapter continued even during this period. Since the beginnings of this chapter members have come and gone. By 2000, regular membership at Cape Town Chapter was 17 women.[54] The chapter at this stage was still inter-religious, being composed of Muslim, Hindu, Jewish and Christian women. Sarojini Nadar, who later on becomes a right-hand woman of Isabel Apawo Phiri during her time as Continental Circle Coordinator was also a member of the Cape Town Chapter at this time. Sarojini Nadar describes herself as a fourth generation South African Indian. Her parents converted from Hinduism to Christianity when she was only two or three months old.[55] Isabel Apawo Phiri had started this chapter with the help of

---

[53] Isabel Apawo Phiri, "African Women's Theologies in the New Millennium," *Agenda* 61, 2004, p. 19.

[54] Denise M. Ackermann, "Claiming our Footprints. Introductory Reflections," in Denise M. Ackermann, Eliza Getman et al (eds), *Claiming Our Footprints. South African Women Reflect on Context, Identity and Spirituality*, Matieland: EFSA Institute of Theological and Interdisciplinary Research, 2000, p. 5-15 [6].

[55] Sarojini Nadar "Emerging from Muddy Waters. For the Man in My Life - My Inspiration to Soar," in Denise M. Ackermann, Eliza Getman et al (eds), *Claiming Our Footprints. South*

Denise Ackermann. When she moved from Cape Town, Denise Ackermann coordinated the Circle. She is a white South African and an Anglican. Apart from Denise Ackermann, Prof Elna Mouton is also instrumental in the life of the Circle during this time. She is a white South African from the Reformed tradition.

The context of South Africa is complex because South Africans outside the Academy (particularly women) live under the triple oppression of race, gender and class.[56] Black theology has limitations in that it has been unable to deal with the popular struggles of the black working class who are the most exploited.[57]

South African chapters are reflective of the multi-racial aspect of the Circle. Since apartheid was also cemented by religion, Circle women in South Africa face many challenges in writing theologies that will serve all women in this context. The reality is that of conflicting theologies.

Non-white Circle women feel white Circle women have enjoyed better positions in life, and participated in the oppression of others. In this, women from non-white ethnicities reinterpret the Bible with the view that colonial interpretations deployed by whites, who sought to oppress women of colour, must be unveiled. Such tensions are sometimes felt among South African women in the Circle and sometimes even verbalized.

The Circle in Cape Town continued to publish during this period. The first book to be published in this period was in 1997 "Claiming Our Footprints," which was edited by Denise Ackermann, Eliza Getman, Hantie Kotzé and Judy Tobler.[58] The chapter had published also: "After the Locusts: Letters from a

---

African Women Reflect on Context, Identity and Spirituality, Matieland: EFSA Institute of Theological and Interdisciplinary Research, 2000, pp. 15-31 [15-17].

[56] Sarojini Nadar, "Power, Ideology and Interpretation/s: Womanist and Literary Perspectives on the Book of Esther as Resources for Gender-Social Transformation," PhD, University of KwaZulu Natal, 2003, p. 2.

[57] Ibid., p. 3. Also see Itumeleng J. Mosala, *Biblical Hermeneutics and Black Theology in South Africa*, Grand Rapids: Eerdmans, 1989.

[58] Denise M. Ackermann, Eliza Getman et al (eds), *Claiming our Footprints. South African Women Reflect on Context, Identity and Spirituality,* Matieland: EFSA Institute of Theological and Interdisciplinary Research, 2000.

Landscape of Faith."[59] This was followed by yet another book by the time Isabel Apawo Phiri became Continental Coordinator. The book was edited by Azila Reisenberger. The title was "Women's Spirituality in the Transformation of South Africa." Denise Ackermann was the coordinator for the Cape Town Circle at this time when Isabel Apawo Phiri had left Cape Town.

Although Isabel Phiri started the Circle, Denise Ackermann has become the leading force of the Cape Town Chapter. Another African Women Theologian in this chapter who was actively involved is Prof Elna Mouton.

When I visited Cape Town in 2002, it was an exciting time to meet Prof Elna Mouton in her splendid office at the Presbyterian/Dutch Reformed Theological Faculty of Stellenbosch University. She was most delighted when she found that the aim of my visit was to talk to her as one of the African Women Theologians. She was grateful that even though she is a White South African, I had singled her out as an African Woman Theologian.[60] White African Women Theologians have sometimes felt alienated because of colour and religion. Prof Elna Mouton is probably one among many white South African women who feel alienated from the black African Women Theologians or vice versa. This is because Black African Women Theologians are predominant in the Circle. The other reason is that South Africa went through apartheid that alienated black, coloured and white South Africans from each other. A similar reaction was evident when I visited Denise Ackermann, a retired Professor at the University of Western Cape. She showed concern over the fact that she has been involved in the Circle for a long time, but was not told of the meeting on the Biographies of Women of Faith that was held in Johannesburg.

Other significant women involved in the Cape Town Chapter are Sarojini Nadar and Eliza Getman. Eliza Getman joined the Cape Town Chapter in 1998 while she was still a student at the University of Cape Town, doing her Master's in Religious Studies. Wilma Jacobson, an Anglican Minister, introduced her to the Circle. Wilma is one of the editors of "Women Hold Up

---

[59] Elna Mouton "After the Locusts: Letters from a Landscape of Faith," in Denise M. Ackermann et al (eds), *Claiming Our Footprints. South African Women Reflect on Context, Identity and Spirituality,* Matieland: EFSA Institute of Theological and Interdisciplinary Research, 2000.

[60] Int Prof Elna Mouton, Stellenbosch University, International Office.

Half the Sky."[61] Eliza Getman is an American married to a South African.[62] Thus she is a member of the Circle through marriage. She is committed to writing and publishing. She is also a grassroots person and is very much involved in her local congregation of the Anglican Church. She preaches on Sundays and helps with other duties within her church. She is also a seasoned editor and helped to edit one of the Circle books: "Claiming Our Footprints."[63]

By 2001, regular membership at Cape Town Chapter was about 20 women. Eliza Getman moved from Cape Town to Edinburgh where she met Olivia Nasaka, a Ugandan who is also a member of the Circle. Olivia Nasaka was doing her PhD then at the University of Edinburgh. Olivia is now back in Uganda and is an ordained minister of the Anglican Church.

Pietermaritzburg

Isabel Apawo Phiri launched the Pietermaritzburg Chapter in 2001.[64] The role of the Pietermaritzburg Chapter in the Circle is far reaching. Members of the Circle: Isabel Apawo Phiri, Devakarsham Betty Govinden and Sarojini Nadar have been involved in editing Circle books. One of such books is "Her-stories: Hidden Stories of Women of Faith."[65]

Eliza Getman joined the Pietermaritzburg Chapter in 2004. It was very encouraging for her to see some of the familiar faces at the chapter, such as Sarojini Nadar, whom she had known from the Cape Town Chapter.

Pietermaritzburg Chapter, by 2005, had around 40 members with about 50% attendance at most meetings of the local chapter. The chapter is very

---

[61] Denise M. Ackermann, J.A. Draper and E. Mashinini (eds), *Women Hold Up Half the Sky – Women in the Church in Southern Africa*, Pietermaritzburg: Cluster, 1991.

[62] Eliza Jane Getman, "Ground Cover" in Denise M. Ackermann et al (eds), *Claiming Our Footprints. South African Women Reflect on Context, Identity and Spirituality*, Matieland: EFSA Institute of Theological and Interdisciplinary Research, 2000, pp. 62-67.

[63] Denise Ackermann, Eliza Getman et al (eds), *Claiming Our Footprints. South African Women Reflect on Context, Identity and Spirituality*, Matieland: EFSA Institute of Theological and Interdisciplinary Research, 2000.

[64] Isabel Apawo Phiri, "African Women Theologies in the New Millennium," *Agenda* 61, p. 19.

[65] Isabel Apawo Phiri, Devakarsham Betty Govinden and Sarojini Nadar (eds), *Her-stories: Hidden Histories of Women of Faith in Africa*, Pietermaritzburg: Cluster, 2002.

creative in its form of leadership. It follows a rotational style of leadership where, every six months, new leaders are elected. The leadership team is made up of a coordinator and a secretary. Their effort to build strong relationships is shown, for example, in the way that they are able to organize a yearly celebration in the form of a dinner, towards which members of the Circle contribute. Some of the key players at the chapter in 2005 were Isabel Phiri, Beverly Haddad, Lilian Siwila, Sarojini Nadar and Fulata Moyo.

Mercy Amba Oduyoye was invited to this Circle and even planted a tree to commemorate the occasion. The chapter has had many projects such as being involved in engendered theological training. They even published a book titled: "In Her Name." The chapter tries to meet once a month, except during holidays of the University, since many members come from this neighbourhood. The chapter also has inter-Circle meetings. In 2005, their aim was to have a joint Circle project with the Cape Town Chapter.

Botswana

The local chapter in Botswana started only in 2003. Botswana's well-known African woman theologian Dr Musa Dube is one of the key Women Theologians on the continent of Africa. Though Musa Dube has become popular in the Circle, she was not one of the first participants at the International Planning Meeting or at the 1989 Convocation in Accra. Further no one from Botswana was at the Convocation meeting. Therefore, the message derived at the Convocation, where Women Theologians were challenged to start local and national chapters, could only have come to Botswana women indirectly. This goes a long way to explain the delay Botswana has experienced in organizing itself into a local Circle. At the 2002 Circle meeting, therefore, a Botswana woman, who was in attendance then, could only say that there was no local chapter in Botswana. "Only a year later was the Circle in Botswana organized." According to Musa Dube, the road to establishing a Circle in Botswana was important. She decided to embark on mentoring Botswana Women Theologians who could participate in the Circle. At this time, although there was no organized Circle in Botswana, Musa Dube was very active in researching and writing. Her contributions are found in several Circle books and other works in Africa and abroad.

According to Musa Dube, training is key to establishing the Circle. Musa Dube facilitated the beginning of the Circle at the end of 2003. When referring to her writing skill, she dates her dream to write not to her Circle involvement but to her early childhood years. She narrates that even in her primary school days she won a price for writing.[66] Her writing skills have been developed further through her teaching career at the University of Botswana. Her passion to write has been slightly different from many African Women Theologians. As a New Testament scholar, she was faced by the challenge that most New Testament books were written by white people and prescribed to Africans. To her, the conscientization to research and write was a political agenda: to make a contribution to books and scholarship that would not only be for Circle readership but also in-depth research and reading that would be referred to in NT scholarship beyond the borders of the Circle. Apart from New Testament scholarship, she has been widely involved in the fight against HIV/AIDS. In this fight, she has been able to utilize her New Testament scholarship to develop resources that would be used in the fight against the epidemic across Circle boundaries.

Thus, through the WCC, Musa Dube has been much involved in theological training, especially in constructing syllabi mainstreaming HIV/AIDS. Through this involvement she has influenced not only women but also men, especially in theological institutions.

Namibia

Isabel Apawo Phiri established a local chapter in Namibia between 1996 and 1997. She was then a lecturer at the University of Namibia. Women from the Lutheran Church were predominant in this chapter.[67] The progress of this chapter has been limited judging from the participation of Namibian women at regional and study commission conferences. The factors that have led to a low vitality of the chapter in Namibia are highlighted in the testimony by one member of the Namibian Circle. She argues that the departure of Isabel Apawo Phiri left them without one who could really develop the Circle. The second reason is that although there are many women who consider themselves Circle members, they find the goal of the Circle, which is research and writing, a challenge. The last reason given was that some women feel

---

[66] Int Musa Dube, 2005.

[67] Int Isabel Apawo Phiri, Kempton Park, 14.7.2005.

they like to meet as a group and share about their ministry experiences rather than writing for publication.[68]

State of Chapters and Leadership

There is a remarkable picture showing the developments of local or country chapters under different leadership over the years. This pattern shows an increase in the number of chapters during the period of Mercy Amba Oduyoye and a decrease in the vitality of some of the local chapters organized earlier, but then a wave of new local chapters during Musimbi Kanyoro's period, some of which had collapsed by the time Isabel Apawo Phiri became Continental Coordinator. Yet even then new local chapters continued to develop. There were many contributing factors to this. The task of this section is to show this remarkable pattern and suggest possible reasons as to how local chapters at different times were positively or negatively affected. A recap of the developments of the Circle will show that during the reign of Mercy Amba Oduyoye local chapters were many. The earliest are those already pointed out: Ghana, Nigeria, South Africa, and Kenya. Of course, at this earlier period Kenya was with Uganda and Tanzania part of East Africa because of the limited number of African women theologians then. This was in the years from 1989, after the Convocation, to 1992. After 1992, more local chapters were developed. Zambia, Malawi and Zimbabwe chapters are examples of those organized between 1992 and 1994.

During the period after Musimbi Kanyoro became continental coordinator, some of the earlier chapters organized in the first phase began to lose vitality and some even stopped being operational. These were the Tanzania, Uganda, Zimbabwe and Zambia chapters, because of reasons already shown. Surprisingly, even though some chapters became non-functional, there were new chapters that got organized during this period. These were the Namibia Chapter, which started in 1996, the Durban chapter, which organized itself in 1997 and the KwaZulu Natal chapter in 2001. What is interesting in this new development is that almost all the new chapters in Southern Africa were organized under the influence of Isabel Apawo Phiri, a Malawian. She kept establishing chapters as she moved in these areas in Southern Africa after leaving Malawi in 1996. In this endeavour she was, of course, assisted by

---

[68] Int member of Namibia Circle, Kempton Park, 14.7.2005.

other Circle members. The pool of Circle members that Isabel brought together in Namibia, for example, were the result of the influence of Musimbi Kanyoro. The majority of them came from the Lutheran Church at the time when Musimbi Kanyoro was working as Executive Secretary for Women in Church and Society with the Lutheran World Federation (LWF). About this time, she writes:

> Through my involvement I was also able to garner the participation of the Lutheran World Federation (LWF) and recruited as many Lutheran women theologians as I could. I persuaded them to write, facilitate a process whereby they could meet and think together, as well as mentor one another.[69]

In the period when Isabel Apawo Phiri was Continental Coordinator, the chapters that were at the brink of dying during Musimbi Kanyoro's period faced the same threat. These were the Tanzania, Uganda, Zimbabwe and Zambia chapters. The reasons for this situation are beyond continental leadership, as they mainly relate to the availability of theological training to the women in these countries. There are of course new chapters that have been developed. Botswana chapter was started in 2003 by Musa Dube, and Pietermaritzburg chapter was launched in 2002. These chapters were still in operation by the year 2007.

Among the earlier ones, the local chapters that seem to have grown from strength to strength were Ghana, Nigeria and Kenya. Further, the newly established chapters like Pietermaritzburg were also growing strong. During the reign of Lusungu Fulata Moyo, the chapters had become less active. This is the reason why the current continental leader, Helen Adekunbi Labeodan has on her agenda to revive the Circle. What are the possible reasons for this landscape? I would suggest the following:

Circle chapters are established around personalities. It is clear that those local chapters that thrive are built around personalities that keep to the vision of the Circle to establish local chapters and make them operational. Firstly, all the local chapters that have a long history of viability: Nigeria, Ghana, Malawi, Kenya, Pietermaritzburg, are linked to such personalities. Mercy Amba Oduyoye has been an inspiration to Nigeria and Ghana circles. In fact, Elizabeth Amoah spends much time with Mercy Amba Oduyoye to

---

[69] Isabel Apawo Phiri and Sarojini Nadar (eds), *African Women, Religion, and Health: Essays in Honour of Mercy Amba Ewudzi wa Oduyoye*, Pietermaritzburg: Cluster 2006, p. 30.

lobby women around Ghana to join the Circle. In Nigeria, Mercy was assisted much by Dorcas Akintunde, the Linguistic researcher for the Anglophone region. In Kenya, Musimbi Kanyoro and Nyambura Njoroge have inspired the Circle for a long period of time, even though, for the most part, both had to maintain an active link with the Kenya Circle through email, visitation and even practical projects such as supplying women's liberative books to the Limuru local chapter. For the Malawi Circle the same can be said of Isabel Apawo Phiri. She saw to it that the Malawi Circle was vibrant. In Malawi, Isabel has been assisted much by Fulata Moyo and Rachel Fiedler, who were local coordinators of the Circle and maintained its viability. In Kenya, Musimbi Kanyoro and Nyambura Njoroge were assisted much by the able leadership of Ester Mombo at Limuru chapter, and Mary Getui and Grace Wambui at Kenyatta University. By 2007, Nyambura Njoroge had returned from Switzerland to live in Kenya.

When we look at the case of Botswana, Zimbabwe and Zambia, the late development of local African Women Theologians had an impact on the development of the Circle. It is clear that the fact that the local chapters lost able leaders to study abroad or to migration to other countries has impacted negatively on the vitality of the local circles from which these women came. Bella Mukunyora left Zimbabwe, and in Botswana, Musa Dube was busy developing women theologians by mentoring them.

While the reasons why Ghana, Kenya and Nigeria got organized faster into chapters can also be linked to these countries' progress in education, it is also true that these countries were privileged in having one of their country women represented at the International Planning Committee (IPC) that became a back up to the women to start local chapters in these countries. In the case of South Africa, there were already emerging Black theologies that were present because of apartheid. This had already generated a fertile environment within which to theologize concerning African women in Culture and Religion. Women's theologies and Black theologies all belong to Liberation theology. South Africa, just as Kenya, Ghana and Nigeria, was also advantaged with progress in accessibility of education to women. This is how as early as the 1980s, Brigalia Bam became the General Secretary of the Council of Churches in South Africa. In addition, South Africa had an advantage equal to Ghana and Nigeria because Brigalia Bam, who shared the vision of the Circle with Mercy Amba Oduyoye, came from South Africa.

From this analysis, it is clear that several factors influenced the development of local or country chapters. These were greatly inspired by those that belonged to the IPC. They had received the vision and could easily relay it into their own countries of origin. Formation of chapters in countries that did not have a representation at IPC was usually done by those that caught the vision from those that were at IPC. Some caught the vision at the first Convocation. However, it is clear that in those countries where there was no woman that was part of the IPC, the genesis of the country's chapters was delayed.

That some local chapters are vibrant, even though some of the leaders have migrated to other countries for various reasons or even passed on, has been possible because the remaining leaders were able enough to carry on with the Circle. Of course, it is clear that this is also linked to the number of African women theologians in a particular area. Kenya, Ghana and Nigeria have high numbers of theologically trained women. This, of course, depends on the level of training these women have. From the evidence of this history, it is clear that if in a local chapter there are women who have attained at least Master's level in theology, there is a possibility that the local chapter will continue. This level of education is strategic in maintaining the Circle, in that one is able to mentor others in the process of research and writing, which they have already passed through. This may explain why the Circles in Zambia, Zimbabwe and Tanzania are less active. It can already be envisaged that if a woman with a Master's degree, who is a member of the Circle, goes back to these countries, the vitality of those local Circles will improve. This is why, for example, the return of Lilian Siwila to Zambia after writing her PhD will definitely improve the momentum of the Circle in Zambia.

These factors varied from chapter to chapter as described above. The factors that influence the vitality of chapters are diverse and vary from one country to the other. I show this by including a detailed analysis of factors that influenced the birth and growth of the Malawi chapter in chapter 4.

Chapter 4: Birth and Growth of the Circle in Malawi (1993 – 2017)

The Beginnings

The official genesis of the Circle in Malawi is by Isabel Apawo Phiri, a Presbyterian of Nkhoma Synod in Central Malawi. She had also been one of the participants at the Convocation of the Circle in 1989, but only started the Circle in 1993 because before that time she was doing her PhD in South Africa at the University of Cape Town.[218] She established the Circle when she came back to Malawi. She was then a lecturer at Chancellor College of the University of Malawi in the Department of Theology and Religious Studies. However, there had been awareness on gender issues in Blantyre and Livingstonia Synods before then. Rev Dr Silas Ncozana had organized an awareness meeting in 1990 at Chigodi Women's Centre near Blantyre.

Isabel Apawo Phiri started the Circle at Chancellor College in 1993. Here she even had support from women academics in other fields that were interested in researching and writing concerning women's issues. These were Nyovani Madise, Flora Nankhuni and Linda Semu, all from the Sociology Department. She even did research together with them. In the experience of beginning the Circle in Malawi it is clear that one of the reasons why local chapters struggle to start in some areas in Africa is that of "cultural conservatism." In Malawi, this was visible when people were angered by the research findings of Isabel Apawo Phiri and her friends regarding sexual harassment on Chancellor College campus. Her house even got stoned for this research.[219]

The chapter at Chancellor College started with a bang when about 50 women came together at its launch.[220] The first meeting consisted of students, staff members and also church women from the surrounding community. Not all

---

[218] Her PhD has been published as Isabel Apawo Phiri, *Women, Presbyterianism and Patriarchy. Religious Experience of Chewa Women in Central Malawi* Blantyre: CLAIM-Kachere, 1997, ²2000.

[219] For details about this incident see: Isabel Apawo Phiri, "Marching, Suspended and Stoned: Christian Women in Malawi 1995," in Kenneth R. Ross (ed), *God, People and Power in Malawi: Democratization in Theological Perspective*, Blantyre: CLAIM-Kachere, 1996, pp. 63-105.

[220] Isabel Apawo Phiri and Fulata Moyo, Focus Group, Malaka-le Theologies, 14.7.2005.

who participated were trained in theology, there were others who were there simply because they were women concerned from a faith perspective. There was also a student that spoke. Isabel Apawo Phiri then organized the second Circle conference. At this time Fulata Moyo was also present. She had just finished her Master's course at the University of Zimbabwe. The meeting took place at Isabel Apawo Phiri's house in Chirunga. This was a follow up meeting to the first one because at the first meeting women had been challenged to do more research on the theme: "Violence against Women."[221] In 1995, the Circle presented the findings from the research that had been done. The research was on rape and sexual harassment in educational institutions with Chancellor College as a case study.[222] Isabel and three other Circle members, Linda Semu, Flora Nankhuni and Nyovani Madise, presented the paper at the University of Malawi research dissemination conference. The four had done this research together. Although this was a joint paper, it was Isabel Phiri who was attacked most. Her house was damaged and also her name. Since this time the Malawi Circle did not hold any further meeting till 1996. In 1996, Fulata Moyo started the ball rolling again capitalizing on her post as the Secretary of the Board for Theological Studies.[223] From this vantage position she was able to lobby women to participate in the Circle. This was after Fulata Moyo had attended the 1996 Nairobi Circle meetings.[224]

From 2004 to 2005 Rachel Fiedler was the coordinator of the Chancellor College chapter. At the 2004 meeting, there had been more women from the Presbyterian side than before. However, in 2005 the number of women from the Evangelical side increased. This could have been due to the fact that Rachel Fiedler is from the Evangelical tradition. The theme for the 2005 meeting was Gender, Health and Religion.

---

[221] Ibid.

[222] Isabel Apawo, "Stand up and be Counted. Identity, Spirituality and Theological Education in my Faith Journey," in Denise M. Ackermann et al (eds), *Claiming Our Footprints. South African Women Reflect on Context, Identity and Spirituality,* Matieland: EFSA Institute of Theological and Interdisciplinary Research, 2000.

[223] This Board relates theological colleges and seminaries through the Department of Theology and Religious Studies to the University of Malawi, so that the diplomas and degrees are awarded jointly by the University and the Board.

[224] Isabel Apawo Phiri and Fulata Moyo, Focus Group, Malaka-le Theologies, 14.7.2005.

Fulata Moyo went to Pietermaritzburg to do her PhD, which she completed in 2009.[225] She did not return to Malawi, though, as she accepted the appointment to the Women's Desk of the World Council of Churches in Geneva. In 2008, she was elected as the Continental Coordinator of the Circle.

Key factors that influenced the Circle

Although Circle chapters in different African countries are influenced differently, there is a high chance that many factors I highlight in this section have a bearing on the formation of chapters in other countries in Africa as well.

It is a fact that the establishment of the Circle in Malawi lagged behind, compared to some countries, although it is not at the bottom of the scale. Other countries such as Zimbabwe and Zambia are worse off than Malawi in terms of Circle development and growth. The factors I highlight below, shed light on this.

Exposure

Exposure takes place in many ways. Firstly, entry into the academic world provides exposure. To be a Circle member one must have an academic interest. This is a license that opens doors to liberation, feminist issues and methodologies. These equip one to either become a member or open Circle chapters in one's area. In Malawi such an academic world would be unveiled to any individual upon stepping into the doors of a secular University that promotes feminist ideas. Currently Chancellor College (of the University of Malawi) and Mzuzu University are the key secular academic institutions that do this. To the contrary, most church based theological colleges and seminaries in Malawi do not promote such ideas to their students. At Chancellor College, the genesis of the Circle was only possible through Isabel Apawo Phiri who had been exposed to feminist and liberation theologies when she went to study abroad for her MA in Lancaster and for her PhD in

---

[225] Fulata Moyo, "Women, Sexuality Envisioned as Embodied Interconnected Spirituality and Sexual Education in Southern Malawi. A Quest for Women's Sexual Empowerment in the HIV/AIDS Context. The Case of *Kukhonzera Chinkhoswe Chachikhristu* (KCC) among Mang'anja and Yao Christians of T/A Mwambo in Rural Zomba", PhD, University of KwaZulu Natal, 2009.

Cape Town.²²⁶ It is this exposure that energized her to start the Circle. In the recent years, Mzuzu University has introduced courses in feminist theologies, liberation theology as well as gender studies. This has created a fertile ground for the genesis of the Circle at Mzuzu University in the coming years.

Globalization also enhances exposure to Circle theologies. Among Circle women in Malawi, those that have led the Malawi Circle have been in touch with the World Council of Churches. Thus, Fulata Moyo and Isabel Apawo Phiri were both exposed to WCC activities. Isabel Apawo Phiri, the mother of the Malawi Circle, was exposed to "women's issues at the consultations and meetings of the programme on Theological Education (now called Ecumenical Theological Education) of the World Council of Churches from 1983 to 1989."²²⁷ In fact, the inspiration to study the religious experience of the Chewa women of Nkhoma Synod she received at the 1989 Continental Conference.²²⁸ At that time she was lecturer at the University of Malawi, Chancellor College. In terms of further studies, Isabel Apawo Phiri benefited from a WCC scholarship when studying for her PhD, and she acknowledges it in her book.²²⁹ The WCC was also a key in the development of women's theologies since its beginnings.

Although this was the period when Mercy Amba Oduyoye "was finding others," Isabel Apawo Phiri was not at this stage a likely candidate to participate in the International Planning Committee because she did not belong to EATWOT to which members of the International Planning Committee belonged.

Isabel Apawo Phiri later did her PhD at the University of Cape Town. Her supervisor was Prof John Walter de Gruchy. Fulata Moyo also benefited from her connection with WCC in her development of Circle theologies. She also received her first PhD funding from WCC. Such WCC connections connected

---

[226] Isabel Apawo Phiri, "Women in Theological Education in Malawi," *Religion in Malawi* no. 2, 1988, pp. 24-28. Isabel Apawo Phiri, "A Convocation of African Women in Theology, Trinity College, Legon, Accra, Ghana 24-30th September, *Religion in Malawi*, no. 3, 1991, pp. 39-41.

[227] Isabel Apawo Phiri *Women, Presbyterianism and Patriarchy. Religious Experiences of Chewa Women in Central Malawi*, Blantyre: CLAIM-Kachere, 2000, p. 7.

[228] Ibid.

[229] Isabel Apawo Phiri, *Women, Presbyterianism and Patriarchy. Religious Experiences of Chewa Women in Central Malawi*, Blantyre: CLAIM-Kachere, 1997/2000.

women to feminist and liberation theologies that prepared them to write Circle theology. Since connection to WCC in the early years was more available to member churches, women that belonged to non-WCC member churches did not have such a privilege of being exposed to feminist and liberation theologies unless they studied at secular universities. This reality had a negative impact on the development of the Malawi local chapter. The pioneer women of the Malawi Circle were inspired by the theologies of Isabel Apawo Phiri and Fulata Moyo. However, this exposure was just 'the tip of an iceberg', what they really needed to know was how to construct Circle theologies. The mentors did not have enough time to expose fellow women to the theological frameworks of feminism and liberation theologies that were required to develop Circle theologies within a wider theological context.

Attending international Circle meetings brings exposure. At one of the Malawi Circle meetings, members acknowledged that there are fewer women in the Circle because of insufficient publicity. This tallies well with that when Isabel Apawo Phiri visited Chancellor College Circle on 13th July 2006, there was a stronger commitment among women to belong to the Malawi Circle. The aspect of 'who explains the Circle to others' is important. When Isabel Phiri talked to the Circle at Chancellor College at that time, there was much interest, not because new things were explained, but because of who talked about this Circle message. Since Isabel Phiri is much respected academically, people were able to receive the message from her much more easily. The other aspect of publicity women in Malawi are looking for is in relation to Circle conferences abroad. They see that the Malawi Circle is not growing because only a few individuals have attended Circle conferences outside Malawi: Fulata Moyo, Rachel NyaGondwe Fiedler, Getrude Kapuma and Isabel Apawo Phiri. This implies that if more Malawi Circle women were given the chance to attend regional meetings, the vitality of the Circle would greatly improve. The fact that the same women have attended Regional and Continental Conferences has tended to make the Circle the property of the few. This in turn has not been conducive to the growth of the Circle. However, the goal to have more women attend Circle meetings shall only be realized with increased mentoring of the Circle women in research, writing and publishing. Regional and Continental Circle meetings are key modes of publicity as they inspire women to develop theologies of women which are informed about what is happening within other African contexts. The privilege to travel and present papers would also be an added motivation.

Exposure also takes place, when women get in touch with others that advocate women's liberation. In the Zambezi Evangelical Church (ZEC), the beginning of the women's organization known as Chiyanjano in 1945 was a breakthrough for the women of this church. Through this organization the women saw themselves as deaconesses, missionary interpreters and leaders of the organization.[230] Part of their fulfilment was the fact that Chiyanjano was also very centralized and women felt some achievement in the event that they got elected to important positions. Further they played important roles at funerals, during Sunday worship and at girls' initiation ceremonies.[231] The establishment of ZAWO (Zambezi Women's Organization) gave opportunity for women to learn vocational skills.[232]

However, contact with other women that were conscientized on women's liberation has made women to be less contented with participation at church women organizational level alone. They look for more. This, of course, attracts resistance from men. This was felt by women both during theological training and after.[233] It is interesting that, after Mrs D. Makupola's graduation, she was given the responsibility to coordinate Chiyanjano in 1981. Mrs Alice Khota, who was the second to enroll in theological training, became her assistant Chiyanjano coordinator in 1999. Mrs M. Chilembwe, the third to join theological training, became the deputy coordinator for Chiyanjano replacing Mrs A. Khota, who became Deputy Youth Coordinator. She also became a lecturer, but only for women, at Evangelical Bible College of Malawi.[234]

Whereas the other three women accepted whatever positions were granted to them, even though they would have loved much better positions, the fourth woman to enrol in theological training did not want to settle for less.

---

[230] See Anthony Nkhoma, Women in Search of Identity. The Case of Women's Ordination in Zambezi Evangelical Church, BA, University of Malawi, 2005.

[231] Ibid., pp. 8-9.

[232] Ibid., pp. 10-13.

[233] Ibid., p. 15.

[234] Ibid., p. 16-17. – There are female lecturers, though, also in the general programme at EBCOM.

After graduating in 2003, she said that her vision had then widened. She was prepared to serve in any capacity, even as a pastor, if she would be given the opportunity. In 2004, she was appointed to coordinate the women's programmes to replace Mrs M. Chilembwe. She went to train with a South African College in early childhood development and still aspires to be an ordained pastor one day.[235]

As time goes on, women are less content to settle for subservient roles in the Zambezi Evangelical Church. Mrs Mary Chaomba, the fifth woman to enrol at EBCOM, graduated "with a vision to serve the church in pastoral roles."[236] In fact she enrolled in the college to train as a pastor; however, she has been appointed to serve as coordinator for Chiyanjano in the North.[237]

There is enough evidence that the desire for ordination which started with the first woman who enrolled at EBCOM is a hotbed for further training and Circle membership.

It was, however, in 2002 when Chiyanjano, defying all odds, boldly stood up to challenge the church's stand on the ordination of women.[238]

The awakening call has been heard and men are slowly heeding the call. They have at the moment allowed three women to be "set apart" for ministry.[239] These women were set apart on June 22, 2003 at a function named "Mapatulidwe a Makodineta (Setting aside/ordaining [Women's] Coordinators)." This minimal decision cannot be maintained for long. Time is approaching when ZEC will fully ordain women. This desire for ordination in Zambezi Evangelical women seems to go together with their search to upgrade their theological training. If this trend continues, there will be an increase in the number of women in the Malawi Circle from Zambezi Evangelical churches.

Exposure also takes place when women learn about feminist movements. I put this factor in establishing the Circle in Malawi last because there are few women that are exposed to liberation and feminist movements. Delving into

---

[235] Ibid., p. 17.

[236] Ibid., pp. 17-18. She graduated with a certificate in Biblical Studies (Chichewa).

[237] Ibid., p. 14.

[238] Ibid., p. 15.

[239] Ibid., p. 17. The three women are: Mrs D. Kumpoola, Mrs M. Chilembwe, and Mrs A. Khota.

feminist and liberation theologies is viewed as delving into non-orthodox teachings. Women view such theologies as alien to the African way of theologizing. One of the reasons why two female students at Chancellor College refused to join the Malawi Circle was that they were afraid that the Circle would make them "lukewarm Christians." They both came from a Charismatic background, one from Calvary Family Church, the other from Living Waters. Throughout their days in Chancellor College they resisted the challenge to join the Circle. This is contrary to the wishes of the Malawi Circle which is looking forward to the time when Charismatic women would desire to be part of it. However, the position Charismatic women pose shows that although Malawi Charismatics are among the first to provide theological training to women that are not pastors' wives, it does not follow that they would be interested in the Circle's agenda to research, write and publish. Women such as Rose Morleene Mbewe from Calvary Family Church or Bertha Chunda from Living Waters are happy just to take up their double roles of being pastor and pastor's wife. These have gone through a theological training that is not just a wife's course, but the same as that of men in their churches. The kind of theology that these women are exposed to is that of men being 'heads' and women as supporters to these men. To begin a theology of re-imagining such roles will require in depth mentoring from those representing Circle theology. This is unlikely to be achieved in the near future because there has not yet been Circle convert among women in Calvary Family Church.

The other important exposure is being in touch with members of IPC. These are the women that got first-hand information on the Circle and therefore can encourage leaders of local chapters. Circle history shows this reality in that the earliest members of the Circle, who became part of the International Planning Committee, were mostly those that taught at secular Universities. These were oriented towards feminist and liberation theologies and became fertile to catch the vision for the Circle early. These were likely to digest the Circle's agenda and establish Circle chapters at their institutions of learning. Such exposure had to be at a certain academic level where one is able to research and write publishable papers.

The projected role of what Malawi academic women could have achieved, if present at the IPC and at the First Convocation in 1989, is justified by the history of the Circle documented earlier in this book where it is clear that countries that had such representation are thriving better than those that did not. Some examples of this trend are: Kenyatta University chapter, Legon chapter and Accra chapter, among others, where academic women became the agents for establishing and developing chapters.

Similarly, Malawi women might have caught the wind of liberation and feminism had they been present at the First Convocation. Isabel Apawo Phiri participated in the 1989 Convocation, but was still undergoing postgraduate training at Cape Town University and so was not living in Malawi to begin the Circle. The other lady, Christine Manda, who attended the Convocation, was not an academic and therefore, even though she got involved with this feminist and liberation movement, she probably was more interested in keeping her church position as the early winds of liberation were too radical for some women. She was a church worker in the Synod of Livingstonia (Church of Central Africa Presbyterian). For Circle history, engaging in research and writing was crucial and this goal was probably less appealing to someone who was working in a non-academic setting, the church. If she were an academic in a University college, research and writing a publishable paper would have been compelling to her since such papers are important in one's staff development.

Individual Conviction

The history of the Malawi Circle shows that although women may be exposed, there are other intrinsic factors that influence them to promote the Circle in their countries or not. The rejection of the Circle by some women in Malawi, for example, is a reaction to the conflict a feminist re-reading of missionary Christianity brings in the lives of women. The origin of such readings of Christianity is the achievement of the missionary churches. In their ambitious project of Christianizing Africans, they imported their own cultures and weaved them into that of their African converts. The Africans have learnt that well, including an androcentric reading of scriptures that shaped missionary Christianity for some time. The Circle is right in re-reading such missionary interpretations that have supported or promoted the oppression of women in church and society. However, when such reading is made public or exposed to grassroots women, these women are shocked because such re-readings disturb their earlier "colonial" readings of Christianity.

Women reported that there was fear to join the Circle because those that were related to it faced much ridicule. There was also fear to join a setup that was "feministic" because such feminism was seen as a threat to women's family units. These Circle theologies sought to transform gender roles that are traditionally conditioned as roles for women. The women that joined the Circle were viewed to implore men to cook for families just as women do. To some women who have internalized cooking roles as only for women in the home, and that this is central to keeping their Christian vows of marriage, this reversal of roles was a threat. It also contradicted some missionary teaching that the man is the "head" of the family, so that discouraging women from cooking for their families opposed the central teaching that man is the head of the family. Such reversal of roles in cooking meant that women were "heads" as well. The local women do not interpret headship as responsibility, but as power to rule. Whatever the man has put in place, the woman should respectfully adhere to it. Feminist re-reading of "headship" was probably in conflict with popular local women's notions of the word. The meaning of the word implies that it is not being male or female that makes one to be head. The head of the family is the person that is responsible in the family. Thus, there are families where women are heads and even where children are heads of families.

One's convictions at different levels influence one's commitment to the Circle goals. Regardless that some women are exposed to a theology that does not encourage them to write about patriarchal hegemonic relationships between men and women in their churches, through their day to day experiences in their church, these women are coming to grips with the challenge. Rose Morleene Mbewe is an example of such women who are awakened about patriarchal hegemonic relationships between men and women in the church through their own experiences. She was born on the 9th of October, 1956 in Zimbabwe. Her grandparents happened to be in Zimbabwe because they worked on the mines. Her parents were Christians.

Some of the issues of patriarchal oppression against women that she has observed are that women in her church have been influenced by the one-party system and fail to speak out on crucial issues affecting their lives in the church. One of the issues Rose Mbewe brings out is that women in her church are looked down upon by the church (men and women). She bases this observation on her own experience as a pastor's wife, but also as someone that is married to an Apostle of the church. She notices that more often than not, members of her church follow decisions made by her husband more than by her.

Her reaction to such an experience is passive. She has chosen not to confront these oppressive members of her church and concentrates on what she considers as more important in her ministry. What she forgets is that it is not just the service that is important in a person's life but also her or his dignity before God and men. This disrespect by church members concerning her wisdom on church matters robs her of dignity before people and God.

Since in research and writing women are breaking the pattern of suffering silently, these women can easily be attracted to the Malawi Circle if they are made aware of it. Since these women love their churches and their faith, the Circle is a safe place to speak out concerning women's issues. Further, in the Charismatic tradition, it is the Holy Spirit that unsettles patriarchal hegemonic relationships between men and women. The Holy Spirit gives gifts to both men and women as He wills regardless of gender. Further, the church's view on theological training for women is supportive to women. In fact, the necessary qualification for one to train in theology is that she or he has a calling from God. Therefore, there are, in the Charismatic churches in Malawi, growing numbers of women pastors.[240]

Pastor Carol Chaponda's experience helps us to highlight the latter argument. Her conversion experience has been the only thing that has earned her pastoral duties. Her conversion experience is attributed to the prayers of her husband who was already a dedicated Born Again Christian. Her husband based his prayers on 1 Corinthians 7:16 which reads: "How do you know, husband, whether you will save your wife?" Although Carol Chaponda was brought up in a Christian family, she had not yet known the Lord personally. One day she went to attend "Lunch Hour Fellowship" at Red Cross in Blantyre.[241] There she was converted to Christ through the founder of Living

---

[240] Richard Gadama, Women in the Charismatic Churches in Malawi: A Historical and Theological Perspective, PhD, Free State University, Bloemfontein, 2016. - The same applies to the Assemblies of God, the largest Pentecostal denomination in Malawi, which currently (2017) has a female General Secretary.

[241] For these Lunch Hour Fellowships as part of the Blantyre Awakening see: Bright Kawamba, The Blantyre Spiritual Awakening 1969 to 1986: An Antecedent of the Charismatic Movement in Malawi, MA, University of Malawi, 2013.

Waters Church, Stanley Ndovi.[242] When he preached, she was so troubled in her heart that she decided to give her life to Christ.

Her walk with the Lord amazed many people because of her transformed life after committing her life to Christ. Although theological training in some churches is seen as a prerequisite for ministry, Pastor Carol Chaponda began her ministry right away after her conversion, without theological training. The first pastoral responsibility was doing charity work, where she gave people clothes, food and many other things according to the prompting of the Holy Spirit. At one time, she gave away all her dresses except one. Since she did not run a paid ministry, she relied on her business to earn a living. Her giving out things at the prompting of the Holy Spirit made her break rules of running a business and as such she was left with only a small capital that was insufficient to cater for her family. Even in this situation, the spirit of God continued to ask her to give away items from her small business. This made the business to go down and brought financial problems to her family. Her children found it difficult to survive on this small income. This was the kind of life she lived from 1986 until 1990.

The role of the Holy Spirit was very central in her charity work. She sought to be obedient to the prompting of the Holy Spirit even when it was difficult to do so. She recalls one such instance when a mentally disturbed woman perpetually visited her begging for food. This was a test to her because it was during the time that she did not have much to live on. She thanked God that she did not resist the prompting of the Holy Spirit and gave her food. In fact, the woman's visits became so frequent that she became part and parcel of the family. Mrs Chaponda stayed with the woman from 1991 till 1994. At the end, the woman confirmed to Pastor Carol Chaponda how right she had been in following the leading of the Holy Spirit.

"Woman, God has tested you but you have passed the tests. He has given you wisdom and on this place, he has established a fountain of healing. Never let any jar draw water from it." These sayings resonated well with what Mrs Chaponda had seen in her dream. "This place has been opened and set free,

---

[242] About him see Khetwayo Banda, "Apostle (Dr) Stanley Ndovie's Contribution to Malawi's Socio-Religious Development," MA module, Department of Theology and Religious Studies, Mzuzu University, 2009.

many people will come to this place to seek your help."[243] This was the beginning of her healing ministry. Because she had been obedient to the Holy Spirit, her ministry was widened. The first fruit of this ministry was her own healing from breast cancer after failing to receive any help from the hospital. It was only through prayer and fasting that she got healed in a dream, in which she saw people singing. On the other side, she saw people crying and yelling "Have Mercy on her, Lord."[244] When she woke up, she saw a group of people surrounding her, requesting her to go to the hospital. She saw a big opening on her breast and told the people that there was no reason for her to go to the hospital because she had already been healed in the dream. This healing was however not instant, it was only after a few months that the condition really got better.

Again, this ministry of healing got widened and not only did she run a healing ministry, but she was also engaged in witnessing and teaching people about prayer. This is what led to the establishment of the "Chisomo School of Prayer." She prefers the word "school" to "church" because she did not limit the ministry to members of the church. The school attracted people from all walks of life (the rich and the poor). When new members came to the school, she first told them about Christ. After this, when one accepted Christ into their life, she taught them Christian foundation lessons such as prayer and the Bible. She also emphasized the Baptism of the Holy Spirit. Thus, she encouraged people that the Holy Spirit is the revealer of all truth.[245]

In Africa, cultural values are viewed as important for survival. When establishing a local Circle, the goals of the Circle must be in harmony with the women's communitarian survival. This requires that, when someone joins the Circle, she should not become the black sheep of the community. In the Christian community, belonging to a fellowship of believers is important and if this is at stake, it threatens one's survival in terms of emotional and spiritual support. When Isabel Apawo Phiri launched the Circle at Chancellor College, there were about 50 women who were part of this group. The

---

[243] See J. Banda, Student TRS, End of Year Essay, 2004.

[244] Ibid.

[245] For a more recent description of her life centering on her ministry as a prophetess see: Richard Gadama, Women in the Charismatic Churches in Malawi: A Historical and Theological Perspective, PhD, Free State University, Bloemfontein, 2016.

number gives an impression that possibilities of having a thriving Circle in Malawi were evident. However, not all women that attended the meeting were academics. The Circle's goal to research and write publishable papers was submerged by the goal to fellowship among believers.

Many of the 50 women were church women interested in the deepening of their faith, and as such, they considered themselves to have a mission to encourage other women in the group in their faith. They came as members of the 'Zomba Action Group'. These women came from within the Chancellor College neighbourhood. Although some of the members came from the academic staff of the college, their goal to research and write was overshadowed by the confessional focus of having an evangelistic mission to their neighbours.[246] When the central goal to research and write publishable papers on women's issues threatened this fellowship with other believers, women distanced themselves from the Circle. This was when some academic women in the group were viewed as using a "hammer approach"[247] in dealing with women's issues on Chancellor College campus. This was when work on sexual harassment on Chancellor College campus was done. The work was researched and written by Isabel Apawo Phiri, Linda Semu and Flora Nankhuni, and then presented at a University research conference at Lake Malawi, where the national radio picked up (largely wrong) bits of information broadcasting that 50% of the girls were raped on Chancellor College campus. At this time, the environment in Malawi had not opened up to speaking overtly about sexual matters. This research therefore was culturally sensitive. Surprisingly, even the educated at Chancellor College were still dressed in this cultural conservatism. This incited Chancellor College staff and students. The stoning of Isabel's house by students was the climax of the staged violence. They were not angry because there was sexual abuse and even rape on campus, but because this woman had the guts to speak about such a taboo.[248] This incidence scared some members off the

---

[246] Bishop Kalilombe suggested in a comment at a Circle seminar in 2006, that if the Circle is confessional, it faces lack of progress in achieving Circle goals.

[247] Isabel Apawo Phiri and Sarojini Nadar (eds), *On Being Church: African Women's Voices and Visions,* Geneva: World Council of Churches, 2005.

[248] Isabel Apawo Phiri, "Marching, Suspended and Stoned: Christian Women in Malawi 1995," in Kenneth R. Ross (ed), *God, People and Power in Malawi: Democratization in Theological Perspective,* Blantyre: CLAIM-Kachere, 1996, pp. 63-105.

Chancellor College Circle and drove Isabel Phiri into exile, first to Namibia and then to South Africa. However, Isabel Apawo Phiri's migration to South Africa became a blessing to the Circle, as she pioneered the opening of several Circle chapters in South Africa.

Apart from the academic staff members there were also students. These became part of this group because they were involved with Isabel Apawo Phiri in Charismatic circles.[249] Isabel Apawo Phiri and her husband, Marx Phiri, were at that time working with the Students Christian Organization (SCOM) that was linked to the Evangelical Fellowship of Students (IFES). At this time, she received much encouragement from such students.

Although these students were involved in some researching, they were more interested in issues of faith. Further, as undergraduates, they were less prepared academically to write and publish. In fact, even if they did, they would probably not have produced quality papers deserving publication. The confessional element of the group likely stifled the growth of the Circle and commitment to the Circle objective of researching and writing.

The Role of Discipleship

For the Circle to develop to the stage where it is self-perpetuating there is need that the one leading the Circle must teach the members of the Circle to research and write. This requires much time for the mentoring process to yield results. The Malawi Circle would probably have been one of the best stories of Circle chapters if Isabel Apawo Phiri had remained a lecturer at Chancellor College. It would have given her enough time to mentor other women. This is seen in her ability to start and strengthen Circle chapters in Southern Africa when she moved to that region. The fact that Isabel Phiri left for Southern Africa before Chancellor College could have a Circle member that was well discipled into the vision for the Circle, had a negative impact on the development of the Circle in Malawi.

When Fulata Moyo re-joined Chancellor College in 1996, it was difficult for her to consolidate the group as a research and writing group. The group had

---

[249] Isabel Apawo Phiri, "Stand up and be Counted. Identity, Spirituality and Theological Education in my Faith Journey," in Denise M. Ackermann et al (eds), *Claiming Our Footprints. South African Women Reflect on Context, Identity and Spirituality,* Matieland: EFSA Institute of Theological and Interdisciplinary Research, 2000.

not been given enough time to learn Circle methodologies since Isabel Phiri had left abruptly to go to Namibia after the negative reaction to her research on sexual abuse at Chancellor College. Fulata Moyo had to re-start the Circle, as at her first Circle chapter meeting held at Chancellor College in 1998, there was no one from Isabel Phiri's earlier group. Fulata Moyo's group was different. It comprised women from other colleges such as Evangelical Bible College of Malawi, Blantyre, Baptist Theological Seminary and Zomba Theological College or former students from such colleges. At this time, her main influence was within the theological colleges that were members to the Board of Theological studies. Fulata Moyo was secretary to this Board and was therefore in a good position to mobilize women for the Circle.

The composition of the Circle group, which Fulata Moyo started, had its limitations, too. It had a high dose of Evangelical women that were products of theological institutions that did not study the kind of feminism and liberation theologies promoted by the Circle: Rachel NyaGondwe Banda, Molly Longwe, Late Mrs Banda, Martha Chirwa from the Baptist Convention; Myra Wilson, Ruth Folayan and one student from EBCOM. There was only one lady (Mrs Chinangwa) who came from the Presbyterian Church. She was at that time a student of Zomba Theological College.

The other limitation to this group was the 'Evangelical theology' itself. It tended to be conservative and uncritical to women's oppression in church and society. This was clear from their writings. Even though these women wrote concerning women's leadership in the Church, their papers were non-critical of the patriarchal hegemonic relationships that existed within their churches. Most of them, apart from Mrs Chinangwa, were very much at home with the roles they filled in their particular churches. Molly Longwe was a lecturer at the Baptist Theological Seminary and a pastor's wife. Although she is a trained theologian, she had no inclination of becoming a pastor, which would have required her to articulate a theology of transforming gender inequalities that addressed her church which did not and does not ordain women pastors.[250] Martha Chirwa and another Baptist woman (the late Mrs Banda) were pastors' wives. Martha Chirwa was at that

---

[250] For a critical analysis of the issue see Hany Longwe, "Democratization of the Christian Faith: The Influence of the Baptist Doctrine of 'Priesthood of All Believers' on the History of the Baptist Convention of Malawi (BACOMA)," PhD, University of Malawi, 2008.

time still in training. Mrs Chinangwa was the only lady that sought a feminist theology that would affirm her in her passion to be a pastor.[251]

The EBCOM group was definitely comfortable where they were. It is also clear that some papers presented at the Circle meeting hosted by Fulata Moyo were unpalatable to them. Since this particular meeting, they have not attended later Circle meetings organized by Rachel NyaGondwe Fiedler. This is a clear sign that developing a theology of transforming gender inequalities is not for women such as these, so that Fulata Moyo's initiative to develop the Chancellor College Circle dwindled. The group would have gained momentum probably if Fulata Moyo had mentored these women for a longer period of time. However, she left Chancellor College to do her PhD at the University of KwaZulu Natal in South Africa. Worse still, the leadership of the Circle was handed over to Rachel NyaGondwe Fiedler who was also just learning about Circle research and writing. The limitation was that she had less time and also less knowledge of feminist theologies to mentor women in the Circle. She was also more involved in community work, running the Lydia Foundation and writing her PhD. Even though she taught TRS courses part time, she had limited opportunities to encourage women to join the Circle. The increase in interest in Circle writings was mainly due to the exposure Chancellor College students had through the reading of Circle books. Isabel Apawo Phiri's books and Rachel NyaGondwe Fiedler's books have often been referred to as among those that have inspired Chancellor College students to get interested in joining the Circle. These books have caught the attention of the students as they have been included in their literature list by lecturers that mainstream gender issues in their courses.

With the return of Getrude Kapuma from South Africa, it was envisaged that another local chapter would start in Blantyre under her leadership. However, this did not happen. It should be noted that rarely have Circle chapters survived if they were not attached to an academic institution. Since Getrude Kapuma is a minister and the possible candidates to join the Circle are also pastors in her own church (CCAP), the composition of the group already presented a challenge to beginning a Circle chapter committed to research, writing and publishing.

---

[251] She achieved this after the CCAP Blantyre Synod finally lifted the restrictions on the ordination of women.

The Role of Isabel Apawo Phiri and Getrude Kapuma

The case, in which Getrude Kapuma and Isabel Apawo Phiri were involved in the march against the Blantyre Synod because of the restrictive stand on ordination of women, was a deterrent to women in ministerial formation to join the Circle in Malawi.[252] To be a Circle member was seen as being aggressive towards one's church. The actions of the church which resulted in suspending Getrude Kapuma, which was followed by her leaving for South Africa, did not encourage women in ministerial formation to join the Circle either. The fact that both Isabel Apawo Phiri and Getrude Kapuma left Malawi because of reasons connected to being members of the Circle negatively impacted the Circle in Malawi.

The Role of the Ecumenical Association of Third World Theologians (EATWOT)

It seems that the World Council of Churches had more influence in contributing to women's consciousness of their liberation than EATWOT did. Women that have joined the Circle in Malawi belonged to WCC member churches. Isabel Apawo Phiri recollects that there were sixteen women who responded to the invitation to participate in the first Women in Theology Consultation held at Chigodi in Blantyre in 1990. These were foremost Presbyterians from Blantyre Synod. Livingstonia Synod sent three participants, Mrs E.C. Munthali, Mrs M. Mwale—products of Zomba Theological College—and Mrs Phiri, a product of Livingstonia School. Nkhoma Synod sent only one participant, Mrs E. Kagundi, a product of Yoswa School (in Nkhoma Synod) for wives of theological students.[253] There were no women from the Roman Catholic Church. This situation differed with East and West Africa where Catholic women were pioneers of the local Chapters.

---

[252] Blantyre Synod has since changed its position and has started to ordain women pastors, Getrude Kapuma being one of them (Getrude Aopesyaga, Kapuma; "'Troubled but not Destroyed': Women of Faith Reclaim their Rights," in Isabel Apawo Phiri, Devakarsham Betty Govinden and Sarojini Nadar (eds), *Her-stories: Hidden Histories of Women of Faith in Africa*, Pietermaritzburg: Cluster, pp. 348-369.)

[253] Isabel Apawo Phiri, *Women, Presbyterianism and Patriarchy. Religious Experiences of Chewa Women in Central Malawi,* Blantyre: CLAIM-Kachere, 1997/2000, pp. 138-139.

It is not clear as to why there were no Malawian Roman Catholic sisters who were members of EATWOT in Malawi. Such Malawi Catholic women would have joined the Malawi Circle if they had belonged to EATWOT. Through this movement they would have likely caught the wind of feminist theologies. Since Roman Catholic women who were members of EATWOT formed the highest number in the IPC it suggests that there was the possibility that Roman Catholic Sisters would have been part of the Malawi Circle. Further, one of the leading figures of EATWOT was Bishop Patrick Kalilombe, a Malawian. It is interesting that Malawi Roman Catholic Sisters, even with this vantage point, were not found in EATWOT and hence at the Malawi Circle. One of the reasons for this would be that Bishop Kalilombe, who would have encouraged Roman Catholic Sisters to join EATWOT, fell out of grace with the then Malawi dictator, Kamuzu Banda. This happened when he got involved in the establishment of Small Christian Communities following the Vatican II Council. These activities of Small Christian Communities were seen to be subverting Kamuzuism. So, he was forced to leave Malawi. I can imagine that Roman Catholic Sisters would not have been free to join EATWOT where Bishop Kalilombe was active; for fear that they would also become "wanted people" by the Kamuzu government.

Further, Malawi Roman Catholic Sisters were unlikely to be part of EATWOT even without the Bishop Kalilombe factor, because the agenda of EATWOT would unlikely have been supported by the government of the day. Before the referendum to have multiparty democracy in Malawi took place in 1993, it was dangerous to get involved in a movement that was connected to Liberation. EATWOT as a forum for theologies of the underside (liberation theologies) was unwelcome to Malawians who wished not to be in trouble with the government. In fact, there were so many oppressive structures then that EATWOT would become a threat to. Further, Malawi Roman Catholic Sisters would have had problems travelling to EATWOT meetings from Malawi, because during Kamuzu's reign there was much scrutiny and restriction in terms of international travel.

Availability of and Access to Circle Books

The lag in the development and growth of the Malawi Circle is also attributed to the limited availability of and access to Circle books. Circle books have contributed to the sensitization of women in Africa to join the Circle. Through these books women are exposed to similar experiences of women in Africa that are of concern to women. Circle books also expose women to Circle methodologies and frameworks that women can use to write Circle publications. However, for a long time, the only Circle book which students at Chancellor College were exposed to was the one written by Isabel Apawo Phiri.[254] Access to Circle books published elsewhere was difficult. On this Musimbi Kanyoro writes:

> We hope that our books will receive wider readership now that they can easily be accessed, (through the Web) but this will not happen if we continue to use publishers who are themselves unknown. The first Circle book, "The Will to Arise", published by Orbis in 1992,[255] is in its fifth printing and easily purchased abroad, but not in Africa. Musa Dube's two books, "Other Ways of Reading"[256] and "Post-Colonial Feminist Interpretations of the Bible,"[257] are as easily available in Africa as they are in the West. Those published on our continent are not easily available and consequently not widely read.[258]

Apart from the logistical problems in delivering books to Malawi and other countries, the lack of a course on "Feminist Theology" in the Department of Theology and Religious Studies does not encourage the Department and the University to stock books on the Circle. This point is verified by how other departments in Africa have attracted Circle books to their libraries through running "Feminist" studies in the department. St Paul's Theological Seminary in Limuru, Kenya, the Institute of Women in Religion and Culture in Accra, Ghana, as well as the School of Religion in KwaZulu Natal University at Pietermaritzburg are key departments that have attracted Circle books to their libraries through running Feminist courses. It is by reading such Circle books that women in Malawi would have been sensitized to join the Circle. The introduction of Feminist Courses at Mzuzu University points to the

---

[254] Isabel Apawo Phiri, *Women, Presbyterianism and Patriarchy. Religious Experiences of Chewa Women in Central Malawi*, Blantyre: CLAIM-Kachere, 1997/2000.

[255] Mercy Amba Oduyoye and Musimbi Kanyoro (eds), *The Will to Arise: Women, Tradition, and the Church in Africa*, Maryknoll: Orbis, 1992.

[256] Musa W. Dube (ed), *Other Ways of Reading. African Women and the Bible*, Atlanta/Geneva: Society of Biblical Literature/WCC, 2001.

[257] Musa W. Dube, *Postcolonial Feminist Interpretation of the Bible*, St Louis: Chalice Press, 2000.

[258] Isabel Apawo Phiri and Sarojini Nadar (eds), *African Women, Religion, and Health: Essays in Honour of Mercy Amba Ewudziwa Oduyoye*, Pietermaritzburg: Cluster, 2006.

possibilities that Mzuzu University might be a home of Malawi National Chapters in the years to come. It is at this University where Circle books are read widely as they are part of the requirement for the African Feminist Theology Course.

Access to Theological Training

Although there is now a steady rise of women studying in the Department of Theology and Religious Studies of the University of Malawi and of Mzuzu University,[259] there has been low enrolment of women in the Departments. That has impacted negatively on the establishment and growth of the Circle in Malawi. Since the history of the Circle shows that Circle chapters attached to institutions of learning have a better chance of living the ideals of the Circle, it is important to have an increase in the enrolment of women in these institutions both as students and as lecturers in the Department. Some scholars such as Kenneth Ross[260] and Isabel Apawo Phiri[261] have pointed out the problem of low enrolment of female students in Chancellor College. Isabel Apawo Phiri lists, among other factors, low literacy levels of women, lack of opportunities to do theology, and lack of opportunities to utilize theological training in churches.[262]

Kenneth Ross agrees with Isabel Apawo Phiri on the bearing other church-instituted theological colleges have on the enrolment of female students in the Department of Theology and Religious Studies. He shows the relationship of these theological colleges to the enrolment of students in the Department of Theology. He argues that the bulk of students must have earned their Diploma in Theology with a 55% mark or above to qualify for entry into the Department of Theology at 3rd year level. However, there is also a minority of students in the Department from those with a Diploma in Education who had Religious Studies as a major subject.[263]

---

[259] Since a few years, several of the new universities have introduced theology courses and they are also open to women.

[260] Kenneth R. Ross, "Theology and Religious Studies at the University of Malawi 1993-1998," *Religion in Malawi*, no. 9, 1999.

[261] Isabel Apawo Phiri, "A Convocation of African Women in Theology, Trinity College, Legon, Accra, Ghana 24-30th September, *Religion in Malawi* no. 3, 1991, pp. 39-41.

[262] Ibid.

[263] In the last years, their numbers have grown considerably.

The relationship between church-instituted theological colleges and the Department of Theology is that recruitment of students into the latter hinges a lot on the former. From this background, it can be argued that the low enrolment of female students in the Department of Theology and Religious Studies is dependent on the enrolment of female students in theological colleges. Since these theological colleges are owned by churches and the selection of students to them is by the churches or sanctioned by them, low enrolment of female students in these colleges will also produce low enrolment in the BA (Theology) degree at Chancellor College. This in turn explains some of the lag in the development and growth of the Circle in Malawi.

The general record of graduates from the Department of Theology and Religious Studies shows that the first graduates in BA (Theology) graduated in 1993, even though the University of Malawi started in 1967.[264] From 1973 to 1991, students in the College could only take Religious Education offered within the Faculty of Education and then moved to the Faculty of Humanities.[265] During these years students were being trained to be teachers of Bible Knowledge in secondary schools, which was a popular subject among pupils because it was usually scored highly at Form Four level.[266]

The table below shows the enrolment ratios between female and male students in the Department of Theology and Religious Studies during selected years.

The table of results from 1992 to 1998 shows that the enrolment of women students in First Year was a significant hope to increasing the enrolment of women students in the Department of TRS. In the first year 1992, when the course was instituted, 50% of the students enrolled in the course were female.[267] In 1993 the percentage of women students in the course rose to 100%. In 1994 the percentage of women students in the BA (Theology) course was 66%. In 1995 this enrolment percentage, although it dropped, was at 33%, and 33% seems to have been the average from 1995 to 1998.

---

[264] Document, Graduates of the University of Malawi 1992-1993, accessed 2001.

[265] See Isabel Apawo Phiri, "Department of Religious Studies 1973-1988," *Religion in Malawi*, no. 2, 1988.

[266] Ibid.

[267] Assessment Record, University of Malawi, Chancellor College, 1992, accessed 2001.

Academic Year	Programme	Women	Men	Total
1992	Mature entry[268]	0	4	4
	First Year[269]	2	1	3
1993	Mature entry[270]	2	0	2
	First Year[271]	1	8	9
1994	Mature entry[272]	0	15	15
	First Year[273]	2	1	3
1995	Mature entry	0	0	0
	First Year[274]	1	2	3
1996	Mature entry	0	9	9
	First Year	0	0	0
1997	Mature entry	1	2	3
	First Year	0	0	0
1998	Mature entry	0	0	0
	First Year	1	2	3

This observation is in line with the views of Kenneth Ross, that First Year recruitment during the period of 1993 to 1998 was most promising because

---

[268] Ibid.

[269] Ibid.

[270] See Assessment Grade Reports 1993, Chancellor College, accessed 2001.

[271] Ibid. The students enrolled in 1st year in 1993 graduated in 1995. See 1967-1997.

[272] See Assessment Grade Reports 1994, Chancellor College, accessed 2001.

[273] See Assessment Grade Reports, 1967-1997, Chancellor College, accessed 2001.

[274] See Assessment Grade Reports 1995/96, Chancellor College, accessed 2001.

at each entry about half of the students were women.[275] Against this positive development, the University of Malawi decided to squash the slot for registering First Year BA (Theology) students after 1998.[276] This change has contributed to low enrolment of women students in the Department of Theology. It is therefore observed that

(a) The four students enrolled in 1992 all graduated in 1993 because this mature course takes only two years. Those enrolling in the course already have a diploma and stay in college for two years to finish their BA (Theology) course. Two other students were enrolled in the programme as first years, registering 50% enrolment of women in that year.[277]

(b) Even though in 1993 only two students enrolled as mature students in the course, by 1994, 4 students graduated in this course. The other two had been enrolled in 1992 as first years. Both of the students had a pass at the end of their first year, the BA 3rd year.

(c) In 1994, out of 15 enrolled in the course at third year, 0% were women.

(d) The record of graduates in 1996 shows that all the 15 male students enrolled in 1994 graduated in 1996. However, enrolment of new students in the third year in 1996 was 9 and 0% were women. The low enrolment of women students in TRS at third year deserves a thorough discussion.

Isabel Apawo Phiri rightly argues that low literacy levels of women have a bearing on their access to theological education.[278] This implies that even though the University of Malawi would put in place recruitment procedures that students of theology enrol at the first-year level, there would still be few women getting admitted to the Department of TRS. The underlying reasons

---

[275] Kenneth R. Ross, "Theology and Religious Studies at the University of Malawi 1993-1998," *Religion in Malawi* no. 9, 1999, pp. 3-9 [4].

[276] This slot has now been reintroduced, after much lobbying, and in 2007 the course has 7 students, an all-time record for first year entry. The lengthy omission of 1st year entry to the BA (Theology) had most likely been due to administrative inertia. The same year Mzuzu University also started its first BA (Theology) course, with 28 students in First Year, five of them women. Third Year entrance had three students, all women.

[277] These were the two women from Blantyre Synod selected by their church to study theology which would prepare them to work in the women's work in their church.

[278] See Isabel Apawo Phiri, "Department of Religious Studies 1973-1988," *Religion in Malawi*, no. 2, 1988.

for this have widely been applicable to secular disciplines of study as well. It is a problem that is not specific to theological training but to a wider range of disciplines. Sociologists have attributed the difficulty of accessing higher education to the way girl children are socialized. Girl children are socialized differently from boy children with the girl children's paradigm for training traditionally being repressive in the area of accessing higher education. Theologians have also pointed out the fact that women are socialized in churches to occupy junior positions to men. The latter has been shown in earlier paragraphs.

Local Church Participation

Some women in Malawi have sought or not sought liberation because of the experiences within their churches. The experiences of women from two Evangelical churches: Zambezi Evangelical Church and Baptist Convention, reinforce an old paradigm that women's experiences per se are a reservoir for conscientization.

From the first women's issue Alice Khota mentioned at the Circle meeting, it is clear that she is concerned about roles ascribed to women after graduating from theological college. She is concerned about power balance in this church that is tilted towards men and not women. Alice Khota has never gone abroad to attend women's meetings that would spark this attitude. She had never read any of the Circle books. Her conscientization about women's issues is from her own struggles with power balance in her church. This paradigm is clearly seen in the experiences of women in the Zambezi Evangelical Church that have attended the Evangelical Bible College of Malawi (EBCOM). The following is a sample of women that have attended the college in relation to the space that is given to them in the Zambezi Evangelical Church.

All the women that graduated from this college served in women's work. They did not become pastors or coordinators of ministries that comprised men and women. In this church, Mrs Deborah Kumpoola, the first woman to graduate in theology from this college, appeared in 1977.[279] She attended the main stream programme where both women and men learn the same

---

[279] See Anthony Nkhoma, "Women in Search of Identity. The Case of Women's Ordination in Zambezi Evangelical Church," BA, University of Malawi, 2005, p. 5.

subjects. She came to this college not as a wife of a "would be" pastor. If she had, she would have followed the wives' programme which follows a

Name	Marital status	Year	Role in Church as of 2005
1. Mrs Deborah Kumpoola	Widowed	1980 Diploma	Coordinator of women's group (Chiyanjano)
2. Miss Jennie L.C. Makapola	Single	1986 Certificate in Biblical Studies	What she is doing is not known.
3. Mrs Alice Khota	Widowed	1995 Certificate in Biblical Studies	Coordinator of Girls' Brigade
4. Mrs Mercy Chilembwe	Widowed	1996 Certificate in Biblical Studies	Coordinator of wives' programme at EBCOM
5. Mrs Monica Frank	Married	Withdrew for maternity	
6. Miss Grace Kasenda	Single	Withdrew, reasons not known	
7. Mrs Mkwezalamba	Widowed	2003 Certificate in Biblical Studies	Coordinator of wives' programme at EBCOM

different (and lower level) syllabus. If she had been in the latter course, serving in women's work would have been more acceptable to her. The problem is that the training she went through aimed at producing pastors, evangelists and Christian workers. Her question is how come, women who have undergone such training are not given the chance to serve in these posts?

Even if the levels of literacy could be raised and scholarships be arranged for women to study theology, women desire to further their theological training if they see women who have gone through theological training engaged in key leadership positions in the church. In the Baptist Convention, the beginnings did show a paradigm shift from junior and missionary conditioned roles to more prominent ones. However, this development was no cause for women in this church to aspire for further training in theology. Most of those that occupied key positions in the church were much less educated than women who had earned theological degrees in the later years. Lack of theological training did not limit them to serve as pastors in different churches. Mrs Mellia Makina never even went to a high school but was the pastor of Mwanafumu Baptist Church. Mrs Agnes Lufani just received a theological training related to being a pastor's wife, attending a six weeks' "wives course." She, however, became a renowned church planter and leader of women's groups.[280]

The other roles that women occupied in the church were those of being *alangizi* (counsellors) and holding administrative posts such as treasurer or secretary of the church. Such roles were not linked to higher theological achievements. Added to this, even in the highest post, that of General Secretary for the Convention, which women in the Baptist Convention could wish to occupy, the first woman that occupied it did not have theological training of any sort. She is a nurse by profession. Her name is Margaret Nyika. She became by chance the first woman to be the Acting General Secretary for a few months. She was appointed to stand in the place of Akim Chirwa, the General Secretary of the Convention, in 2000 when he went abroad for a time.[281]

The other aspect to the relationship between theological training and women's roles in the Baptist Convention is how women who have theological training are sidelined by the church. By the time Margaret Nyika was Acting General Secretary, there were women such as Rachel Banda, Molly Longwe and Grace Matupi who had theological training. Whereas it is a policy for the Baptist Convention that the General Secretary should always be a pastor, it

---

[280] See Rachel NyaGondwe Banda [Fiedler], *Women of Bible and Culture. Baptist Convention Women in Southern Malawi*, Zomba: Kachere, 2005, p. 186.

[281] Ibid.

is interesting that even in the event this rule was broken,[282] the Convention did not choose a woman with theological training. Sidelining women who had theological training was not only happening at this level but at other levels as well. Women who graduate from theological colleges, even those that went through the Baptist Seminary, are not given positions even at the lowest level of working in the women's department. These women end up being self-employed. These usually work hard to do things on behalf of the church through their own self-initiated projects with little remuneration. It is possibly true that women are sidelined in employment within the church because of the question whether it is worthwhile for a woman to receive money for doing a job in the church.

When women are offered employment in the church, it is usually not attached to a salary. Rachel Fiedler was appointed as "Development Desk Worker" and the letter of appointment said that she will not receive any income from the Convention until she raises money for the projects and will then obtain her salary from there. Such actions do not attract women in this church to seek theological training. Ordination for women who have attained the required theological training could promote women's interest to do theology. The General Secretariat led by Rev Fletcher Kaiya as General Secretary and Rev Emmanuel Chinkwita as the President tabled the motion to allow women's ordination but it was rejected.[283] Some of the arguments against this were that the Baptist Convention should not emulate what other churches are doing but should consult Scriptures regarding women's ordination. A committee was set up to construct papers on the issue. Until now this committee has not met and deliberated on the issue. At the 2008 Annual General Meeting the issue came up again, as Sigelele Baptist Church in Blantyre had called a woman, Mrs Kachere, as their pastor. The issue was

---

[282] A recent General Secretary, Simon Mkamanga, never had any theological education; in Baptist polity that is not required.

[283] See Hany Longwe, Democratization of the Christian Faith: The Influence of the Baptist Doctrine of "Priesthood of All Believers" on the History of the Baptist Convention of Malawi (BACOMA), PhD, University of Malawi, 2007, published as: Hany Longwe, *Christians by Grace – Baptists by Choice. A History of the Baptist Convention of Malawi,* Mzuzu: Mzuni Press, 2011.

discussed and in no way decided.[284] In 2009 at each of the six Regional Annual Conventions the issue was discussed again with one speaker opposing and one supporting the ordination of women. Again, no conclusions were reached.[285] In December 2011 the issue was picked up again, this time by the women's association at their annual conference in Mzuzu.[286] Two male speakers presented the case for women's ordination and Bridget Mwenefumbo, the President of Umodzi wa Amayi a Baptist, asked those women, who wanted to be ordained pastors, to come forward.[287] After this the issue was taken up by the Baptist Convention's Pastors' Fraternal, who requested that the Women's Union should not raise the issue any more as it had the potential to divide the church.

The wave of women pastors in the Jali area in the 1970s and 1980s has all vanished. They became pastors without theological training and neither were they ordained. They were not even chosen to be pastors of the congregations; they became pastor by starting churches and by members affirming their mission work by ascribing the title of pastor to them. This is why, while they were widely accepted as pastors by women, many male pastors did not recognize them.[288] These therefore did not encourage others to do theological training.

An important role model that has inspired women in the Baptist church to study theology at a higher level is that of Molly Longwe, who was a lecturer at Lilongwe Baptist Theological Seminary, where formation of pastors that can play a role in accepting women as pastors is done. Some of the pastors

---

[284] Klaus Fiedler could not attend the meeting since the date was moved, so he published his plea for ordination of women: Klaus Fiedler, *Baptists and the Ordination of Women*, Zomba: Lydia Print, 2008.

[285] At the South East General Assembly Funwayo Mafuleka, pastor of Zomba Baptist Church, spoke in support of women's ordination, Rev Chipande of Liwonde Baptist Church spoke against it, and I was given the opportunity to speak from the women's perspective.

[286] Hany Longwe presented on the practical side, Klaus Fiedler on the biblical side. For his views see: Klaus Fiedler, *Baptists and the Ordination of Women,* Zomba: Lydia Print, 2008.

[287] Nine women came forward, all experienced over years in the work of the church, including Bridget Mwenefumbo, who was looking forward to become a pastor after retirement from her position as the manager of a macadamia estate.

[288] For details see: Rachel NyaGondwe Banda [Fiedler], *Women of Bible and Culture. Baptist Convention Women in Southern Malawi,* Zomba: Kachere, 2005, pp. 132-136.

that studied under her did not at first accept to be taught by a woman. This attitude changed quickly and she became a model to the Baptist Convention women to study theology and the students (almost all male) rated her as probably the best teacher there.[289]

Lack of Openness to Women's Leadership in Churches

Some of the major trends in Evangelical theology are negative to seeking women's liberation. The following elements in many Evangelical theologies shape a patriarchal hegemonic relationship between men and women in church and society: (1) Assigning lower positions in church to women than to men, based on a wrong interpretation of scripture. (2) Training men and not women in theology because of the belief that it is men that are called to be pastors. The UMCA trained women in education related to lower roles in the church and society.[290] Being nursing teachers to local women was one of such junior roles. Miss Simpson, for example, worked very hard at the Medical College writing medical text books in Chinyanja for teaching nursing to local women. She died on Christmas day 1935 and a new brick hospital was opened in remembrance of her hard work.[291] The mission also operated a Leper colony which was being funded by the British Empire Leprosy Association and by the Nyasaland Government. By 1931, it had a hundred patients.

Thus, Malawian women were discipled into such subordinate roles portrayed by missionary women. Often those that were educated chose to be teachers. Even then fewer women compared to men qualified to teach. In the 1930s, for example, Mrs Katherine Mkwasho was the only woman who qualified as a teacher in the Anglican Church.[292] It is clear that missionary education

---

[289] She did her PhD with the University of KwaZulu Natal in Pietermaritzburg: Molly Longwe, A Paradox in a Theology of Freedom and Equality: The Experiences of Pastors' Wives (Amayi Busa) in the Baptist Convention of Malawi (BACOMA), University of KwaZulu Natal, 2012 (Supervisor Prof Isabel Phiri). Her MTh from the same University has been published as: Molly Longwe, *Growing Up. A Chewa Girls' Initiation*, Zomba: Kachere, 2007 (available through African Books Collective, Oxford).

[290] Monica Kishindo, "A Survey of Likoma Island from Early Times to 1935," Final Year History Paper 1969/70, University of Malawi.

[291] Ibid.

[292] Ibid.

programmes were many but this education privileged men more than women.

This subjection of women in church also extended to Post-classical mission churches in varied forms with Charismatic and Pentecostal groups being more progressive in leadership than women in mainline Evangelical churches.[293]

It is sometimes assumed that African Instituted Churches, because they are seen as more culturally relevant,[294] would have more women leaders in the church; but this is not the experience of earlier indigenous churches in Malawi. The major reason is that many early Independent churches were not much different from mainline churches. They were break away groups from mainline churches and in many cases behaved very much the same as their mother churches. So, whether one is a member of a mainline, non-mainline, Evangelical or Charismatic church, women are subjected to a theology that has defined women as subordinate to men. This situation of women in churches prevent them from articulating a theology of women's liberation as such deters them from joining the Circle.

Participation of Men in Women's Issues of Liberation

Against the above restrictions imposed on women to do theological training, it is clear that there is a clear voice from some men in key positions in the church who are encouraging women to have theological training at a higher level. Of these men, it is those that allowed and supported their wives to study theology at a higher level. In the Baptist Convention, Akim Chirwa, Hany Longwe and Klaus Fiedler are examples. Akim Chirwa allowed Martha Chirwa to study theology even as an independent student at Zomba Theological College. Apart from encouraging Molly Longwe to do theological training, Hany Longwe opened space at the Baptist Seminary for women to do theology. This is what enabled Liddah Kalako to go through Seminary

---

[293] Pentecostal and Charismatic Churches are often more open to female leadership due to their Holiness heritage (Barbara Cavannes, "God Calling: Women in Pentecostal Missions" in Grant McClung (ed), *Azusa Street and Beyond*, Gainesville, Bridge-Logos, 2006, pp. 53-66).

[294] This concept is disputed by Hilary Mijoga, *Separate but Same Gospel. Preaching in African Instituted Churches in Southern Malawi*, Blantyre: CLAIM-Kachere, 2000, pp. 167ff.

training.[295] Since then, more women have studied theology at the Baptist Theological Seminary.[296] From the discussion above it is clear that enhancing the number of women from Baptist churches to enrol in a Department of TRS of one of the universities or in other colleges of higher learning cannot be arrived at with one approach.[297] The increase in the number of women studying theology would not have materialized without the sponsorship Klaus Fiedler organized for some of them from Germany.

The increase in the number of women trained in theology in Blantyre Synod (CCAP) can be traced to the time when Rev Silas S. Ncozana was the General Secretary from 1985 to 1995.[298] It was during his time that the first meeting of "Women in Theology" was convoked in Malawi. It was also during this time that Blantyre Synod deliberately invited Female Reverends from abroad to work in their Synod with the intention of sensitizing women to positions of leadership even at the level of the ordained ministry. Some of these women were Peggy Reid, a Canadian minister, and Rev Jane Kamau from the Presbyterian Church of East Africa.[299]

Since the period of Silas Ncozana, Zomba Theological College has contributed positively to the development of Malawi Circle leadership through involving women at leadership level and recruiting them as students. Isabel Apawo Phiri was recruited to teach some courses at this college. Fulata Moyo taught courses on sexuality together with her late husband, Solomon Moyo. Rachel NyaGondwe Banda (Fiedler) taught at the wives' course but was also enrolled at the college in the Diploma course. Martha Chirwa earned her first degree (BDiv) from the same college. Climax to this is that two Circle members, Mrs Mercy Mgeni and Mrs Jannie Chalimba, were employed in the Women's

---

[295] Before entering the Seminary, she was an evangelist, church planter and pastor. She entered the Seminary as a widow and died two months after completing the course (Hany Longwe, *Christians by Grace – Baptists by Choice. A History of the Baptist Convention of Malawi*, Zomba: Kachere, 2010, pp. 114, 174, 245, 268-273).

[296] Currently (2017) there are eleven women among the 65 students.

[297] Several women studied at the African Bible College in Lilongwe, which since then has become a university.

[298] See Isabel Apawo Phiri "1995: The Struggle of Women in the Church and the University of Malawi" Paper, no date, no publisher, accessed 2.3.2006, p. 1.

[299] See Isabel Apawo Phiri, *Women, Presbyterianism and Patriarchy*, Blantyre: CLAIM-Kachere, 2000, p. 138.

Department as staff. They were both very active in the Circle.[300] Getrude Kapuma became a lecturer at Zomba Theological College.

Key Determinants in Establishing the Circle in Malawi

This chapter has shown that the establishment of the Circle in Malawi has been determined by: (1) Women's exposure to feminist and liberation movements. (2) Discipleship work of Circle women leading Circle chapters: if these leaders had been able to give ample time to the discipleship of local women, the Malawi chapter would have developed more strength. (3) The church affiliation of women in Malawi also contributes to their freedom to join the Circle. Since the Circle is preoccupied with unsettling patriarchal hegemonic relationships, some women, because of their church backgrounds, do not see this Circle objective as important for their lives in church and society. Most of these women have suffered from indoctrination into support roles by the leaders of their churches. (4) Low participation at joint meetings of the Circle either locally or abroad. These are avenues where women are exposed to the Circle objectives and approaches that would inspire the women to join the Circle.[301] (5) Low enrolment of female students at Chancellor College has also contributed to the lag in the development of the Malawi Circle. At the continental level, it has been shown that Circle chapters that are attached to academic institutions have more vigour than those chapters that exist away from such institutions. The women theologians at Chancellor College would have inspired the Circle to be committed to its goals of research and publishing. (6) Local experiences in church and society have also barred women from aspiring to write regarding unsettling relationships in the church and society. For some women in such churches, women do not need theological training for them to be leaders at higher levels of church government. (7) Contact to winds of change in general has a bearing on women joining the Circle. (8) Survival considerations: Christian women in Malawi view survival in personal faith, church and society

---

[300] She has completed her MA by now: Jannie Chalimba, Daughters of the King. Women in CCAP Blantyre Synod. MA, University of Malawi, 2011.

[301] Chimwemwe Katumbi, a lecturer at the Department of Theology and Religious Studies of the University of Malawi attended for the first time a Circle meeting in Ghana in 2009, but she did this from Scotland where she was on a 9 months teaching assignment of the Scottish – Malawian Partnership.

as an important aspect of their lives. If such survival has been established, it must be sustained regardless of changing circumstances, unless other alternatives present them with the same or better ways of survival. (9) Pneumatological considerations: whereas the Circle is seeking liberation through cultural reinterpretation, biblical reinterpretation, and redefining patriarchal power relations, some women, especially those in Charismatic and Pentecostal churches, rely on the Holy Spirit to transform patriarchal hegemonic relationships between men and women in church and society. The above factors are not conclusive but highlight the real struggles the Malawi faces in its efforts to establish a live chapter. Further, these factors are an eye opener to positive factors that are repressive to Circle chapters in different countries in Africa.

Chapter 5: The Role of Zones, Regions and Study Commissions in the Growth of the Circle

At the 1989 Convocation the women were challenged to establish local (country) chapters as well as to hold Zonal meetings (meetings that call together delegates from more than one country) in different areas as part of inculcating transformation of gender inequalities. The role of the local chapters has been described in chapter 3 as well in chapter 4.

These local circles and Zonal meetings became coals of fire upon which pots of transforming gender inequalities were placed. These pots boiled at different intensities depending on the place, but most especially on the personalities that managed the pots. The climax of the Zonal Circles is the Institute for Religion and Culture established by Mercy Amba Oduyoye in Accra, Ghana.

Zones

The other push in the genesis of country chapters was through group work. This was especially done through Zonal meetings where two or more countries collectively engaged in research and writing and presented their work at one chosen venue. This was most beneficial to countries that were not so well established in terms of having their own local chapters. Such meetings became a learning environment and an inspiration for establishing chapters in their own countries. The other advantage of these Zonal meetings was that the countries that met were close by in terms of geographical proximity. This allowed a larger number of women to attend these meetings than if the meeting had been held far from them, as was the case with the Convocation. After the Zonal meetings, it is clear that there was much learning that took place in terms of research and writing to the point that other countries were stimulated to do research and writing in their own countries as a chapter.

There were four meetings of this nature and because they were meetings that took place in the middle before the following continental meeting in 1996, they were called Biennial meetings. All of these meetings took place in 1993 and 1994. Before the Zonal conferences, there was a main Planning Committee that took place in December 1992 in Accra, Ghana. Here the International Planning Committee was involved. It was given the mandate to coordinate the Zonal conferences with the local Circle women. Thus, before each Biennial Institute there was again another Planning Committee. This Planning Committee was usually composed of one or two people from the International Committee and the others were from the country where the meeting was to be held. Such arrangements also provided opportunities of mentoring new members of the Circle into how they can organize institutes.

The other task of the planning meetings was to set up the agenda of the institutes as well as the particular issues to be addressed. The theme and proposed list of issues were always sent before the actual institutes because the delegates to the institutes had to research and write papers to read at the institute where they would be subjected to intellectual scrutiny to improve their quality for publication. This process required editorial work of those that were experienced in writing quality papers that would qualify for publication. The writing of a paper was a condition for being selected to attend a conference. It is because of this that some Circle members have not attended institutes even though they are registered members.

In Southern Africa, Rev Phina Olga Kgosana was chosen as leader of the Zonal meetings there. She had not been a member of IPC. Southern Africa here includes the Anglophone countries of the south: Malawi, Zambia, Botswana, Namibia, Swaziland, South Africa and Zimbabwe.

In 1992 the first Zonal meeting took place when there was a Regional meeting in Manzini, Swaziland.[1] At this conference, the Circle cooperated with EDICESA, an organization that later on also cooperated with the Eastern and Southern African Conference that took place in Nairobi in 1994. Other three Zonal/Regional conferences followed. The theme for these meetings, with the exception of the one for Francophone Africa, was 'Women in the Household of God.'[2]

Rev Grace Ndyabahika was chosen to lead the Eastern Africa Zone.[3] She also had not been a member of the IPC. Her area included Uganda, Kenya and Tanzania.

---

[1] Ibid.

[2] Ecumenical Information and Documentation Centre for Eastern and Southern Africa.

[3] She contributed: Grace N. Ndyabahika, "Women's Place in Creation," in Musimbi Kanyoro and Nyambura Njoroge (eds), *Groaning in Faith: African Women in the Household of God*, Nairobi: Acton, 1996, pp. 23-30.

For the Western Africa Zone, Dr Rabiatu Ammah, a Muslim, was chosen. She was already a lecturer at the University of Ghana in Legon. She too had not been a member of the IPC. In the West African Zone, Rhodah Ada James and Margaret Umeagudosu became prominent leaders. Their inspiration came mainly from the late Sr Rosemary Edet who was a Nigerian and a member of the International Planning Committee. In Ghana, the women had the advantage of having the founder of the Circle, Mercy Amba Oduyoye and a key member of the International Planning Committee, Dr Elizabeth Amoah.

Through the guidance of Mercy and Elizabeth Amoah, Rev Rachel Entrue Tetteh, Rev Dora Ofori-Owusu and Ms Rebecca Iwuchukwu became prominent leaders. While less is heard about Rhodah Ada James, Margaret Umeagudosu has contributed a lot to the growth of the Circle in Nigeria. She is the founder of the local chapter in Nigeria.

The West African Zonal Meeting was set to take place in 1993 in Lagos, Nigeria. However, because of political strife in Nigeria, the venue shifted to Accra, Ghana. The meeting date also shifted to December 16-21, 1993.[4] Mercy Amba Oduyoye, who was the coordinator of the Circle then, led the planning group. However, as she usually does not work in isolation, her sisters accompanied her from Nigeria as well as from Ghana. From the Nigeria side, Rhodah Ada James and Margaret Umeagudosu were responsible for the local arrangements in the earlier place when the meeting was to take place in Nigeria, Lagos. The suggested number of participants was firstly 15 and then it climbed to 27.[5] In fact the list presented to Mercy at the end of it all was 33. At this occurrence, Mercy Amba Oduyoye did not hesitate to hammer on what the agenda of Circle is, namely to research and write. She presented her view to the local organizing committee there in this way: "But please stick to our decision that only those that have written papers should attend the conference, otherwise the reason for our existence will be defeated."[6] She also highlighted the difference between what the Circle and other Church women groups are doing. In this she was referring to the fact that if the Circle held conferences where all women are welcome

---

[4] John Pobee - Elizabeth Amoah, 10.9.1993.

[5] Ibid.

[6] Mercy Amba Oduyoye - Margaret Umeagudosu and Rhodah Ada James, Geneva, 16.6.1993.

whether they write or not, there would be no difference with other church women groups. This is also why she explains that even though in the beginning women who did not write were invited to the meeting in Nigeria, it was only to enable them to get to know one another as women face to face but also to identify writing African women theologians.[7]

Even when the venue changed, they worked hard in making sure that the women from Nigeria came to the meeting. The women were really brave to come to the Convocation in spite of the political upheaval in Nigeria then. But even then, some women from the Calabar region that earlier wanted to attend the meeting could not come because of the war there. The cancellation was a disappointment to some but this is where Mercy also demonstrated her leadership abilities and concern for others. To her, to pray for the peace of Nigerians was crucial and she was willing to postpone the meeting to a later date and even change the venue.[8] The key person on the Nigerian side was Sr Rosemary Edet, but by that time she was very sick and had been flown to USA for medical treatment. The meeting was to take place at the Eucharistic Heart of Jesus Generalate, 7 Amore Str. off Toyin Str, Ikeja, Lagos.

On the Ghana side, Dr Elizabeth Amoah led the planning committee. Having been in the International Planning Meeting meant that she had experience in organizing meetings of this nature. She worked with Rev Rachel Entrue Tetteh and Rev Dora Ofori-Owusu. However, in terms of communication, Mercy often wrote to Dr Elizabeth Amoah and Rev Rachel Entrue Tetteh.[9] In the end, it was decided that only 30 delegates come to the conference because of reasons related to the cancellation of the earlier venue and postponement of the meeting in Ghana. Mercy Amba Oduyoye wrote: "You will recall that it has been proposed to hold in Nigeria a consultation on 'Women in the Commonwealth of God' Unfortunately the political developments of last July did not make it wise to go ahead with it. Consequently, it lost a substantial part of the deposit made on board and lodging. We now propose Ghana as venue. There will be 30 persons maximum." At that time Ghana was planning to send 17 and many were

---

[7] Ibid.
[8] Letter to Sisters by Mercy Amba Oduyoye, 24.3.1993.
[9] Mercy Amba Oduyoye - Rachel Tetteh, Geneva, 3.6.1993.

already working on their papers. But just as in the case of the Nigeria chapter, Mercy insisted that the local organizers of Ghana limit the number of delegates. Mercy wrote: "My heart bleeds to think we cannot say to all that are interested: come."[10] The conference was in the end held in Accra, Ghana. According to the programme made by the planning committee, Sr Rosemary was to take a major role. She was the moderator of the conference. Apart from that she was to speak on the topic 'The Household of God: Biblical Exegesis on the Place of Women in the Kingdom of God.' She was also supposed to close the session, as it was customary that the host country carries out that function. However, the fact that she was picked to close the session amidst other Nigerian Circle women shows the respect she commanded from the Nigerian Circle as well as those from other countries to come to the conference. Sr Rosemary Edet has since passed on to be with the Lord soon after. To signify her importance, there was a special call at the 1996 conference to remember her death.

The other key player on the programme was to be Mercy Amba Oduyoye. Rebecca Iwuchukwu was to speak on 'Women and Religion in Africa.' She was to present this paper on the second day of the conference, on the 19th July 1993. Rev Rachel Tetteh was to lead worship and do a Bible Study on 'Participation and Inclusiveness in the Commonwealth of God.' Other Circle women were to lead the five workshops planned for the Institute. The workshops were heavy on issues of Culture and Religion. In terms of Religion, African Traditional Religion was more pronounced than Christianity and Islam. Three sessions were on African Traditional Religion. These were: 'Women Rituals,' to be presented by Ms Rebecca Ganusah, 'Religion, Taboo and Women' to be presented by Dr Margaret Umeagudosu, and finally the one on 'Witchcraft and Spirit Possession from the Women's Perspective' by Dr Elizabeth Amoah.[11]

There was only one workshop that alluded to the Christian Religion and the Muslim Religion. The topic for this workshop was 'The Earth Belongs to God: Women's Response' to be presented by Sr (Dr) Rosemary Edet. The high dosage of African Traditional Religion in the discourses at the West African

---

[10] Conference Programme, The Circle of Concerned African Women Theologians Biennial Institutes Project, Session Zonal Conferences (West Africa), 18-23 July 1993 Lagos/Nigeria.

[11] Conference Programme, 18-23 July, Nigeria/Lagos.

Zonal conference resonates well with the common perceptions by Africans that Western Africa is strong on African Traditional Religions. This might have been very attractive to the participants. The last workshop: 'Violence against Women' was a crosscutting theme for all religions. Deaconess Ekundayo presented this seminar.[12]

The Institute of the East African Zone took place in 1994, January 4-8 in Nairobi, Kenya. The venue of the conference was the Methodist Guest House, a place that hosts many ecumenical meetings. The theme of the conference was 'Women in God's Kingdom.' The title of the theme reads differently from the one adopted by the West African English-Speaking Conference, but in essence they both mean the same. The interpretation of 'Commonwealth of God' is that religious women have a common right and responsibility to the World. Further, since we belong to God, the earth is a common home. The word Commonwealth is also Kingdom.[13] Again at this conference, cooperate leadership was visible in the Circle in both working as a team but also cooperating with other groups. The cooperating organization at this time was the Ecumenical Information and Documentation Centre for Eastern and Southern Africa (EDICESA). The conference attracted women from 11 African countries and women from two Nordic countries to set the Institute in process.

Just as at the West African Zonal Meeting, the main focus of the Institute was African Traditional Religions. The papers were to hinge on the theme of environment and women's health. In addition to this there was a strong emphasis on the Bible. In fact, there were already suggested passages on which the women needed to theologize. The following were the topics: a workshop was to deliberate on the sub theme 'Environment'. The suggested topics under this theme were: The Earth Belongs to God: Women's Perspective; the Sacredness of Nature in African Religion; Christianity and Islam; the Symbolic Living of Africans in their Traditional Natural Environment; the Goddess in African Religions and their Influence on Women; Women's Priesthood in Relation to Nature; Totemism; Sacred Places and Objects (like rivers, hills, mountains trees, etc).

---

[12] Ibid.

[13] Memo from WCC to Musimbi Kanyoro from Mercy Amba Oduyoye.

In the second workshop, again Traditional Religion relating to women's well-being was tackled. The topics under this theme were: Religion and Women's Health, Taboos and Women's Well-being; Effects of Rituals on Women's Well-being; Sexuality and Women's Well-being; Women and Spirit Possession; Witch Craft and Witch Hunting: Women's Perspective; African Symbols of Hospitality: the Place of Women; Women in the African Traditional Religions; Religious Pluralism in Africa: Women's Experience.

The last workshop was on 'Biblical Perspectives on the Commonwealth of God.' Under this theme, the following topics were suggested: Participation and Inclusiveness; Dignity and Worth; Justice; Biblical Exegesis of the following texts: Proverbs 9:1-6; Wisdom's Feast; Gen 16 and 21:1-2; Gen 22:1-19, Sarah and Hagar; Isaiah 55:1-3 (Mt 11:28-30); 1 Kings 17:8-16; Mt 25: 31-41, the Last Judgement; 1 Corinthians 11:17-34; Hospitality in Corinthians; Romans 8, Creation and Groaning; Eph 2:11-12 Breaking down the Walls.[14]

The picture shown in the various issues that the women dealt with in the area of tradition and the Bible confirms that the perception that these women were mainly writing to vie for positions in the church is wrong. In fact, topics on women's participation in the church at this institute were few and at the Western Africa Zonal meeting, there were no topics to that end. Papers for this conference were sent to Dr Nyambura Njoroge and Musimbi Kanyoro who at that time were already working in Switzerland.

The participants at this meeting came from Swaziland, South Africa, Tanzania, Angola, Zambia, Uganda, Namibia, Zimbabwe, Malawi, and Kenya.[15] There were about 50 women who attended the Institute. The funds for the conference were raised both locally in Nairobi and internationally.

The key player for this conference was Mary Getui Nyanchama, as Teresa Hinga, who had started with her, had left for the USA. Mary Getui Nyanchama joined the Circle in 1994.[16] Her role in coordinating the Anglo African Institute in Kenya is crucial.

---

[14] Musimbi Kanyoro - Mary Getui and Teresa Hinga, 21.9.1993.

[15] Document, Circle of Concerned African Women Theologians, Process of Creating Biennial Institutes of African Women in Religion and Culture, nd, no author, The Institute of Religion and Culture, Ghana, 14.9.2005.

[16] Int Mary Getui, The Institute of Religion and Culture, Ghana, 14.9.2005.

For the Francophone Africa Zone Ms Hélène Yinda was chosen.[17] Francophone countries include all countries that are French speaking. These countries include Cameroon, Ivory Coast and Congo.

The Institute was held in Douala, Cameroon, 25 - 31 July 1993.[18] The theme of the conference was "African Hospitality and Christian Women," different from the two other Zonal institutes in other regions. The Institute attracted 40 women from Francophone countries: Senegal, Ivory Coast, Togo, Benin, Madagascar, Burundi, Rwanda, Zaire and Cameroon. Interesting at this conference was also the use of drama in theologizing. There was a drama on men's solidarity with women and what the church could do about it. The coordinators of the Institute were Rev Louise Ngo Tappa and Dr Rose Zoë-Obianga from the International Planning Committee. Again, the spirit of cooperative leadership was strong here in that the organizers worked with FEMEC and WCC. The papers at this conference were being prepared for publication by Ms Colette Bouka–Coula and by Rev Sr Justine Kahungu who had been a key presenter at the 1989 conference. Each Zonal Institute was also undertaking the process of editing. There were three teams in total doing the editorial work, but also two teams coordinating the publication of AMKA.[19] Out of this, two issues of AMKA were published.[20]

For Lusophone Africa, Ms Eva Gomez was chosen as leader. Circle women that were part of the IPC whether within the country or abroad always assisted these leaders.

Regions

Apart from local chapters and Zones, the 1989 Convocation instituted the regions to facilitate Circle work in the different regions. This meant that the Continental leaders through collaboration were to coordinate the work in Zonal/Biennial Institutes/Regional Conferences in different areas. According to the decision, these regional meetings were to take place before the continental meeting to be held in 1996. The interchangeable usage of the

---

[17] She wrote, among others, Hélène Yinda, *Cercle des Théologiennnes Africaines Engagées: Femmes Africaines. Le Pouvoir de Transformer le Monde*, Yaoundé: Editions Sherpa, 2002.

[18] Mercy Amba Oduyoye, WCC, 16.7.1993 - Monsieur le Pasteur Harry Henry.

[19] Document "1996 Institute of African Women in Religion and Culture," no date, no name.

[20] Ibid.

words: Regional Institutes and Zonal Institutes is neither confusing nor giving opposing meanings. They are appropriate. These meetings are Institutes because they were vehicles of learning. This learning was achieved through group mentoring, through lectures and group discussions. Those members that were knowledgeable of the issues and how best to tackle them became mentors for the beginners. These meetings were Zonal as well as Regional because they involved more than one country and more or less followed language and geographical position of the particular countries.

In addition to the Zonal leaders, the Convocation also elected communication secretaries for the particular regions. Regions were bigger than Zones. For example, the Anglophone Region included countries that are in West Africa, East Africa and Southern Africa. Whereas Regions were organized along the lines of colonial languages, Zonal meetings were different. They were organized in accordance with their proximity to each other. That some Zonal areas were grouped along colonial language lines was just a coincidence.[21] Communication secretaries were appointed to work together with the Zonal coordinators in communication of activities of the Circle within their particular regions. In the Francophone region, the communication's secretary was Sr Bernadette Mbuy-Beya, who had been a member of the IPC. For the Anglophone Region the communication secretary, Dr Teresa Mbiri Hinga, had not been a member of the IPC.[22]

The inclusion of members of the IPC was crucial in the development of the work during this period so as to enforce a process of mentoring between those in the IPC and the new leaders involved in the Zonal conferences. Indeed, this process of mentoring produced many able leaders.

In the Eastern and Southern African regions, Nyambura Njoroge, Isabel Apawo Phiri, Denise Ackermann and Mary Getui Nyanchama became prominent. Although it was Teresa Hinga who was elected to be Communications leader for the Anglophone region, her move outside Africa is the reason that her involvement in the Circle activities in this region at this time was short-lived. Mary Getui Nyanchama played a major role in the Zonal

---

[21] A product of such cooperation between Zones along language lines is: Musimbi Kanyoro and Nyambura Njoroge (eds), *Groaning in Faith: African Women in the Household of God*, Nairobi: Acton, 1996, in which the Eastern and Southern African Zones cooperated.

[22] Provisional Addis Ababa Circle Report, p. 3, accessed 6.3.2006.

meetings in the absence of Teresa Hinga. She was greatly assisted by Nyambura Njoroge. Contributions of Nyambura Njoroge after the Zonal meetings have been in the area of editing Circle books as well as leading a study commission on ministerial formation, which will be discussed in the upcoming chapter. Isabel Apawo Phiri became a key catalyst in the Southern Region Circle but also at the continental level. Her life story and contributions to the Circle will be found in the story of the Circle in her country of origin, Malawi, in South Africa where she has been a considerable number of years, and in the context of her being the continental coordinator of the Circle from 2002 to 2007.

Study Commissions

At the 1996 Convocation, when Musimbi Kanyoro became Continental leader, it was agreed that women would also promote their Circle objectives through thematic groupings. These were called Study Commissions. Since the establishment of these groupings there has been an increase in theological literature. In this book, I elaborate on the Study Commission in chapter 6 to give a special space on their contribution to theological education.

However, the drastic decision to have study commissions, using a thematic approach, seems to have killed the momentum of chapters, Zonal meetings, and regions with their geographic approach. Since the role of Zonal meetings and regional meetings was to encourage and strengthen local chapters, a laxity in conducting them has cost the Circle the possibility of having more vibrant local chapters. Zonal meetings developed leadership in different geographical regions to the benefit of local chapters in that particular part of Africa. In fact, the dream at the 1989 Convocation was to have Biennial Institutes before the next continental conference. With the institution of Study Commissions, Zonal meetings could hardly take place. Musimbi Kanyoro outlines one of the reasons why it was hard for Zonal meetings to take place, in this way:

> Zonal leaders found it difficult to function because the Circle had no financial infrastructure to support their travel. Some of the newly elected leaders were not fully aware that all Circle work is voluntary, and when they realized they were expected to volunteer long hours, their commitment decreased.[23]

---

[23] Ibid., p. 34.

The Circle meetings were mainly those specialized in different areas of theologizing in relation to the Study Commissions. Such conferences were those held in Johannesburg: firstly on "Biographies of Women" and later "On Being Church." It is only those Circle members who could research and write within the particular Study Commission that would take part. Other Study Commissions did not even hold a meeting. This led to Circle members in different localities being inactive.

The Institute of Women in Religion and Culture

Hereafter, I describe the Institute of Women in Religion and Culture in Ghana. I have chosen to give it a special treatment because it stands out in the way chapters and zonal meetings operate elsewhere. Since it was started by Mercy Amba Oduyoye, it has the potential to illuminate her vision of how a typical local chapter and zone would operate.

Mercy Amba Oduyoye founded the Institute in 1999 at Trinity College Campus in Legon, Ghana, with the intention of promoting research on women in religion and culture, and of developing a theology in which women and men are equal.

The time she was convener of the Study Commission on Religion and Culture, she committed her life to this. The starting point was when she convened a meeting, held in Johannesburg, South Africa, with her colleagues in the Study Commission. After this meeting, she began the Institute in Ghana primarily for Ghanaian women.[24] Though the Institute started in 1998, it was only officially inaugurated on 13 October 1999 at Trinity College.[25] The college had been requested to provide eight rooms for the conference in the women's hall.[26] This was in the year 1998. She was given room number 25. By 1999, the number of women participating in the programme had increased and she had to ask the college for an additional room. The college again considered her request and granted her an additional room, number 21. The work continued to grow, and in 2002, Mercy again approached the College Board to provide another room for the women. The college now was alerted to the

---

[24] Int Mercy Amba Oduyoye, Institute of Women in Religion and Culture, Accra, 14.9.2005.

[25] Circular Letter, Mercy Amba Oduyoye to Persons Invited to the 2003 Institute of Women in Religion and Culture Meeting, 8.9.2003.

[26] Mercy Amba Oduyoye - Rev Dr Dan Antwi, Principal, Trinity College, 12.8.1999.

need for more space for the Institute. Mercy Amba Oduyoye decided that a centre for the women should be built on a separate location within the Trinity campus to cater for the growing numbers of women participating in the Institute. The Board of Trinity College agreed to this proposal and the building began in 2003. The Board asked Mercy Amba Oduyoye about the name of the building and she decided that the building be called Talitha Qumi Centre. This name was chosen so as to keep its relationship to the vision of the Circle.[27]

The name had its origin from a Bible study on the story of the centurion's daughter. This story is about Jairus' daughter who was brought back to life by Jesus. This Bible study was done at the 1989 Convocation and since then the title Talitha Qumi has appeared in different places, including in titles of Circle books. The funding for the building largely came from the Presbyterian Church of USA and individual donors.[28]

The first Institute was the inauguration in 1999. Apart from women from Ghana, there were about 15 who were invited internationally to the meeting as guests. These were Sallie Cuff, Denise Ackermann, Daisy Nwachukwu, Mercy I. Omoigi, Anneke Geesense-Ravestein, Omega Bula, Gae Han, Christina Landman, M.I. Oguntoyinbo-Atere, Grace Ereme, Mbenda Ngo, Hélène Yinda, Justine Kahungu Mbwiti, Hannah Wangeci Kinoti, Sr Annie Wasike Nasimiyu, and Puleng Lenka-Bula.[29] Already at this juncture, the issue of women's health was of primary concern.[30]

The next Pan African Meeting took place in 2001, again at Trinity Theological Seminary.[31] In 2003, another Conference took place from 4-9 October, also at Trinity Theological Seminary.[32] The conference had women from three main groups: African Women Theologians, ethicists and other women theologians.[33] There were 44 invited guests, who can further be grouped into

---

[27] Oral Presentation, Rev Afo Blay, Pan African Conference, 12.9.2005.

[28] Ibid.

[29] Document, International Arrivals, Institute Correspondence, 8.9.2003.

[30] Mercy Amba Oduyoye to Elizabeth Calvin, 17.9.2005.

[31] Mercy Amba Oduyoye, the Director, Institute of Women in Religion and Culture, Trinity Theological College, addressed to all participants, 8.9.2003.

[32] Ibid.

[33] Ibid.

three main groups: Africans, Ghana locals, those of African descent and partners. The African group was made up of Bernadette Mbuy-Beya, Helen Labeodan, Dr Musa Dube, Betty Govinden, Mabel Katahweire, Rev Dr Teresa Okure, Dr Christina Landman, Dr Mary Gouty, Dr Musimbi Kanyoro, Prof Isabel Phiri, Dr Vibila Vuadi, Nyambura Njoroge, Ms Hélène Yinda, Felicidade Cherinda, and Mary Tusuubira. From the Local Ghana Group, there were: Rev Dorothy Akoto, Dr Elizabeth Amoah, Dr Rabiatu Ammah, Angelina Wood, and Mrs Rosemary A. Among–Otego, Sr Paulette Ankara, Dina Abbey Mesh, Mabel Katahweire, Lydia Adajahwah, Patience Dickson, Araba Ata Sam, Ama Afo Blay. Women of African descent were Prof Katie Cannon, Detaili Kpodza, Eleanor Scarlet, Hazel A. Camayne, Kathryn Addo, and Elsa Tamez. Women who came as partners were: June Rogers, Anne King, Elizabeth Calvin, Margaret Farley, Letty M. Russel, Shannon Clarkson, Shawn Madigan, Esther Suter and Barbara Schmid.[34]

Whereas the Circle took up the issue of HIV/AIDS after the 2002 Convocation, the Institute of Women in Religion and Culture started efforts on the issue of HIV/AIDS already in 2000. It also held a national conference and collaborated well in the implementation of the Circle Pan African Conference that took place in Addis Ababa, Ethiopia.[35] After this 2002 Institute, the Institute participated in the Yale Divinity School Initiative on HIV/AIDS in Africa.[36] The Institute held another Pan African Conference in 2003 in Ghana.[37]

From 1999 to 2003, "be it retreat, workshop, seminar, national conference or Pan African Conference gathering, has featured the concern of women's health with specific emphasis on HIV/AIDS."[38] In 2003, the theme of the Conference was "Theological and Ethical Resources to Face the Challenge of the HIV/AIDS Pandemic."[39] The organizer of this institute was Mercy Amba

---

[34] Document, Correspondence File, accessed 15.3.2005.

[35] Mercy Amba Oduyoye to Elizabeth Harding, 17.12.2002.

[36] In 2003/2004 Sr Annie Nasimiyu and Dorothy Ucheaga were the first fellows of this programme (Regional Circle Report 2005, p. 24).

[37] Letter of Invitation to Elizabeth Calvin, 17.12.2002.

[38] Letter of Invitation Mercy Amba Oduyoye to all Participants, 8.9.2003.

[39] Letter of Invitation, Mrs Hannah Agyeman, National Women's Secretary, Apostolic Church, Ghana, 21.7.2003.

Oduyoye, the Director of the Institute.[40] Joyce Boham was key in making contacts by email as well as phone calls.[41] Prominent women were: Lt.-Col. Mrs Doris Afoul (League of Mercy Secretary) and Captain (Miss) Agatha Easel (Alum Medical Clinic).[42]

Mercy Amba Oduyoye likes to cooperate. She demonstrated this as mother of the Circle in many ways, but also as director of the Institute of Women in Religion and Culture. The Institute's board had the following members: Rabiatu Ammah, Mercy Amba Oduyoye, Lorene Nyaka, Isabel Phiri, Elizabeth Amoah, Dinah Abbey Mensal, Esther Offer–Abusage, Irene Dottie, A.A. Akron, J.A. Add, Kwesi Sam Woode, Lilly Oteng-Yeboah, Fr Paul Beke, Sam Addo and Redd Emmanuel Asante.[43]

Lessons from the Institute

The institute traces its origin to the Study Commission on Religion and Culture where Mercy was one of the conveners.[44] Mercy Amba Oduyoye implemented the vision of how these local institutes would look like by developing an Institute that is locally owned and managed without missing the link to the other Circle women and religious women in general who are involved in either written or practical theology. The pattern of involving women in religion from all walks of life, although the Circle's main emphasis is research and writing, is not meant to sideline women who cannot do academic research, writing and publishing. At the Convocation itself, there were church women that did not or could not write academic papers. At Zonal meetings, it was common to have such church women participate in the meetings.

The advantage in the inclusion of non-academics is that it is a learning process for both sides. At the 2005 institute, for example, there were women from different churches and from the Muslim community, mostly from the

---

[40] Letter of Acknowledgement from Angela Dwamera Aboagye, Executive Director, The Ark Foundation, Ghana, 18.08.2003.

[41] For example, Acknowledgement Letter, Anne Harding, Col Territorial President of Women's Ministry, to Mercy Amba Oduyoye, 9.9.2003.

[42] Ibid. The military titles refer to Salvation Army officers.

[43] List, Institute of Women in Religion and Culture, accessed 15.9.2003.

[44] Int Mercy Amba Oduyoye, Institute of Women in Religion and Culture, 14.9.2005.

women's groups that participated in the institute. Some of them were leaders of women's groups, others were pastors' wives. The result of this pattern is that theological reflection is also adjusted to the level of the participants. Discussions, for example, were conducted in groups according to language familiarity. The varieties of local Ghanaian languages were also taken into account. Those who did not understand any of the Ghanaian languages were put in a group that used English for the discussions. The deliberations, although carried out in different languages, were reported to the group in English because in each group someone who knew English was included. Both the lectures and the reports from the group discussions were in English, and there were always summaries in vernacular languages.[45] The approach was that the participants were not obliged to articulate theology through an academic paper; sharing experiences orally was also an acceptable form of doing theology. In one of the invitations to the 2003 Institute the invited persons were asked to come and share their experiences.[46] This, of course, applied only to local Ghanaian participants. On the other hand, international guests, unless advised otherwise, were required to write a paper as a condition for them to attend the conference. Should this practice not be followed by local chapters elsewhere? This way of doing theological reflection together with those that are not academics but practitioners of religion would be energizing and fruitful in many countries in Africa. Those in the academy would be able to learn from those that are not but are involved in grass roots programmes such as Home-Based Care. The Ghana Circle, through the Institute, creates awareness in women about the Circle through regular programmes of the Institute that take place about three times a year and are called "Forward Seminars." These seminars are held in different parts of Ghana and they are followed by national conferences alternatively to the Pan African Institutes.[47] If such a strategy was adopted and emulated by other local chapters, there is a possibility that these local Circle chapters would increase their vitality.

---

[45] Personal Observation, Institute of Women in Religion and Culture Meeting, Ghana 12.-16.9.2005.

[46] Circular Letter, Mercy Amba Oduyoye, 2003 Correspondence File, accessed 15.9.2005.

[47] Mercy Amba Oduyoye - Prof Amoah from Correspondence File, accessed 15.9.2005.

Editorial Work

Editorial work was important even at this stage of Zonal Institutes. Nyambura Njoroge, as regards the East Africa Zonal Conference, insisted that there should be a workshop entitled "Revisiting Circle Writing Style." She suggested Ms Joyce Tsabede and Isabel Apawo Phiri to lead this workshop.[48] Nyambura Njoroge's role at this meeting was also to make sure that brief updates of local chapters were given. Using a cooperative model of leadership, she decided that a specific Circle member would prepare each local update and that each one would present the brief report for 10 minutes at the conference. The presenters were: Musimbi Kanyoro, who would present an update on the Circle and its Historical Background; Denise Ackermann who would present South Africa (Cape Town and Johannesburg Chapters); Teresa Hinga on East Africa; Ms Kathindi on Namibia and Mercy Amba Oduyoye on West African Circles.[49] There has also been publishing in Francophone Africa.[50]

Conclusion

The Circle has developed geographically and yet, from this history, it is true that the change in focus from Zones and Regions to Study Commissions derailed the opening of new chapters. On the other hand, there was an increase in theological literature which is an issue that this book tackles in the following chapter.

---

[48] Letter for Nyambura Njoroge, World Alliance of Reformed Churches, 19.11.1993.

[49] Ibid.

[50] One of the titles is Hélène Yinda and Kä Mana, *Pour la Nouvelle Théologie des Femmes Africaines. Repenser la difference sexuelle, promouvoir les droits des femmes et libérer leurs energies créatives*, Yaoundé: Editions CLE-CIPRE, 2001. Another title is Hélène Yinda, *Cercle des Théologiennnes Africaines Engagées: Femmes Africaines. Le Pouvoir de Transformer le Monde*, Yaoundé: Editions Sherpa, 2002.

Chapter 6: Contributions of the Circle to Theological Education

In this chapter, I outline some of the contributions of the Circle to theological education in the period from its conception to 2007. The Circle is not the only mouth piece that has made the contribution. Thus, I do not claim that the contributions I include in this chapter are solely the achievements of the Circle. I am aware that there are other fora that have contributed to the same cause. I also do not claim to present all the contributions of the Circle in this area, because the Circle is geographically widespread and it would have been financially impossible to collect all the achievements of the Circle in the area of Theological Education. It should be recalled that at the first Circle convocation, the Circle clearly outlined areas of its focus.[1] I have taken these ambitions into perspective as I present some of the contributions of the Circle to theological education in this chapter.

Production of Literature

One area where the Circle has made notable contributions is in the academic world. One of the concerns for organizing the Circle was that there were few books in the academic arena of theology that were written by women. This created what African women theologians called 'the dearth of literature on African women by African women.'[2] The women sought to change this situation by committing themselves to publish for the academic study of religion and culture.[3] Over the years, Circle women have published theological books or articles that have transformed this landscape of theological literature in Africa. With such literature on women available,

---

[1] These goals were well summarized. They included the following areas: To create a forum for women's issues, to publish women's theologies, to research on women's issues, to include women's issues in academia, to promote cross cultural studies on contemporary women's issues and so on. See Mercy Amba Oduyoye and Musimbi Kanyoro (eds), *Talitha Qumi. Proceedings of the Convocation of African Women Theologians 1989*, Accra: Sam Woode, 2001, p. 3.

[2] Ibid.

[3] Ibid.

some theological institutions have introduced women studies. Mzuzu University has developed a full course on African Feminist Theology.[4]

Mercy Amba Oduyoye is one of the earliest African women that wrote such theology even before the inception of the Circle. One of the earlier women during this time that wrote was Chief (Mrs) Ogundipe, who wrote on the ordination of women in the Methodist Church in 1977.[5] At the same time Mercy Amba Oduyoye wrote the book "And Women, where do they come in?"[6] This is another testimony that shows that there were movements before the Circle that promoted women's liberation. Major fora that did this were EATWOT and the World Council of Churches.

Mercy Amba Oduyoye's contribution to writing theology has inspired many to embark on the same. Many women would never have written a book or an article had they not been inspired by the Circle and its theological literature. At a special Circle conference "Malaka-le[7] Theologies: Women, Religion and Health in Africa," held in Johannesburg at Kempton Park from 12th to 15th July 2005, one could not doubt that Mercy Amba Oduyoye' writings had made a profound impact on the participating women and their lives, but also on men and other women in Africa in general. This was shown at a round table meeting that was aimed at celebrating the life of Mercy Amba Oduyoye in a special way. Nyambura Njoroge, the mother of a Theology of Lament, chaired this meeting. Mercy's literature was seen to have visibly encouraged other Circle women to write.

---

[4] The main courses are: Religion and Feminist Theology (year 1), African Feminist Theologies (year 2), Gender and Human Justice (year 3) and African Feminist Theologies and Development (year 4). In addition, other courses like New Testament, Church History or Missiology contain clear feminist elements.

[5] Chief (Mrs) G.T. Ogundipe, *The Ordination of Women*, Lagos: Methodist Church Nigeria Literature Bureau, 1977.

[6] The full titles of the books are: Mercy Amba Oduyoye *And Women, where do they Come in?* Lagos: Methodist Church Nigeria Literature Bureau, 1977; Chief (Mrs) G.T. Ogundipe, *The Ordination of Women*, Lagos: Methodist Church Nigeria Literature Bureau, 1977. See Mercy Amba Oduyoye, *Daughters of Anowa, African Women and Patriarchy*, Maryknoll: Orbis, 1995, p. 223.

[7] At the conference Mercy told the story that one day she had problems opening a drawer and decided to break it open. Her housemaid told her: "Malaka-le," use a gentle approach. And she opened the drawer without breaking anything.

Miranda Naomi Pillay from Tanzania, for example, encountered Mercy's writings way before she met her in 1995, the year when Mercy went to the University of Western Cape where she was given an honorary doctor's degree.[8] Mercy's book was for Miranda Naomi Pillay the first work from the Circle she ever read. Thus, when Denise Ackermann, the pillar of the Cape Town chapter, introduced to her to Mercy as a person and as the author of the Circle, it made sense to her. She is now a strong member of the Circle.

The other Circle woman that read Mercy's writings before becoming a Circle member is Beatrice Okeyere-Manu. Beatrice was inspired by Mercy Amba Oduyoye's book "Daughters of Anowa," through which she nurtured her heart regarding issues of gender inequalities.[9] She read this work between 1989 and 1996. After this period, she was privileged to meet Mercy personally in 2003 at the same time as Lilian Siwila.[10] This was the time when Mercy came to Pietermaritzburg and came to Isabel Apawo Phiri's class as a guest.

Philomena Njeri Mwaura from Kenya was also introduced to issues of gender inequality through Mercy's writings. For her, it was Mercy's book "Hearing and Knowing" that stirred her to be engaged in issues of gender inequality.[11] After this, she met Mercy Amba Oduyoye personally at the 1996 Convocation in Nairobi, Kenya. She then met her again in 1998 at a conference in Nairobi. Then she has been meeting her at EATWOT as well as at Circle meetings.[12] Mercy's encouragement to other Circle as well as non-Circle women can ably be expressed in these words by her close companion, Elizabeth Amoah:

> She is indeed a wise African woman theologian who has contributed tremendously in the area of theology, the study of religion and culture, missiology, and to the academic world in general. – Mercy has written, and

---

[8] Int Miranda N. Pillay, Kempton Park, South Africa, 14.7.2005.

[9] Mercy Amba Oduyoye, *Daughters of Anowa. African Women and Patriarchy*, Maryknoll: Orbis, 1995.

[10] Lilian Siwila is from Zambia and played a major role in the period between 2002 and 2007 while Isabel Apawo Phiri was the Continental Circle Coordinator.

[11] See Mercy Amba Oduyoye, *Hearing and Knowing: Theological Reflections on Christianity in Africa*, New York: Orbis, 1986.

[12] Int Philomena Njeri Mwaura, Kempton Park, South Africa, 15.7.2005.

published several books and articles on a variety of themes in these areas. She has ... mentored several scholars in and outside the African continent.

By 2002 the Circle had published 31 books.[13] This shows that the Circle's commitment to publish was taken seriously. The 31 books were celebrated in style at the Addis Ababa Convocation. The Circle women treated themselves to traditional dances led by an Ethiopian dance group. They also displayed the books under the leadership of Dr Dorcas Akintunde.[14] The women were so energized with the production of these books that they encouraged each Circle chapter to have at least one publication presented at the following 2007 Pan African Circle conference.[15]

The number of publications continued to grow after 2002. Papers presented at the 2002 Convocation formed the first additional books to the list.[16] In addition to this, there were many manuscripts either at the printer or nearly off the printer during this period.

This track record of publishing would have not been there without able and committed Circle women who edited the many manuscripts. The manuscripts were usually those that were presented at Circle conferences or workshops. Some originated apart from such events. These arose from occasional appeals for papers by the Circle leadership. Some of the notable editors of Circle books are as follows.

Mercy Amba Oduyoye

She has edited four monographs: These include: "The Will to Arise,"[17] "People of Faith and the Challenge of HIV and Aids,"[18] "Talitha Qumi,

---

[13] See Provisional Addis Ababa Circle Report, p. 7, accessed on 6.3.2006.

[14] I was present at the display.

[15] See Circle Newsletter no. 9, 2006, p. 3.

[16] One of them was, Isabel Apawo Phiri, Beverly Haddad et al, *African Women, HIV/AIDS and Faith Communities*, Pietermaritzburg: Cluster, 2003.

[17] Mercy Amba Oduyoye and Musimbi Kanyoro, *The Will to Arise: Women, Tradition, and the Church in Africa*, Maryknoll: Orbis, 1992.

[18] Mercy Amba Oduyoye and Elizabeth Amoah (eds), *People of Faith and the Challenge of HIV/AIDS*, Ibadan: Sefer, 2004.

Proceeding of the Convocation of African Women Theologians 1989."[19] While the above three books were edited with others, she was the sole editor of one book. This monograph is "Transforming Power: Women in the Household of God. Proceedings of the Pan-African Conference of the Circle of Concerned African Theologians."[20] Through cooperative editing, Mercy Amba Oduyoye was able to mentor others in this art.

Musimbi Kanyoro

Musimbi Kanyoro has edited a number of books. In this book, I have referred to the following: "Grant Me Justice. HIV/AIDS and Gender Readings of the Bible,"[21] "Groaning in Faith: African Women in the Household of God,"[22] "The Will to Arise,"[23] and "Talitha Qumi! Proceedings of the Convocation of African Women Theologians."[24]

Nyambura Njoroge

Nyambura Njoroge has edited several Circle publications. In this book, I refer to three books edited by her. These are: "Talitha Cum! Theologies of African Women,"[25] "There were also Women Looking from Afar"[26] and "Groaning in

---

[19] Mercy Amba Oduyoye and Musimbi Kanyoro (eds), *Talitha Qumi, Proceedings of the Convocation of African Women Theologians 1989,* Accra-North: Sam-Woode, 2001.

[20] Mercy Amba Oduyoye, *Transforming Power: Women in the Household of God. Proceedings of Pan-African Conference of the Circle of Concerned African Women Theologians,* Accra-North: Sam Woode, 1997.

[21] Musa W. Dube and Musimbi Kanyoro (eds), *Grant Me Justice. HIV/AIDS and Gender Re-readings of the Bible,* Pietermaritzburg: Cluster, 2004.

[22] Musimbi Kanyoro and Nyambura Njoroge (eds), *Groaning in Faith: African Women in the Household of God,* Nairobi: Acton, 1996.

[23] Mercy Amba Oduyoye and Musimbi Kanyoro (eds), *The Will to Arise:* Maryknoll: Orbis, 1992.

[24] Mercy Amba Oduyoye and Musimbi Kanyoro (eds), *Talitha Qumi, Proceedings of the Convocation of African Women Theologians 1989,* Accra-North: Sam Woode, 2001.

[25] Nyambura Njoroge and Musa Dube (eds), *Talitha Cumi! Theologies of African Women,* Pietermaritzburg: Cluster, 2001.

[26] Nyambura Njoroge and Irja Askola (eds), *There were also Women Looking from Afar,* Geneva: World Alliance of Reformed Churches, 1998.

Faith: African Women in the Household of God."[27] Of these monographs, "There were Women Looking from Afar," is not a Circle book although it is addressing women's issues. This work also shows the multiple organs that have promoted women's issues apart from the Circle. In this case, the World Alliance of Reformed Churches also played a role in promoting women's liberation in Africa.

Musa W. Dube

Musa Dube is a seasoned editor. This book refers to only a few of the works that she has edited. However, even though she is a seasoned editor, much of her editing work has been to non-Circle monographs. Here I only present Circle books that she has edited and are included in this book. These are: "Grant Me Justice. HIV/AIDS and Gender Readings of the Bible,"[28] and "Other Ways of Reading."[29] Musa Dube edited the latter on her own. Other book she co-edited include: "Talitha Cumi! Theologies of African Women."[30]

Denise Ackermann

Denise Ackermann is one of the first women in the Circle that edited Circle Books. In this book, I include the following titles: "Claiming Our Footprints"[31] and "Women Hold Up Half the Sky."[32] Denise is among the Circle women that have mentored Isabel Apawo Phiri into Circle research and writing.[33]

---

[27] Musimbi Kanyoro and Nyambura Njoroge (eds), *Groaning in Faith: African Women in the Household of God,* Nairobi: Acton, 1996, pp. 23-30.

[28] Musa W. Dube and Musimbi Kanyoro (eds), *Grant Me Justice. HIV/AIDS and Gender Re-readings of the Bible*, Pietermaritzburg: Cluster, 2004.

[29] Musa W. Dube (ed), *Other Ways of Reading - African Women and the Bible,* Atlanta/Geneva: Society of Biblical Literature/WCC, 2001.

[30] Nyambura Njoroge and Musa W. Dube (eds), *Talitha Cumi! Theologies of African Women,* Pietermaritzburg: Cluster 2001.

[31] Denise M. Ackermann, Eliza Getman and Hantie Kotzé, Judy Tobler (eds), *Claiming Our Footprints. South African Women Reflect on Context, Identity and Spirituality,* Matieland: EFSA Institute of Theological and Interdisciplinary Research, 2000.

[32] Denise M. Ackermann, J.A. Draper and E. Mashinini (eds), *Women Hold Up Half the Sky - Women in the Church in Southern Africa,* Pietermaritzburg: Cluster, 1991.

[33] I got this impression when I visited Denise Ackermann in South Africa.

Isabel Apawo Phiri and Sarojini Nadar

In this section, I have deliberately treated the two Circle editors above together because they have collaborated in editing some of the Circle books I have used. I start with the book on "African Women, Religion and Health: Essays in Honour of Mercy Amba Ewudziwa Oduyoye,"[34] "Her-Stories: Hidden Stories of Women of Faith in Africa,"[35] and "On Being Church."[36] However, there is one book that I use which Isabel Apawo Phiri did not co-edit with Sarojini Nadar. This is: "African Women, HIV/AIDS and Faith Communities."[37]

Other Circle Editors

Under this heading I include names of Circle women who edited only one book that I have used. Mary Getui edited "Conflicts in Africa."[38] Other Circle editors in this category include: Hazel Ayanga,[39] Christina Landman,[40] Devakarsham Betty Govinden,[41] Elizabeth Amoah,[42] Beverly Haddad and Madipoane Masenya (ng'wana Mphahlele).[43]

---

[34] Isabel Apawo Phiri and Sarojini Nadar (eds), *African Women, Religion and Health: Essays in Honour of Mercy Amba Ewudziwa Oduyoye,* Pietermaritzburg: Cluster 2006.

[35] Isabel Apawo Phiri, Devakarsham Betty Govinden and Sarojini Nadar (eds), *Her-stories: Hidden Stories of Women of Faith in Africa,* Pietermaritzburg: Cluster, 2002.

[36] Isabel Apawo Phiri and Sarojini Nadar (eds), *On Being Church. African Women's Voices and Visions,* Geneva: World Council of Churches, 2005.

[37] Isabel Apawo Phiri, Beverly Haddad, Madipoane Masenya (ng'wana Mphahlele) (eds), *African Women, HIV/AIDS and Faith Communities*, Pietermaritzburg: Cluster, 2003.

[38] See Mary Getui and Hazel Ayanga (eds), *Conflicts in Africa: A Women Response*: Nairobi: Circle, 2002.

[39] She co-edited with Mary Getui the monograph *Conflicts in Africa: A Women Response*: Nairobi: Circle, 2002.

[40] She edited this book in the same year the study commissions were set up. Christina Landman (ed), *Digging up our Foremothers. Stories of Women in Africa,* Pretoria: UNISA, 1996.

[41] Isabel Apawo Phiri, Devakarsham Betty Govinden and Sarojini Nadar (eds), *Her-stories: Hidden Stories of Women of Faith in Africa,* Pietermaritzburg: Cluster, 2002.

[42] Mercy Amba Oduyoye and Elizabeth Amoah (eds), *People of Faith and the Challenge of HIV/AIDS,* Ibadan: Sefer, 2004.

[43] Isabel Apawo Phiri Beverly Haddad, Madipoane Masenya (ng'wana Mphahlele) (eds), *African Women, HIV/AIDS and Faith Communities*, Pietermaritzburg: Cluster, 2003.

The record of editorial work in the Circle seems to have been achieved through much collaboration. It is also true that some of the Circle Women have done more editing than others. This is equally true with the establishment of Circle chapters, where some Circle members have helped to start more Circle chapters than others. This is natural in any field of expertise.

Study Commissions

The source of some manuscripts that were edited into books was from study commissions that were organized at the 1996 Convocation. The Convocation elected leaders for the commissions with the mandate to encourage research related to their commission and make publications from researched papers of academic quality.[44] The Commissions were organized based on four specific themes with their specific objectives as detailed below.

African Biblical and Cultural Hermeneutics

Musa W. Dube Shomanah and Musimbi Kanyoro were to coordinate this study commission on African Biblical and Cultural Hermeneutics. Musa Dube comes from Botswana and is another prolific writer, especially in the discipline of New Testament. In relation to this objective of the Circle, Musa Dube presented a paper outlining the importance of developing African women theologians that would acquire enough prerequisites to be efficient Biblical interpreters. Musa Dube asserted that Biblical languages were important in the exercise.

The success of this commission on Biblical Reinterpretation is seen, for example, in the production of "New Ways of Reading," edited by Musa Dube and others.[45] The book provides some insights on how a re-reading of the Bible can bring about the transformation of gender inequalities in church and society. Works on biblical interpretation are also found in other Circle books, in the form of chapters.

One of the earliest Circle contributions on biblical interpretation came from Sr Rosemary Edet. In her article "Language of Endearment: An Asset for

---

[44] See Report by Nyambura Njoroge, 13.4.1998.

[45] Musa W. Dube (ed), *Other Ways of Reading-African Women and the Bible*, Atlanta/Geneva: Society of Biblical Literature/WCC, 2001.

Women and Theology,"[46] she argues that women enjoy a more affirming language than men. She argues how the Bible talks about how men must love women in Solomon's Songs of Songs, and where God is likened to "a hen that gathers her chicks." This means that God has favour with women. In this theology women are active participants in doing theology. They are mothers and caregivers; hence they should be allowed to participate in the decision-making processes of the church. She proposes that there should be a move from emphasizing notions that are oppressive to women to notions that affirm them. Again, a selective approach to cultural reinterpretation is reflected here. This approach emphasizes how cultural elements that are liberating should be affirmed to promote women's dignity and transformation of gender inequalities in church and society. Other notable contributors in this area include Cheryl Barbara Anderson, Dorcas Olubanke Akintunde, Denise Ackerman and Sarojini Nadar.[47]

African Women in Religion and Culture

The other study commission was on "African Women in Religion and Culture." The coordinators were Hélène Yinda Mbenda from Francophone and Mercy Amba Oduyoye. There was Teresa Tinkasiimire and also Nokuzola Mndende, a professing African Traditionalist from Zimbabwe. The study commission reminded itself that the subject of Religion and Culture was not new to the Circle. It was there in the beginning, but the challenge facing the commission was to research in this area within an interreligious context as not all women in the Circle were Christians. This was a new thing to the commission. In fact, at the International Planning Committee, none of the members was a Muslim or a Traditionalist, and the subject was approached only from the Christian point of view. With the growth of the Circle, which included an increasing number of women from other religions, interreligious dialogue had to take place.

The study commission decided that they would take the dialogue on "Religion and Culture" beyond the private to the public dialogue. A classic example where such a public dialogue took place was in instances where

---

[46] Ibid., pp. 194-196.

[47] For their perspectives on this subject see Rachel NyaGondwe Fiedler, Johannes W. Hofmeyr, Klaus Fiedler, *African Feminist Hermeneutics. An Evangelical Reflection*, Mzuzu: Mzuni Press, 2016, pp. 44-47.

African women theologians from non-Christian backgrounds led the worship in the presence of Christian Circle women.

A contribution from the Christian perspective is by Musimbi Kanyoro, who is renowned in the Circle for pioneering a theology of Cultural Hermeneutics (Cultural Reinterpretation). Her specific area in this discipline, however, is Feminist Cultural Hermeneutics.[48] She looks at transformative theologies of women in the context of reading women's traditional culture.

Approaches of transformation depicted by Musimbi Kanyoro can best be understood by referring to her own testimony, in this way:

> In my home village, I learned that culture must not be romanticized. It was necessary for us to come to terms with identifying in our cultures those things that were beautiful and wholesome and life-affirming and to denounce those which were denying us life and wholeness.[49]

In this, Musimbi Kanyoro asserts herself as one of the first Circle women to deploy a selective approach to how women in Africa must interpret culture. She is not of the opinion that culture should be completely denounced, as some earlier missionaries supposedly did. She believes that there are certain elements in culture that are good and must be harnessed by African women. On the other hand, she admits that certain elements are dangerous to the life and wholeness of women and that these must be rejected.

For Musimbi Kanyoro the Bible is her starting point in theologizing about culture in Africa, because "rural women in Africa love the Bible and take the Bible seriously. For example, they will argue that Levirate marriages are good because they are in the Bible."[50] In this exercise, Musimbi describes the agenda of cultural hermeneutics as not to legitimize culture just because it is found in the Bible, but that "cultural hermeneutics puts every culture to scrutiny with the intention of testing its liberative potential for people at different times in history."[51] This means that even if culture can be found in the Bible text, if it is not liberative, it must not be followed by those that take

---

[48] See Musimbi R.A. Kanyoro, *Introductions in Feminist Theology: Introducing Feminist Cultural Hermeneutics. An African Perspective,* Sheffield Academic Press, 2002, pp. vii-99.

[49] Ibid.

[50] Ibid., p. 10.

[51] Ibid.

the Bible seriously. The other facet Musimbi Kanyoro points out is how the culture of the one interpreting the Bible influences Bible meaning. Musimbi argues:

> The culture of the reader in Africa has more influence on the way the Biblical text is understood and used in communities than the historical facts about the text. This leads me to suggest that not knowing the nuances of the culture of modern readers of the Bible has more far-reaching repercussions to biblical hermeneutics than is normally acknowledged.[52]

Musimbi Kanyoro's theology of cultural reinterpretation is not proposed by her alone in the Circle. As a cofounder of the Circle, by virtue of belonging to the IPC,[53] she has influenced many women in the Circle to develop this theology of cultural reinterpretation. As a tribute to Musimbi Kanyoro's role in the Circle, this chapter surveys some contributions of women to this theologizing. It is in the same vein that a deliberate effort has been made to include theologies of another cofounder of the Circle, Sr Rosemary Edet from Nigeria.

Circle women in Africa have been inspired by this methodology of cultural reinterpretation. Musimbi Kanyoro and Mercy Amba Oduyoye were pioneers in this methodology. From Nigeria, Circle women wrote on this theme and had a book published on it.[54] Some of the themes in the book included: "Menstrual blood and priestly roles" by Oluwafeni Abosede Okunola, "Cultural attitude to women's education and economic empowerment" by Kehinde Edewor, "Inheritance in Africa and the rights of a female child" by Ruth Oluwakemi Oke, "Women against women" by Martina Atere, "Dynamism in the Bible and Yoruba culture" by Olutundun A. Orebiyi, "No longer be silent" by Dorcas Akintunde, "Reorienting the African woman today" by Helen Adekunbi, "Tradition, poverty and the church as challenges for African women" by Mercy Itohan Omoigui, and "Cultural values" by Oluwatosin Akintan. Esther Lasebikan gave an overview to the book. The keynote address was given by Mercy Amba Oduyoye, who was leader in this field and a member of this commission.

---

[52] Ibid.

[53] Ibid., p. 28.

[54] Dorcas Olubanke Akintunde, *African Culture and the Quest for Women's Rights*, Sefer: Ibadan, 2001.

Sr Rosemary Edet also edited publications on the same theme.[55] One of them was on "Christ and the Nigerian Womanhood," where she is arguing that there is need to relate Christology today to the life of Nigerian women. She argues that the Nigerian woman's theology is affected by the traditional worldview because in their cultural context there are elements that are both affirming and distorting the image of a Nigerian woman. Here she agrees with the theology of cultural reinterpretation proposed by Musimbi Kanyoro. For example, that a Nigerian woman is "to be seen occasionally" and "not to be heard frequently" is a less affirming cultural disposition. This might influence an oppressive Christology that relegates women to silent positions in the church. Rosemary Edet redefines this stand by introducing a liberating theology of Christ Himself. She argues that this must be looked at through the eyes of how Christ dealt with women in the Bible. In Jh 4:27, for example, Jesus did a shocking thing by talking to a Samaritan woman who was considered an outsider; women were also beneficiaries of His power (Lk 8:2; Mk 1:29-31; Mk 12:24-30). She therefore argues that a Christology that will affirm women as complete and acknowledge that male domination is sin, and that this domination came as a result of the fall, should be introduced.[56] Other scholars on African Feminist Hermeneutics include Nyambura Njoroge and Margaret Umeagudosu.[57]

Theological Education

The third study commission (on theological education) was coordinated by Nyambura Njoroge, Vibila Vuadi and Emeline Ndossi. The objectives of the commission were to investigate theological institutions, Seminaries and Bible Schools in the area of curriculum. Are the biblical languages taught there and at what level? To look at members of staff and their areas of specialization; the ratio of women to men, as well as the names of women and years when they started to teach; to look at the number of women students and the years when a particular Institution started to admit women; to check

---

[55] Rosemary Edet and Margaret A. Umeagudosu (eds), *Life, Women and Culture: Theological Reflections: Proceeding of the National Conference of a Circle of African Women Theologians*, Nigeria: MUA Printers 1990.

[56] Ibid., pp. 37-43.

[57] Rachel NyaGondwe Fiedler, Johannes W. Hofmeyr, Klaus Fiedler, *African Feminist Hermeneutics. An Evangelical Reflection*, Mzuzu: Mzuni Press, 2016, pp. 37-39.

whether women are allowed to take all courses leading to ordination. The exercise would also look at what kind of ministry women were involved in after graduation. The goal would be to trace contributions women have made and their challenges to ministry; to check whether the Institution offers gender studies and whether it has accommodation for female students. Does the Institution have women's counters in the Library? In this exercise, a research using a focus group of 10-15 women pastors/theologians would be used to document experiences of women in ministry. The research would also include a survey on what women found most helpful or lacking for their seminary training as regards their practice in ministry. Theological research was also extended to pastors' wives. In this an assessment of the training given to pastors' wives was to be done. This was to be done by studying the curriculum used in training. The commission was also charged to encourage women to write and collect sermons and prepare them for publication.

Again, no particular book from this commission was realized. There have been notable contributions on the issue of what roles women take after theological training included in the book on "Biographies of Women of Faith in Africa."[58] There are also contributions on the themes in the form of articles in other Circle books. An article on pastors' wives by Rachel NyaGondwe Fiedler is an example.[59] Other Circle women already wrote on the themes of this commission before the introduction of the commission. Isabel Apawo Phiri had already written on the enrolment of female students in theology as early as 1988.[60] This was also before the Circle was officially organized, just to show that the transformation that has taken place in the area of gender relations cannot only be credited to the Circle. Other women like Isabel Apawo Phiri were also influenced to write on these issues through others apart from the Circle.

---

[58] From Malawi, see Isabel Phiri, *Women, Presbyterianism and Patriarchy. Religious Experiences of Chewa Women in Central Malawi*, Blantyre: CLAIM-Kachere ²2000(1997). Also, Rachel NyaGondwe Fiedler, "Against the Flow: Stories of Women Pastors in the Baptist Convention in Malawi," in Isabel Apawo Phiri, Devakarsham Betty Govinden et al, *Her Stories: Hidden Stories of Women of Faith in Africa*, Pietermaritzburg: Cluster, 2002, pp. 181-201.

[59] Rachel NyaGondwe Fiedler, "Pastors' Wives and Patriarchy: Experiences of Church Women in Malawi," *Religion in Malawi*, 13, 2006, pp. 23-27.

[60] Isabel Apawo Phiri, "Women in Theological Education in Malawi," *Religion in Malawi*, no. 2, 1988, pp. 24-28.

The other contribution related to the theme of this commission was from Nigeria. Mary Edet, a disciple of Sr Rosemary Edet, wrote on "Church Women Organizations."[61] Her approach to women's groups as offering roles for women is positive. She even sees them as mothers of the Church. She relates this theology to Mariology. The church, according to her, was born of a woman (Mary) because Jesus Christ was born of Mary. Rosemary Edet does not only hail Church women groups as appropriate roles for women, she goes further to hail some roles in the church that other women would consider non-liberating. She argues that Nigerian women are making an impact by involving themselves in Christian child rearing programmes and development work. This to some Circle women would be among the conservative Evangelical Circle theologies. Other Circle women have taken a different approach on issues relating to women's ministry restricted to women's organizations and children. The approach shows two sides to the story of the re-reading of such church women. One is that they are playing a fulfilling role in church but on the other hand that there is need for such women to find ways of more liberation. Notable Circle monographs on church women groups have been written with these two perspectives in mind. One example is Beverly Haddad who wrote on Anglican women in South Africa.[62]

Of the three women who coordinated the commission Nyambura Njoroge has maintained an active role in the Circle. She was best suited for this commission because Nyambura has an extensive experience as an ordained minister of the Word and Sacrament in working with churches, parishes, and in ecumenical, international and cross-cultural contexts. The goal of this commission was to encourage theological and biblical reflections that promote partnership of women and men in God's mission and in church ministry.

Nyambura Njoroge has a record of involvement in leadership development and ecumenical theological education discussions. She has significant communication skills in the area of pastoral ministry, teaching and public speaking including preaching. Apart from editing Circle books, she is also

---

[61] Rosemary Edet and Margaret Umeagudosu (eds), *Life, Women and Culture*, pp. 86-94.

[62] Beverly Gail Haddad, "The Mothers' Union in South Africa. Untold Stories of Faith, Survival and Resistance," PhD, University of KwaZulu Natal, 2000.

involved in team editorial projects of other theological books. She has experiences in gender studies, Bible studies and ecumenical consultations and seminars. She has a record of continuing archival research in the area of women's involvement in the 19th to 20th century missionary enterprise.[63] She holds a PhD in African Theology and Christian Social Ethics obtained at Princeton Theological Seminary in America in 1985.

Biographies of Women of Faith in Africa

The fourth commission was on Biographies of Women of Faith in Africa which culminated into a book: "Her-Stories: Hidden Histories of Women of Faith in Africa."[64] The coordinators of this study were Isabel Apawo Phiri and Devakarsham Betty Govinden. Even after the monograph, Circle women have continued to contribute to this theme. This book is also a product of this commission. I was inspired to write a history of the Circle when I attended the 'Biography of Women of Faith' workshop held in Johannesburg in 2001.

Establishment of Partnerships

Another contribution of the Circle is in the development of strategic partnerships between the Circle and academic institutions in the First World. An example is the partnership (2002-2005) between Yale Divinity School and CIRA (Centre for Interdisciplinary Research on AIDS).[65] The contribution this partnership has brought is enormous in the area of research methodologies. In the beginning the partnership was intended to cater for Circle women who had PhDs. However, two Circle women that went to Yale Divinity School on this programme did not have PhDs.[66] The 2006 Circle Newsletter records the following Circle women as having benefited from the partnership: Fulata Moyo from Malawi, Sylvia Amisi from Kenya, Vuadi Vibila from the Democratic Republic of Congo, Anne Nasimiyu-Wasike from Kenya, Dorothy Ucheaga from Nigeria, Theresa Tinkasiimire from Uganda, Constance Ambasa Shishanga from Kenya, Isabel Apawo Phiri from Malawi, Dorcas

---

[63] Int Nyambura Njoroge, Addis Ababa, 2002.

[64] Isabel Apawo Phiri, Betty Devakarsham and Sarojini Nadar (eds), *Her-stories: Hidden Histories of Women of Faith in Africa,* Pietermaritzburg: Cluster, 2002.

[65] Ibid.

[66] Ibid.

Akintunde from Nigeria and Hazel Ayanga from Kenya.[67] The CIRA partnership continues to cater for Circle members who are registered as PhD students and have reached proposal stage. The first beneficiaries of this programme are Lilian Siwila from Zambia and Bongiwe Dumezweni from South Africa, who were expected to join the programme by December 2006.[68]

Circle and Women Educators

The other contribution of the Circle to the academic world is in the area of improving education for women theologians. This would contribute to an increase in the number of women lecturers and tutors in seminaries and theological schools.[69]

Apart from finding schools and scholarships for students, the Circle has helped sharpen the skills of women theologians that are already in tutoring careers through encouraging women to research and write.

The Circle has also upgraded women's studies by securing scholarships for them. In the first period, such scholarships were provided by WCC. Through this facility, the Circle has made strides in training women to a higher level. In the area of biblical studies for example, key biblical scholars in the Circle emerged in the names of: Sarojini Nadar, Madipoane Masenya, Dorcas Akintunde and Musa Dube. All, apart from Musa Dube, have at one time or the other belonged to a church that is historically classified as Evangelical.

Apart from improving education for women theologians, Circle women have committed themselves to work towards an inclusion of women's studies at African universities and other tertiary institutions.[70] This has been done in institutions such as the University of KwaZulu Natal and Limuru Theological Seminary in Kenya.

---

[67] Ibid.

[68] Ibid.

[69] See Mercy Amba Oduyoye and Musimbi Kanyoro (eds), *Proceedings of the Convocation of African Women Theologians 1989*, Accra-North: Sam-Woode, 2001, p. 14.

[70] Ibid., p. 3.

Conclusion

Although the institution of Study Commissions delayed the development of new Circle chapters, the emphasis on generating women's theologies in the fields of their capabilities, produced specialized theological works in different disciplines of theology. Because of this, theological education has the required books to fit their specific curricula.

Chapter 7: The Circle, Women and Development

My argument in this chapter is that although the Circle cannot claim to transform the evils of the contemporary world, its contribution has been significant in complementing development strategies in different countries. Circle theology has made a deliberate application to contemporary development issues since its inception. This is clear from the activities of the Circle, from its early members until today.

The goal of Circle theology is to promote women's empowerment and gender equality. All its theologies are aimed at empowering women and promoting gender equality in religion and society. Thus, the Circle is in line with the International Protocols that include women's empowerment and gender equality as important for the development of a country.

Circle Theories of Empowering Women in Development

There are two main theories that women propose. One articulates that women empowerment occurs within the framework of women only development projects or programmes. The other articulates that women should be included in development with men in order to realize their empowerment.

Women Only Development Approach

This approach originated in the early 1990s, soon after the inception of the Circle. It was applied to promote women's empowerment within different religious structures. It is within this framework that analyses by some Circle women focussed on the role of women's organizations in the development of the churches. This focus has also included women only development programmes within the churches.

Cecelia Asogwa from Nigeria, for example, shows how instrumental Circle women are in providing practical help to their communities in Nigeria through a "Women Only" project. Her paper "Doing Theology is Empowering the Marginalized to Live their Faith as Persons Created in God's Own Image"[1] is based on this work. She argues that women in Nigeria are being empowered through theology done as envisioned in the programmes stated by the Women Development Education Centre. These projects include: Forty

---

[1] Rosemary Edet and Margaret Umeagudosu (eds), *Life, Women and Culture,* pp. 194-195.

Women Self Help Associations; Training Workshops etc.[2] Although Cecelia Asogwa proposes a theology that accepts roles traditionally ascribed to women by their churches, on the other hand, it is common that women engage themselves in development work not by choice but because they have been squeezed out of the church's prominent roles. Such women who find themselves in this situation are oppressed. On the other hand, those that see these roles as best fitting for them are liberated and must comfortably take up those roles. This can best be explained by this quote:

> Women's liberation should neither aim at forcing women to be leaders, nor should women's liberation be limited to the occupation of leadership roles. It is about attaining their full potential as God has equipped them ... Such support roles were liberating to women, because they did them not out of being oppressed but out of choice.[3]

There are notable "Women Only" development projects that Circle women are engaged in to the extent that it is difficult for me to include them all in this chapter.

Women in Development Approach

This approach also started in the 1990s. It argues that women should be included together with men in development programmes. Since the beginning women have concentrated on increasing women's access to all levels of control in development programmes. This was firstly applied to include women in the development of the church. Circle women singled out exclusion from ordination as limiting their access to controlling processes relating to the development of their churches.

This was done in many ways. One way is in lobbying and advocating for the ordination of women. Women have done this by being ordained themselves, writing on ordaining women and marching against the ban on ordination. This issue began to surface in the Circle with the first Convocation in 1989. Women committed themselves to transforming church policies that barred women from such key positions.[4] It was common in some African churches that church policies deterred women from serving in key positions such as in

---

[2] Ibid., pp. 72-85.

[3] See: Rachel NyaGondwe Banda [Fiedler], *Women of Bible and Culture: Baptist Convention Women in Southern Malawi*, Zomba: Kachere, 2005, pp. 46-47.

[4] See Mercy Amba Oduyoye and Musimbi Kanyoro (eds), *Talitha Qumi. Proceedings of the Convocation of African Women Theologians 1989*, Accra-North: Sam–Woode, 2001, p. 3.

the ordained ministry. This was systematically achieved, for example, by not allowing women to enrol in church related seminaries. If they did, such women often were given a lesser role to play apart from administering the sacraments.

This was against the background that women are equally gifted to do pastoral work. Bassey Ude articulates this in her article on "The Emerging Spirituality of Women in Nigeria."[5] Her argument is that women have spiritualities, spiritual gifts that need to be utilized in the church, and not suppressed. She gives an example of some established churches which bar women from leadership and suppress women's spirituality which is supported in African Instituted Churches and even in the New Testament.[6] This approach is key in redefining traditionally ascribed roles for women that are less empowering.

The case of Mary Chinkwita of Nkhoma Synod, outlined by Isabel Apawo Phiri in her research, is an example of squashed hopes for women's ordination. She was called to the ordained ministry but was only given women's work to do. She was frustrated and left the ministry.[7] The Malawi Circle has registered much progress in this area. A few churches have started ordaining women.[8] Although such a change can not only be attributed to the Circle, it cannot be denied that the Circle has directly and indirectly contributed to this change. Blantyre Synod began to ordain women when women asked the church to do so through a march. Two women in the "march" were members of the Circle. One of them, Getrude Kapuma, is now an ordained minister of the same church. Although such changes are taking place in some churches,

---

[5] See Rosemary Edet and Margaret A. Umeagudosu (eds), *Life, Women and Culture: Theological Reflections: Proceeding of the National Conference of a Circle of African Women Theologians,* Nigeria MUA Printers 1990, p. 209.

[6] Ibid., pp. 147-161.

[7] For details of Mary Chinkwita's case, see Isabel Apawo Phiri, *Women, Presbyterianism and Patriarchy: Religious Experiences of Chewa Women in Central Malawi,* Blantyre: CLAIM-Kachere, 2000, pp. 57-61.

[8] In Malawi, the CCAP Synods of Blantyre and Livingstonia began to ordain women. For a paper on how women pastors are perceived by some see: Joyce Mlenga, Women in Holy Ministry in the CCAP Synod of Livingstonia. A Study of Perceptions, PhD Module, Department of Theology and Religious Studies, Mzuzu University, 2008.

other churches continue to deny women ordination.[9] Some churches that are not ordaining women have started tabling the issue in their assemblies.[10]

The issue of ordination was a cause for concern even before the genesis of the Circle. M.G. Okure wrote on ordination in Nigerian churches under the title: "An Authentic Experience of the Ordained Woman."[11] She herself was an ordained minister of the Presbyterian Church of Nigeria and became the first woman minister in this church in Aba Imo State. As the first woman to be ordained, the road to ordination had not been easy, but after she was ordained in 1982, she has faithfully served the church including being chosen to represent her church in various important fora. From 1982 to 1985, she was appointed to chair the Board of Christian Education for the Synod. In the same year, she was appointed as the Consultant for African Women of the member churches. Her contention here is that the church should be prepared to change in a changing society. Further, that the church must change because it is an institution that has brought the most radical changes in the world. This means that the traditional understanding that only men should be leaders needs to be challenged.[12]

Dr Margaret Umeagudosu presented her paper on: "Gender Warfare in the Church: Debate on the Ordination of Women in Igbo Christian Churches."[13] She argues that those who see women as subordinate misinterpret the Bible, and perhaps their own worldview as regards women is distorted. Her reinterpretation on this issue is from the biblical perspective. She revisits women leaders in the traditional Judeo-Greco Roman culture as models that support women to become leaders in church and society even in cultures that are oppressive to women. She also adds that Paul, who is viewed as suppressive to women, has to be seen in how he worked with women (Rom 16).[14] He treated them as equals, and even taught equality as seen in Gal

---

[9] In the Baptist Convention a church in Blantyre called a woman pastor, but the Pastors' Fraternal has turned down the request to recognize her, as the issue of ordaining women was still being discussed.

[10] Will there ever be a woman priest in the Roman Catholic Church?

[11] Rosemary Edet and Margaret A. Umeagudosu (eds), *Life, Women and Culture: Theological Reflections: Proceedings of National Conference of Circle of African Women Theologians*, Nigeria: MUA Printers, pp. 120-127.

[12] Ibid., pp. 128-146.

[13] Rosemary Edet and Margaret Umeagudosu (eds), *Life, Women and Culture*, pp. 154-155.

[14] See Rachel NyaGondwe Fiedler, Johannes W. Hofmeyr, Klaus Fiedler, *African Feminist Hermeneutics. An Evangelical Reflection*, Mzuzu: Mzuni Press, 2016, pp. 104ff.

3:28.[15] In relation to Igbo churches in Nigeria she argues that women are given freedom to lead churches, but this was not so in most established churches because of the missionary influence from their mother churches.[16]

The other contribution on the same issue of ordination is by E.M. Uka. In her presentation on "Grounds for the Ordination of Women to Priesthood: A Socio-Theological Perspective,"[17] she uses the same approach as Margaret Umeagudosu on how Paul's letters should be understood. His words that suggest oppression should be judged from what he did concerning women and also said about women elsewhere in the Bible. In addition, she tries to argue that the idea of ordination mystifies the office of "ministers," and yet there is no ordination in the Bible. We are all called to serve (1 Cor 4:4). She also adds that in certain mother or missionary churches, women are ordained and therefore it is illogical, when in their daughter churches in Africa, women are refused ordination.[18]

This theory of integrating women in controlling processes of the development of the church has also been applied to women in development in general. Thus, Circle women are making a link between theology and the current development issues. The following section on key areas of developments illustrates this.

The Circle has made contributions in areas such as politics, secular employment and health. I have chosen examples from Nigeria, South Africa, Kenya and Malawi for this chapter. The first area where the Circle has done advocacy work is in the area of politics.

---

[15] Rosemary Edet and Margaret A. Umeagudosu (eds), *Life, Women and Culture: Theological Reflections: Proceedings of National Conference of Circle of African Women Theologians*, Nigeria: MUA Printers, pp. 128-146.

[16] Ibid., pp. 162-176.

[17] Ibid., pp. 10-19.

[18] Ibid.

The Circle and Politics

Sr Rosemary Edet writes about advocating for political transformation in Nigeria. She does this in the monograph "Life, Women and Culture: Theological Reflections."[19] This is the beginning of Circle women linking theology to politics.

Rosemary Edet argues that it is impossible to do theology in Africa without looking at geographical and political issues. Circle theology needs to make a link between its theology and the experiences of women with different forms of government, economic poverty and independence. In her work, she stresses the example of how colonial culture was imposed on African culture and how conflicts that arise from that perpetuate the problem of patriarchy in African cultures. Sr Rosemary Edet argues that this has led to African societies treating women as inferior even in cultures that in the past gave prominence to women. She also highlights how the styles of political leadership imposed on Africans by the colonial cultures have defined the context of women in Africa.[20]

The other contribution in the area of politics is by Sr Mary Juliana Ada. She wrote on: "Nigerian Women in the Making of Nigerian History."[21] She shows how Nigerian women have contributed much to the development of the country. She cements this view by giving examples of women that made a contribution to the country. These include, for example, Princess Moremi of Ile Ife who had a prominent position among the Yoruba and is remembered in history for freeing her people from the hands of enemies.[22]

Circle theologies are able to address political issues because women in secular politics suffer from similar forms of patriarchy as women in religion. Both women in religion and politics often suffer from oppressive elements imposed on them by their culture. On the other hand, many people in Africa are religious and thus it cannot be denied that oppressive elements in religion also contribute to their position in politics.

---

[19] See Rosemary Edet and Margaret A. Umeagudosu (eds), *Life, Women and Culture: Theological Reflections: Proceeding of the National Conference of a Circle of African Women Theologians,* Nigeria: MUA Printers 1990.

[20] Ibid. pp. 177-179.

[21] Ibid.

[22] Ibid.

The Circle, Women and Secular Employment

Another contribution on politics is from Kenya. Philomena Njeri Mwaura explains how globalization and economic policies have contributed to the sufferings of women on Kenya. She justifies this point by highlighting the experiences of rural women in agriculture and their struggle in accessing University education for their children.[23]

Circle women have also lobbied for the liberation of women in secular employment. Mrs A. Akpan, for example, addresses an area in the secular society where nurses and teachers face marginalization. She argues that women in Nigeria are sidelined because of lack of education, as sons are given priority over girls to access education. This has resulted in inequalities in employment opportunities where women have been restricted only to certain jobs. An example where such inequality is seen is in Nursing and Teaching.[24] These remain the option for the majority of women in Nigeria and in Africa as a whole. Again, here Circle thinking provides reasons and solutions for women's oppression in secular employment. It is also true that socialization of boy and girl children impacts on their position in both secular and religious engagements. On the other hand, women's engagement in secular employment can be a religious issue as well as certain forms of religious interpretations discourage women from active engagement in secular work.[25] Circle theology therefore makes a useful contribution here by intersecting religious and cultural perspectives with secular employment.

Women and Secular Literature

Circle women have also lobbied for change in how women are represented in Literature. Bassey Okon for example addresses the issue in her article: "The Portrait of Women in Contemporary Literature." She argues in this paper that the portrait of the Nigerian woman in literature is viewed in the light of what

---

[23] Philomena Njeri Mwaura, "The Lives of Kenyan Women under Globalization", in Philomena N. Mwaura and Lilian D. Chirairo, *Theology in the Context of Globalization. African Women's Response*, Nairobi: EATWOT Women's Commission, 2005, pp. 62-75.

[24] Rosemary Edet and Margaret A. Umeagudosu (eds), *Life, Women and Culture: Theological Reflections: Proceeding of the National Conference of a Circle of African Women Theologians*, Nigeria: MUA Printers 1990, pp. 24-32.

[25] Women in the Bible Believers Church (Branham) in Malawi are discouraged from secular work by their teachings (Richard Gadama, The Bible Believers in Malawi: History, Teachings and Practices [1977-2011], MA, Mzuzu University, 2012).

contribution she makes to the society. In her discussion, she refers to different books such as Chinua Achebe's "A Man of the People," Zaynab Alkali's "The Still Born," Buchi Emecheta's "The Joy of Motherhood;" Nancy Harrison's "Winnie Mandela" and, in passing, to other relevant books. Bassey Okon argues that women in such literature are portrayed as subservient to men, for example, as a fruit to be given to man.[26] Again, the Circle in such discourses creates knowledge how such representations in secular Literature can provide models of oppression to women in Africa.

The Circle, Women and Health

The area where Circle women have done significant advocacy work is in the area of HIV/AIDS. Notable work related to this issue started with the 2002 Convocation. The original theme was: "Religion and the quest for peace, health and wholeness: African women making a difference."[27] The following were the sub-themes: 1. The connection between women, peace and justice. 2. The connection between peace and women's health. 3. The connection between militarism on the continent and its implications on women. 4. The connection between peace and wholeness in sacred texts (both Holy Scriptures and sacred "Orators" of indigenous religions). 5. The role of religion either in healing conflicts or in exacerbating them. 6. The intersection of gender, poverty, racism and religious intolerance. 7. Creating a culture of human rights particularly for children (focus on street children, militarized children [child soldiers], trafficking of children, child enslavement, and sex tourism. 8. Religious resources for overcoming racism, sexism and ethnocentrism on the continent etc.[28]

The Circle wanted to concentrate on the theme of peace because some Circle women were in countries trapped in war. The venue at which the conference was to be held was Yaoundé, Cameroon. However, this theme was replaced by the one related to HIV and Aids. The change was amicably arrived at through discussions between Musimbi Kanyoro and Mercy Amba Oduyoye. Joyce Boham was a key player communicating about changes with Teresa Hinga, who was the Anglophone leader at that time.[29]

---

[26] See Rosemary Edet and Margaret A. Umeagudosu (eds), *Life, Women and Culture: Theological Reflections: Proceeding of the National Conference of a Circle of African Women Theologians,* Nigeria: MUA Printers 1990, pp. 24-32.

[27] Ibid.

[28] Ibid.

[29] See Joyce Boham, Circular Letter to Circle members, 6.11.2001.

The new goals of the conference are well stipulated in the provisional Addis Ababa Circle report in this way: (1) to provide a safe space for in-depth learning about the challenges of HIV/AIDS poses to women within the African social, cultural and religious context. (2) Circle members to present to each other their research on HIV/AIDS from a woman's perspective with a view of preparing some of that research for publication. (3) To use the Ethiopian context as a field for learning about how women are affected by history, religion and culture in Africa. (4) To create safe space for practical learning about stigma and HIV/AIDS and to use collective solidarity to make individual and collective commitment to break the silence on stigma and sexuality. (5) To enable Circle members to hold a business meeting and make decisions for the Circle's future including the selection of new leadership to continue the work of the Circle. (6) To give an opportunity for Circle partners to participate and gain first-hand knowledge of the Circle. (7) To celebrate the achievements of the Circle during the past period.[30] The reason for this change was to allow as much time as possible for deliberations on HIV/AIDS.[31]

Even though the 2002 Convocation launched the focus on HIV and AIDS, other countries were already doing much work in this field. One such example is Ghana through the Institute of Religion and Culture.

Women and Security Issues

There was turmoil due to war in some places in Africa at that time. In fact, the Zonal meeting in Nigeria in 1994 could not take place because of political unrest. The choice of HIV/AIDS over the theme of peace according to Musimbi Kanyoro was "to enable the Circle to prioritize its responses and thereby develop appropriate strategies."[32] The other reason for this change, however, may have been to attract funding for the continental Circle meeting, since projects in the area of HIV/AIDS have easily attracted funding when this issue was very fresh.

The Circle may have felt that it was going to be more difficult to source funding for "peace" projects than for an "HIV/AIDS" project. The easiness in sourcing funds is visible in that the Circle was able to pay for the expenses of

---

[30] See Provisional Addis Ababa Circle Report, accessed 6.3.2006.

[31] See Provisional Addis Ababa Circle Report, p. 7, accessed 6.3.2006.

[32] See Isabel Apawo Phiri and Sarojini Nadar (eds), *African Women, Religion, and Health: Essays in Honour of Mercy Amba Ewudziwa Oduyoye*, Pietermaritzburg: Cluster 2006, p. 36.

the Addis Ababa conference, even including a very expensive accommodation (Hilton Hotel) and conference facilities.

In November 2001, International and African Ecumenical organizations participated in a World Council of Churches (WCC) Global Consultation on the ecumenical response to the challenge of HIV/AIDS in Africa, which was held in Nairobi, Kenya. This consultation produced a plan of action as a guideline for the churches, para-church organizations and ecumenical partners in responding to the plague of Aids. Musa Dube participated in this consultation. It was felt that though many Circle women were doing many good things towards HIV/AIDS, it was time to have a systematic response.[33]

Gender Based Violence

The Circle has been strong in dealing with this issue within its conceptualization of sexuality issues. Some of the issues the Circle has dealt with in this area include violence against women and violence against children. In this section, I only highlight the Circle's role in dealing with violence against women in the context of HIV and AIDS, poverty, family and masculinity. For this I have limited my choice of examples to the works by Isabel Apawo Phiri, a Malawian but writing from the context of South Africa. From my perspective, she is one of the Circle women that have written the most on the subject.[34]

Violence against Women and HIV and AIDS

The following are some of the issues she has covered in her research: in November 2002, her article appeared in the Journal of Theology for Southern Africa dealing with violence against women.[35] In this she argues that violence against women is a result of patriarchy. Isabel outlines some of the beliefs that promote this: the belief that a wife is property; being single is a curse; when HIV infected men have sex with a virgin, they will be cured of

---

[33] Isabel Apawo Phiri, "African Women of Faith Speak out in an HIV/AIDS Era," in Isabel Apawo Phiri, Beverly Haddad, Madipoane Masenya (ng'wana Mphahlele) (eds), *African Women, HIV/AIDS and Faith Communities*, Pietermaritzburg: Cluster, 2003, p. 7.

[34] There are more contributions from Circle women on HIV/AIDS, like Philomena Njeri Mwaura, "Stigmatization and Discrimination of HIV/AIDS Women in Kenya: A Violation of Human Rights and its Theological Implications", *Exchange*, vol 37, 2008, pp. 35-51.

[35] See James R. Cochrane et al (eds), "Overcoming Violence against Women and Children," Special Issue, Nov. 2002, *Journal of Theology for Southern Africa*.

HIV/AIDS.[36] She suggests approaches for overcoming such violence in this way: By telling stories of violence; raising self-esteem in that women, too, are created in the image of God; creating solidarity with each other such as in church women's groups; marching as a group of church women against abuse; acquiring skills to create awareness of gender issues; engendering of theological curriculum provision of counselling and support services to those who are abused.[37] In another paper Isabel Phiri outlines the fact that HIV/AIDS is a gendered pandemic and quotes Philippe Denise and Beverly Haddad.[38]

Marriage, HIV and AIDS

Isabel Apawo Phiri highlights the role of marriage in the spread of HIV and AID. In this She also adds another aspect to Circle theology in this she has dispelled the common understanding that marriage is a safe place for women. Her works have been published in Circle books,[39] and in journals such as the Journal of Theology for Southern Africa.[40] Her works have contributed much to theological issues and approaches that would increase protection and care for married women in the era of HIV/AIDS.

Isabel Apawo Phiri problematizes the conception of masculinity and sexual identity constructed by society based on biological sex characteristics influenced by culture and Bible. She is wise but also as clever as a serpent. She demonstrates this by tactfully redefining notions of Evangelical theology

---

[36] Ibid., pp. 24, 26.

[37] Ibid.

[38] See Isabel Apawo Phiri, "A Theological Analysis of the Voices of Teen Age Girls on Men's Role in the Fight against HIV/AIDS in KwaZulu-Natal, South Africa," in Steve de Gruchy et al, *Special Issue, The Agency of the Oppressed Discourse: Consciousness, Liberation and Survival in Theological Perspective.* 120, November 2004, p. 35. She quotes P. Denis, "Sexuality and AIDS in South Africa," *Journal of Theology for Southern Africa*, March 2003, pp. 63-77 and Musa W. Dube, "Preaching to the Converted: Unsettling the Christian Church. A Theological View: A Scriptural Injunction," *Ministerial Formation,* Geneva: World Council of Churches, April, 2001, pp. 38-50, and Beverly Haddad, "Gender Violence and HIV/AIDS: A Deadly Silence in the Church," *Journal of Theology in Southern Africa*, 11.2003, pp. 93-106.

[39] For example, Isabel Apawo Phiri, "The Church as Healing Community: Voices and Visions from Chilobwe Healing Centre," in Isabel Apawo Phiri and Sarojini Nadar (eds), *On Being Church: African Women's Voices and Visions,* World Council of Churches, 2005, pp. 13-27.

[40] See Isabel Apawo Phiri, "A Theological Analysis of the Voices of Teen Age Girls on Men's Role in the Fight against HIV/AIDS," *Journal of Theology for Southern Africa*, 2004, p. 20.

that often oppress women through a literalistic interpretation of the Bible. She turns such notions around and shows how they can be used to empower women in the fight against HIV/AIDS. She proposes approaches to deal with HIV/AIDS gleaned from such notions. An example is where the social construct that men are heads of the family is turned around to promote a sense of responsibility, so that men can use their power to choose to refrain from risky sex that will infect the wife, other women and their children.

Another central notion that Isabel Apawo Phiri addresses is the conservative Evangelical conviction that "gender issues" or discussion of them are disruptive to families because they concentrate on women alone and not on both men and women. She argues that such convictions are dangerous in the era of HIV/AIDS. Her contribution to this therefore is in developing approaches that would unsettle such convictions.

Masculinity and HIV and AIDS

Isabel Apawo Phiri is also one of the few women who show the danger of ignoring masculinity issues in dealing with HIV/AIDS. She argues that any HIV/AIDS intervention that ignores men and targets only women and girls is not adequate. However, she turns this notion around and refocuses on women. For example, she sides with the girls who object to dangerous forms of socially constructed masculinity such as that being man means having girlfriends. To crown it all, Isabel outlines the approach where both men and women become agents of change seeking justice basing on the character of God who in Jesus sides with the oppressed.[41]

Isabel Apawo Phiri's major work in constructing theologies of transforming gender inequalities is in the area of the family.[42] Here she bases her theologies on Bible studies and focus group discussions with communities in the area of the family. Her works on family relationships are revealing. She has shown through her research the dangers of family structures in Africa in the face of the HIV/AIDS pandemic. In this, she agrees with S. Baden and H. Wach that in Sub-Saharan Africa "marriage is a major risk factor for any African woman to contract the HI-virus."[43] She further argues that it is heterosexual multiple relationships that are crucial in Africa in terms of the

---

[41] Isabel Apawo Phiri, "A Theological Analysis of the Voices of Teenage Girls," pp. 34-45.

[42] Public Seminar, Circle Meeting, Lydia Foundation Building, Zomba, 13.7.2006.

[43] See Isabel Apawo Phiri, "HIV/AIDS: An Anglican Theological Response in Mission," *The Ecumenical Review*, vol. 56, no. 4, 10.2004, p. 423.

spread of HIV/AIDS rather than homosexual relationships,[44] and that as long as literalistic interpretations of the Bible teachings and African cultural practices continue, HIV/AIDS would be difficult to curb in Africa.[45] She therefore advocates a theology of transforming this paradigm to prevent HIV/AIDS infection through marriage. In this discussion, she unveils the key preconceived idea that promotion of "family" or "marriage" is an answer to HIV/AIDS. She actually hits hard on this and shows how family or marriage can be very dangerous spaces in the era of HIV/AIDS.

Isabel Apawo Phiri also proposes a new theology that deals with HIV/AIDS. This theology is the mission-oriented theology which acknowledges the centrality of the Bible as authoritative within the church.[46] An example of this reflection is where she proposes that there should be a shift from a theology that sees HIV/AIDS as a punishment from God to a theology of God who is in solidarity with all who are affected or infected by HIV/AIDS,[47] fighting literalistic interpretations would be such that divorced women or women single from birth would be hotbeds for transmitting HIV/AIDS; worse still that those that are infected are immoral.

The Role of the Church in HIV and AIDS Work Prevention

Theologies of transforming gender inequalities in the Circle have also touched on the role of the church in HIV/AIDS prevention and care. On this front, Isabel Apawo Phiri has also made contributions. She proposes that dealing with HIV/AIDS requires censoring structural sins within the church that promote the spread of the pandemic. On the same front of creating a theology of the church in transforming gender inequalities, Isabel Phiri articulates a "theology of sacredness of life" which mandates taking responsibility to protect those that have already been infected so that the infection is contained. She outlines cases where poverty forces women to have multiple partners and contract HIV/AIDS.[48] The church must devise ways of dealing with poverty issues to discourage transmission of the virus to her members.[49] The underlying theology here is that the church should

---

[44] Ibid., p. 246.
[45] Ibid., p. 426.
[46] Ibid., p. 246.
[47] Ibid.
[48] Ibid., p. 428.
[49] Ibid.

not blame the victim, but that they should also share the blame that they are often perpetrators of this discourse.

One of the prominent theologies of Isabel Apawo Phiri is the theology of healing in the fight against HIV/AIDS. In fact, Isabel's key area of focus is the theology of healing reflected in many of her writings.[50] In this she proposes that prayer is an essential tool in dealing with HIV/AIDS.[51] This also comes in handy when many programmes dealing with HIV/AIDS are donor driven, mostly seeking to help with the physical needs, like through relief programmes for orphans and widows. She advocates that the spiritual side of a person is also important in dealing with HIV/AIDS. However, it should be recognized that spiritual resources alone are not enough in dealing with HIV/AIDS, as those that are infected by their spouses may as well be prayerful. A theology of spiritual healing is important because it gives hope to the dying.[52]

The Circle and Levels of Women Empowerment

From the engagement of women in development described above, it is clear that Circle women have three key levels of empowerment.

Access to control

Circle women argue that full participation in development requires that they take part in the decision-making bodies. For many churches, it is unless one is ordained that he can take part in such decisions.

Access to resources

Circle women have identified education as an important resource in their empowerment. Education provides them opportunity to paid employment. Theological education empowers them to participate in their religion fully.

Conscientization

Women have identified knowledge of gender issues as important in empowering women in development. Through production of Circle literature

---

[50] Comment, Isabel Apawo Phiri, Bible Study Group, Pietermaritzburg 7.3.2006.

[51] See Isabel Apawo Phiri, "HIV/AIDS: An Anglican Theological Response in Mission," *The Ecumenical Review,* vol. 56, no. 4, 10.2004.

[52] Ibid. p. 429.

and increased networking either in Circle for a or other for a that promote women's empowerment, Circle women increase empowerment.

Dignity

Circle women throughout history emphasize that women's empowerment is not only in terms of access to resources and control but that such empowerment should include promotion of women's dignity as those created in Gods image.

Welfare

Although the dominant view is that women should gain access to controlling development of the church, some argue that women must be given chance to engage in positions where they are comfortable to be. If women are satisfied to be involved in women's only projects, they should be empowered to do that work.

Conclusion

This chapter has shown that the Circle makes a link between their theologies and development. This is probably why, there are many Circle women participating in various development programmes of their countries and globally. This is also because the theories of engaging women in development are similar to secular theories of engaging women in development. The Welfare approach and the Women in development approach are particularly similar to those promoted by the Circle. The levels of empowerment are also similar to those in the Harvard framework and those proposed by Sara Longwe.

Chapter 8: Celebrating Maturity: 28 Years of the Circle of Concerned African Women Theologians (1989 – 2017)

In this chapter, I reflect on the Circle with the view of making a summary of the important stages of the Circle and gleaning lessons from the past that can inform the present and future generations. This is important in all history writing. The past of the history has a transformative power for the present realities of history.[1] I will use the birth and growth of human beings for my reflections on the history of the Circle in this chapter. In the first few pages, I retell the story, to capture some of the landmarks in the development of the Circle. I retell the story of the Circle from 1989 to 2007, to show its relevance to the present and the future. Onward, I highlight realities of the Circle after 2007. There is the decline and then there are attempts to revitalize the Circle. Although I do not provide the full picture of what happened between 2007 and 2017, ten years after the end of my PhD research, I highlight important aspects and begin a process of reflecting on such aspects with the intention of opening up a new area of historical research to complement the current one, but also to energize the establishment and growth of Circle chapters in Africa and beyond.

An African Baby Born in Ecumenical Surroundings (1988-1989)

In Africa, the birth of a child is very important. Those that cannot bear children are often stigmatized. The birth of a child entails much preparation requiring many decisions on issues such as where the birth should take place and at what hospital, and who should be at the birth; and most important is the assembly of items that are required for the new born baby. It is through the eyes of these aspects of birth and growth that I provide a reflection on the 28 years of the Circle in Africa.

The Baby's Birth Place

It is now common knowledge that the Circle is an African Baby born in Ecumenical surroundings. She was born in Accra, Ghana from Sept 24 to October 2, 1989. The mother of the Circle is Mercy Amba Oduyoye, a

---

[1] Steven Paas, *From Galilee to the Atlantic. A History of the Church in the West*, Zomba: Kachere, 2004.

Ghanaian married to Modupe Oduyoye, a Nigerian. They both had a track record of ecumenical influences through the many ecumenical bodies such as the AACC (All Africa Conference of Churches) and World Christian Students' Federation they either worked for or associated with. Mercy Amba Oduyoye's father was also in touch with ecumenical associations as a minister (and at one-time President) of the Methodist Church of Ghana.

Since the Circle is about African Feminist Theologies, Mercy Amba Oduyoye's plan on who should be involved in the birth of the Circle, had to include those that were in touch with Feminist Theologies. These were none other than those that were members of EATWOT (Ecumenical Association of Third World Theologians), an organization started by Sergio Torres, a Roman Catholic priest from Chile, in 1976. Women who were involved in this association, were, after all, already seasoned researchers and writers on Feminist Theologies through the Women's Commission of EATWOT. Women involved in this organization had additional exposures to Feminist Theologies through their places of work. Some were working with Ecumenical church bodies like Brigalia Bam, who worked with the South African Council of Churches and Musimbi Kanyoro, who headed the women's desk of the Lutheran World Federation (LWF); some worked in academia, like Sr Teresa Okure, Sr Betty Ekeya of Egerton University in Kenya, Elizabeth Amoah and Rachel Tetteh of the University of Ghana in Legon, Sr Rosemary Edet of the University of Calabar in Nigeria etc, where research was part of their careers. Mercy Amba Oduyoye assembled these women to plan for the birth of the Circle. They met in Geneva, Switzerland in 1988 and formed what is known the IPC (International Planning Committee). These women were of diverse theological orientations and in fact some did not have theological education as their main discipline of study, like Musimbi Kanyoro and Rose Obianga, who had studied linguistics.

Women at the Birth of the Circle

The 1989 Convocation in Accra, Ghana, is the birth date and place of the Circle. Before the Birth of the Circle, there had been a long period of identifying women that would be present at the Birth. This was largely done through independent efforts by Mercy Amba Oduyoye. As an Akan woman and a true African, who treasured collaboration with others, she cooperated in the project of finding women to attend the Convocation by connecting with institutions where African Women Theologians would be found. Key to this project was the World Council of Churches (WCC), where she worked and which helped with funds and opportunities for Mercy Amba Oduyoye to invite others to the Circle. She contacted others beginning in the 1980s, when she worked with WCC in Geneva. The representation at the Birth of the Circle included 16 African and three European countries. From Africa, one woman each came from Cameroon, Congo, Lesotho, Namibia, Sierra Leone, Swaziland, Uganda; two women each came from South Africa, Zambia and Zimbabwe; three women each came from Malawi and Tanzania; five women came from Zaire, eight from Nigeria; nine from Kenya; and 19 from Ghana. From the West, one woman came from the UK, two from Switzerland and five from the United States of America.[2]

Those present at the Birth of the Circle were from different academic backgrounds. Some were University lecturers, others had degrees in various fields, but there were also some without tertiary credentials. These were mainly women belonging to church women's groups in Ghana. This combination of the élite and the grass roots seems to have been at the heart of Mercy Amba Oduyoye's vision of the Circle even beyond the 1989 Convocation. In the 21st century, Mercy Amba Oduyoye's Institute of Religion and Culture in Legon, Ghana, also had the same composition.

Assembling the Essentials for the Birth of the Circle

One of the essentials was inducing the birth to take place. The IPC decided to present well researched papers on women's issues. They chose to research and write on sexuality issues and women's liberation. Apart from these papers, they included other items that would appeal to the non-academic participants. Such items included poetry, worship sessions and Bible studies. This mixed approach was used because presentation of researched papers on women's issues was something new to many women; so, items included those the women were accustomed to.

In addition, the Convocation theme was framed in line with the common hunger Church women have: missions. Thus, the theme, Talitha Qumi! based on the story of Jairus' daughter coming back to life, was appealing to women as it suggested a call to missions.

The Circle Getting out of Chikuta (Seclusion) 1989-1996

In Malawi, when a baby is born, baby and mother remain in seclusion till the umbilical cord falls off. After this the baby is brought out and is introduced

---

[2] Mercy Amba Oduyoye and Musimbi Kanyoro, *Talitha Qumi. Proceedings of the Convocation of African Women Theologians 1989,* Accra-North: Sam-Woode, 2001.

to the community. Some babies die in *chikuta* and others survive. This is similar to what happened to the Circle. Once the Circle was born in 1989, it needed to be independent of the mother (Mercy Amba Oduyoye) and her birth attendants (the IPC). However, such independence also required that the Circle lives in the care of other caretakers, as it was introduced into different African countries.

Time to Grow up (Initiation)

In some African cultures, when a baby reaches seven years, there is an initiation that a child goes through. The introduction of the Circle to different countries was an important stage of initiation into Circle theologies. During this period, it was important that women belonging to the different chapters were socialized into the central tenets of the Circle. Thus, through the leadership of the Circle at different levels, members were socialized in researching and writing African Feminist Theologies. This was the vision of starting the Circle, to deal with the dearth of theologies on women and by women. The test that the women had learnt the skill was the ability to write well researched papers for publication.

The Namkungwi (Advisors)

The skill to write was developed through specially selected advisors at the 1989 Convocation. These were the Chapter leaders, Zonal leaders, Linguistic communication leaders, Continental leaders, and Study Commission leaders who provided an opportunity for the Circle women to learn the trade. During this period, the sustainable efforts to discover and cultivate African women doing theology rested in the hands of members of the IPC and those that got converted to African Feminist Theologies at the 1989 Convocation. This commitment was clearly stated at the 1988 IPC meeting in Geneva:

> So, for the moment, the most important task is to get a couple of people who will make things happen in the countries represented here. There is no need to found new associations at home, but it is important to get a women's caucus of whatever existing Theological Association you belong to. Those who do not belong to any association but would like to do their theology in community need to seek out sisters and work together as a Circle of Concerned Women Theologians. Those who find themselves working or

studying abroad should seek out and assist one another as well as make approaches to women of African descent who are doing theology.[3]

A Matter of Death and Life in Chikuta (Seclusion)

Not all IPC members and those that attended the 1989 Convocation, introduced the Circle into their countries of origin or work place. Only a few did. Some had Circles die within their wombs. Even those that began Circles in their countries began them at different speeds. Ghana and Nigeria introduced the Circle soon after the 1989 Convocation. Ghana had a Circle chapter in 1989, and so had Nigeria. Rachel Tetteh led the Ghana chapter that met at the Methodist headquarters in Accra. Kenya, Tanzania and Uganda established an East Africa Zone Circle in 1989. They did not establish country chapters for a reason. Although Kenya had a group of women theologians experienced in research and writing, among them members of EATWOT, this was not the case with Tanzania and Uganda. Tanzania and Uganda had women clergy from the Anglican Church that were not seasoned in research and writing. Sr Annie Nasimiyu, Mother Superior of the Little Sisters of St Francis (LSSF) in Kampala, introduced the Circle to the three countries as a Zone. Although she was not a member of the IPC, she was a member of EATWOT. Zambia came second in establishing a national Circle in 1990. South Africa came third in establishing chapters. Brigalia Bam, then the general Secretary of the South African Christian Council, organized the first national chapter In South Africa in 1991.[4] The Cape Town Chapter became the fourth to be established on 6th March, 1992. Isabel Apawo Phiri, together with Denise Ackermann, introduced the chapter. At this time, Isabel Apawo Phiri was a PhD student at the University of Cape Town. In 1992, Kenya also had her own chapter, the Kenyatta University Circle chapter introduced by Mary Getui. Two of the three women that attended the Convocation did not bring the Circle to Malawi. They were busy with the practical work of their Presbyterian church. The third woman, Isabel Apawo Phiri, who was studying in South Africa at that time, established the Malawi chapter in 1993 on her return. Kenya established its second chapter in 1996, when Esther Mombo introduced the Circle at Limuru Theological College.

---

[3] Mercy Amba Oduyoye and Musimbi Kanyoro, *Talitha Qumi. Proceedings of the Convocation of African Women Theologians*, 1989, p. 29

[4] Isabel Apawo Phiri, "African Women's Theologies in the New Millennium," *Agenda* 61, 2004, p. 18.

Celebration after an Initiation Ceremony

In Malawi, after a girl or a boy has undergone initiation, there is usually a feast to celebrate the new status of the initiate, and neighbours are always invited. Similarly, introducing the Circle to the neighbours, to meet women doing the same things, was an important step to show that the Circle had reached a new period of growth. The Zonal meetings, also called Biennial Conferences, which took place in 1993 and 1994, were important in meeting this need. The planning committee, held in December 1992, was very important to make this happen. The blend between the members of the IPC and the representatives from the country where the Zonal conferences would meet, made things even more beautiful. The planning meeting set the agenda and defined the issues it would focus its research on. The theme and the issues of focus were circulated to the women before the Zonal meetings to give them a chance for research and the writing of papers.

The Manzini Zonal Meeting (Swaziland) was the first to take place in cooperation with EDICESA in 1992.[5] The second was the West Africa Zonal meeting that took place in Accra, Ghana (December 16 to 21, 1993) after shifting the venue from Lagos, Nigeria, due to political strife there.[6] Dr Rabiatu Ammah was chosen leader of the West Africa Zone. Mercy Amba Oduyoye and Elizabeth Amoah from the IPC together with Rhodah Ada James and Margaret Umeagudosu from the Nigeria Circle and Rachel Entrue Tetteh and Rev Dora Ofori-Owusu from the Ghana Circle arranged the meeting.

The Francophone Zonal meeting took place in Doula, Cameroon, 25-31 July 1993. Hélène Yinda was leader of the Francophone Zone (Cameroon, Ivory Coast and Congo) and organized the meeting. The combined Eastern and Southern Africa Zonal meeting took place in 1994 from January 4-8 in Nairobi at the Methodist Guest House, a home for many ecumenical conferences then. The focus for this meeting was African Traditional Religion. Rev Phina Olga Kgosana was chosen leader of the Southern Africa Zone (Malawi, Zambia, Botswana, Namibia, Swaziland, South Africa and Zimbabwe). Rev Grace Ndyabahika was chosen leader for the Eastern Africa Zone (Tanzania, Kenya and Uganda). The joint Southern and Eastern Zonal meeting was organized by Musimbi Kanyoro from the IPC and Mary Getui Nyanchama and

---

[5] Ecumenical Information and Documentation Centre for Eastern and Southern Africa
[6] Letter by John Pobee to Elizabeth Amoah, 10.9.1993

Teresa Hinga from Kenya.[7] At the 1996 convocation, they elected Zonal leaders.

Apart from Zonal meetings, the Circle was introduced to the neighbours through Linguistic Regional Meetings and the Convocations. Unlike Zones which were organized according to proximity of countries, the regions were organized along the lines of colonial languages: Anglophone (English); Francophone (French) and Lusophone (Portuguese).

At times, different regions would meet together, especially at continental conferences. Sometimes Zones in the same linguistic region would have joint workshops. For example, in 1994, the Southern and East Africa Zones had a joint workshop. Mary Getui, lecturer at Kenyatta University, helped organize the workshop.

Sr Mbuy-Beya became Communication secretary for Francophone, Teresa Mbiri Hinga became Communication Secretary for Anglophone and Ms Eva Gomez became leader of Lusophone. Apart from these leaders, members of the IPC worked with the regions closely, through Linguistic regions and Study Commissions. Women that had vibrant chapters learnt how to research and write through the Circle chapters. Others like those from Malawi, who did not have vibrant chapters, learnt their skill through presenting papers at workshops organized within their Zones, Linguistic regions and or at Continental convocations or through participation in a Study Commission.

The other avenue where the Circle was introduced to her neighbours was through the Study Commissions. The 1996 Convocation instituted four Study Commissions based on thematic areas the women would focus on. These were: (1) *African Biblical and Cultural Hermeneutics*. Musa Dube and Musimbi Kanyoro were elected to coordinate this commission. (2) *African Women in Religion and Culture*. The coordinators for this commission were Hélène Yinda Mbenda from Francophone and Mercy Amba Oduyoye. (3) *Theological Education*. Nyambura Njoroge coordinated this commission. (4) *Biographies of Women*. The coordinators of the commission were Isabel Apawo Phiri and Devakarsham Betty Govinden.

From Childhood to Puberty (1996-2002)

For many countries, the period between 1989 and 1996, was for nursing the baby. This was done through the introduction of the Circle to neighbouring

---

[7] Musimbi Kanyoro - Mary Getui and Teresa Hinga, 21.9.1993.

countries through local chapters and Zonal meetings. But from 1996 onwards the Circle needed to learn how to start to stand, walk and run with encouragement from the local chapter leaders and what their neighbours did. As this process was taking place, it was not uncommon that in other countries the Circle was still in *Chikuta*. In *some* cases, the Circle was born but had only limited childhood development. However, there was much evidence that the Circle reached its puberty during this period. The Circle was thirteen years of age and at this time the girl had reached puberty.[8] The signs of maturity were the production of literature, engagement in editorial work, more women taking up leadership beyond their local chapters and opening up of additional country chapters. However, some chapters had reached the age but showed less signs of maturity. This mixed portrait of the Circle between 1996 to 2002 is described below.

Childhood Steps: Establishing Circle Chapters

While the Circle took root in some countries in Africa, other countries did not have local Circle chapters by 1996. Though there were representatives from Lesotho and Zimbabwe at the 1989 Convocation, there was no Circle chapter in these countries by 1996. The Namibia chapter was only introduced between 1996 and 1997 by Isabel Apawo Phiri, at that time a lecturer at the University of Namibia. Women from the Lutheran Church dominated the Circle. By 2002, the chapter was still struggling because members found research and writing alien to their calling and to their fellowship needs.[9]

The Durban chapter was introduced in August 1997 and was launched in 1998 by Isabel Apawo Phiri. She was by then professor at the University of Westville and Director of the Centre for Constructive Theology. The chapter was vibrant and at one time, 200 women belonged to it.[10] The Pietermaritzburg chapter was introduced in 2001, and the same year Isabel Apawo Phiri launched the KwaZulu Natal Chapter.

Circle Chapters with Limited Childhood Development

In some countries, the Circle chapters did not experience much growth for many reasons. Among those that were stunted, were Tanzania, Uganda, Zambia and Malawi. The first cohort of Circle women in Uganda was

---

[8] I only reached puberty at 16.
[9] Interview, member of Namibia Chapter, Kempton Park, 14.7.2005
[10] Isabel Apawo Phiri, 'African Women's Theologies in the New Millennium' *Agenda* 61, 2004, p. 19.

demotivated to engage in gender research.[11] There were 23 women at the beginning of the Circle in Uganda, but the evangelical influence, characteristic of the Anglican low church tradition combined with the Evangelical wind of the East African Revival promoted by Bishop Kivengere, killed the momentum of the Circle. Among the first women that were members of the East Africa Zone Circle and started the Ugandan Circle were Grace Nyabaika and Mabel Katahweire. The majority of the women considered research and writing on women's issues as secondary to fellowshipping with each other and preaching the gospel to the lost.[12]

In Tanzania, the Circle chapter did not develop because the first cohort of the Circle was dominated by women from the Lutheran Church. The women promoted fellowship at the expense of research and writing on women's issues. The Chapter started to walk again in 1996, with the encouragement of Sr Teresa Okure.

In Malawi, the Circle declined after the 1995 incident when Isabel Apawo Phiri was attacked by students when she, together with other Circle members, Nyovani Madise, Flora Nankhuni and Linda Semu had presented a paper on sexual violence on Chancellor College campus where the Circle was based. In 1996, the Malawi Circle was restarted by Fulata Lusungu Moyo, who was also the secretary for the Board for Theological Studies.[13]

The Zambia chapter had slow growth because the first cohort of the Circle was dominated by women ministers and members of the United Church of Zambia. Among them were Peggy Mulambya Kabonde, Juliet Matembo and Omega Bula. The Circle did not grow because they concentrated on the practical life of the church and not on research and writing on women's issues.

The Circle at Puberty

Puberty is another stage of maturity and in Africa this stage is also celebrated with initiation ceremonies. In some African countries, there are childhood initiation ceremonies: Child hood initiation ceremonies included opening of new chapters and incorporation of more members into the chapters. But

---

[11] Interview, Ugandan Man, Kampala, 28.4.2006

[12] Interview, member of Uganda Circle, Kempton Park, 12.7.2005

[13] This Board relates theological colleges and seminaries through the department of Theology and Religious Studies to the University of Malawi, so that the diplomas and degrees are awarded jointly by the University and the Board.

adolescents undergo another initiation ceremony. Likewise, now that the Circle reached puberty stage, they needed much more than mastering childhood steps. There is need for the circles to participate at regional and zonal workshops and be involved in the study commissions.

Production of Literature and Editorial Work

Although some chapters in South Africa were established later, it had women that had passed the childhood stage in Circle theologies. This was especially true for those that were editors of Circle books not commissioned by the Circle chapter.[14] The many opportunities through the local chapters, Zones, Regions and Study Commissions intensified the Circle's research that led to an increase in Circle publications.

From Puberty to Adulthood (2002-2007)

According to UNICEF, a child is anyone under the age of 18 and beyond this age one is an adult. The road to adulthood meant the Circle relating their theologies to issues of global concerns. During this period, issues of HIV and AIDS and war were some of those concerns. At the 2002 Continental Convocation, the Circle decided to present research papers on the subject of HIV and AIDS. This issue had already been looked at at the Ghana Circle through the Institute of Religion and Culture in Legon. Adulthood meant that one was able to adapt African Feminist Theologies not only to the global issues but to different local situations.

The Circle as a Grandchild: Decline and Growth (2007-2013)

From this history, we have seen that those converted at the 1989 Convocation were Mercy Amba Oduyoye's children. We have also seen how these children have developed at different speed through childhood, puberty and adulthood. At this stage those that were converted early are having their own children. Thus, Mercy Amba Oduyoye is now a grandparent of the Circle. This section describes the grand children of the Circle and how they relate to the grandparent.

Grand children are not often carbon copies of their grandparents. But there are also exceptions where grandchildren can resemble their grandparents. Should the Circle celebrate the difference or reject it and seek resemblance?

---

[14] One of the publications was Isabel Apawo Phiri, Betty Govinden Devakarsham and Sarojini Nadar (eds), *Her-Stories of Women of Faith in Africa,* Pietermaritzburg: Cluster, 2002.

This is a question that is not plausible in this section of the chapter. However, as a historian, my focus is to assess the resemblances and differences between the Circle of 1989-2007 and the Circle of 2007 and 2016. The reality of this period is that the Circle declined as a community of women doing theology together, even though individual Circle projects continued to grow.

By 2013, the number of country Circle chapters had decreased. Some countries had no chapter, while other countries had a limited number of chapters. In South Africa, for example, three Circle chapters still existed. Countries such as Malawi had no live Circle chapters any more. By 2016, some referred to the Circle as a sleeping giant that needed to be awakened.[15]

Conclusion

Regardless of the fact that the Circle has met many challenges to spread to other African countries, the Circle has made significant contributions to theological education and development in general. The Circle has generated theological literature that informs theological education as well as many development initiatives in the world. Circle theology has earned its place even in the mainline theological discourse. It is important that the Circle and the world at large continue to document the contributions of the Circle in engaging women in church and society.

As the Circle plans a revival it has to be cognizant of its history and rethink whether to continue with the modus operandi of the Circle or sketch alternative ways of creating African Feminist Theologies.[16]

Gleaning from the history of the Circle, it is clear that revival must include an aspect of promoting network of Circle members as an important avenue of learning and receiving knowledge about the Circle among the old and new Circle members in order to create leadership that will move the Circle forward in every generation.

Further, since this history has excluded many of the important developments, especially those in Lusophone and Franco phone, it would be good to write a Lusophone Circle History as well as a Francophone Circle History. This would be a great step in writing a full history of the Circle.

---

[15] Nathando Hadebe - Getrude Kapuma, Molly Longwe and Rachel Fiedler, 20.6.2016.
[16] Ibid.

Bibliography

Published

Ackermann, Denise M., "Claiming our Footprints. Introductory Reflections," in Denise M. Ackermann, Eliza Getman et al (eds), *Claiming our Footprints. South African Women Reflect on Context, Identity and Spirituality,* Matieland: EFSA Institute of Theological and Interdisciplinary Research, 2000, pp. 5-15.

Ackermann, Denise M., Eliza Getman and Hantie Kotzé, Judy Tobler (eds), *Claiming Our Footprints. South African Women Reflect on Context, Identity and Spirituality,* Matieland: EFSA Institute of Theological and Interdisciplinary Research, 2000.

Ackermann, Denise M., J.A. Draper and E. Mashinini (eds), *Women Hold up Half the Sky – Women in the Church in Southern Africa,* Pietermaritzburg: Cluster, 1991.

Ackermann, Denise, "Claiming our Footprints. Introductory Reflections," in Denise Ackermann, Eliza Getman et al (eds), *Claiming Our Footprints. South African Women Reflect on Context, Identity and Spirituality,* Matieland: EFSA Institute of Theological and Interdisciplinary Research, 2000.

Ackermann, Denise, Eliza Getman, Hantie Kotzé, Judy Tobler (eds), *Claiming Our Footprints. South African Women Reflect on Context, Identity and Spirituality,* Matieland: EFSA Institute of Theological and Interdisciplinary Research, 2000.

Ackermann, Denise, J.A. Draper and E. Mashinini (eds), *Women Hold Up Half the Sky. Women in the Church in Southern Africa,* Pietermaritzburg: Cluster, 1991.

Akintunde, Dorcas Olubanke, "The Attitude: A Model for Contemporary Churches in the Face of HIV/Aids in Africa," in Isabel Apawo Phiri, Beverly Haddad, Madipoane Masenya (ng'wana Mphahlele), *African Women, HIV/Aids and Faith Communities,* Pietermaritzburg: Cluster 2003, pp. 94-110.

Akintunde, Dorcas Olubanke, *African Culture and the Quest for Women's Rights,* Sefer: Ibadan, 2001.

Anderson, Cheryl Barbara, "Lessons on Healing from Naaman (2 Kings 5:1-27): An African American Perspective," in Isabel Apawo Phiri (ed), *African Women, HIV/Aids, and Faith Communities,* Pietermaritzburg: Cluster 2003, pp. 23-24.

Banda, Rachel NyaGondwe [Fiedler], *Women of Bible and Culture: Baptist Convention Women in Southern Malawi,* Zomba: Kachere, 2005.

Becher, Jeanne (ed), *Women, Religion and Sexuality. Studies on the Impact of Religious Teachings on Women,* Geneva: WCC 1991.

Boff, Leonardo and Virgil Elizondo (eds), *Concilium. Theologies of the Third World. Convergences and Differences,* Edinburgh: Page Brothers, 1988.

Cannon, Ketie Geneva, "The Emergence of Black Feminist Consciousness," in Letty Russel (ed), "Feminist Interpretations of the Bible," in Letty M. Russel, *Feminist Interpretations of the Bible,* London/New York: Basil Blackwell, 1985.

Cavannes, Barbara, "God Calling: Women in Pentecostal Missions" in Grant McClung (ed), *Azusa Street and Beyond,* Gainesville, Bridge-Logos, 2006, pp. 53-66.

Chimombo, Steve, *The Hyena Wears Darkness,* Mzuzu: Luviri Press, 2017.

Cochrane, James R. et al (eds), "Overcoming Violence against Women and Children," Special Issue, Nov. 2002, *Journal of Theology for Southern Africa*.

Denis, Philippe, "Sexuality and Aids in South Africa," *Journal of Theology for Southern Africa*, March 2003.

Douglas, Kelly Brown, *Sexuality and the Black Church. A Womanist Perspective*, Maryknoll: Orbis, 1999.

Dube, Musa W. (ed), *Other Ways of Reading - African Women and the Bible*, Atlanta/Geneva: Society of Biblical Literature/WCC, 2001.

Dube, Musa W. and Musimbi Kanyoro (eds), *Grant Me Justice. HIV/AIDS and Gender Re-readings of the Bible*, Pietermaritzburg: Cluster, 2004.

Dube, Musa W., "Grant me Justice: Towards Gender Sensitive Multi-Sectoral HIV/Aids Readings of the Bible," in Musa W. Dube and Musimbi Kanyoro, *Grant me Justice. HIV/Aids and Gender Readings of the Bible*, Pietermaritzburg: Cluster, 2004, pp. 16-21.

Dube, Musa W., "Preaching to the Converted: Unsettling the Christian Church. A Theological View: A Scriptural Injunction," *Ministerial Formation*, Geneva: World Council of Churches, April, 2001, pp. 38-50.

Dube, Musa W., *Postcolonial Feminist Interpretation of the Bible*, St Louis: Chalice Press, 2000.

Edet, Rosemary and Margaret A. Umeagudosu (eds), *Life, Women and Culture: Theological Reflections: Proceeding of the National Conference of a Circle of African Women Theologians*, Nigeria: MUA Printers 1990.

Fabella, Virginia and Sergio Torres (eds), *Irruption of the Third World. Challenge to Theology*, Maryknoll: Orbis, 1983.

Fiedler, Klaus, *Baptists and the Ordination of Women,* Zomba: Lydia Print, 2008.

Fiedler, Klaus, *Missions as the Theology of the Church. An Argument from Malawi*, Mzuzu: Mzuni Press, 2015.

Fiedler, Klaus, *The Story of Faith Missions. From Hudson Taylor to Present Day Africa*, Oxford et al: Regnum, ²1995.

Fiedler, Rachel NyaGondwe, "Against the Flow: Stories of Women Pastors in the Baptist Convention in Malawi," in Isabel Apawo Phiri, Devakarsham Betty Govinden et al, *Her Stories: Hidden Stories of Women of Faith in Africa*, Pietermaritzburg: Cluster, 2002, pp. 181-201.

Fiedler, Rachel NyaGondwe, "Pastors' Wives and Patriarchy: Experiences of Church Women in Malawi", *Religion in Malawi*, 13, 2006, pp. 23-27.

Fiedler, Rachel NyaGondwe, "Theological Education for Women in Malawi", *Studia Historiae Ecclesiasticae*, vol. 35, 2009, Supplement, pp. 119-134.

Fiedler, Rachel NyaGondwe, Johannes W. Hofmeyr, Klaus Fiedler, *African Feminist Hermeneutics. An Evangelical Reflection*, Mzuzu: Mzuni Press, 2016.

Getman, Eliza Jane, "Ground Cover" in Denise M. Ackermann et al (eds), *Claiming Our Footprints. South African Women Reflect on Context, Identity and Spirituality*,

Matieland: EFSA Institute of Theological and Interdisciplinary Research, 2000, pp. 62-67.

Getui, Mary and Hazel Ayanga (eds), *Conflicts in Africa: A Women Response*, Nairobi: Circle of Concerned African Women Theologians, 2002.

Getui, Mary, "Africa, Church and Theology: Do they Need Each Other?" *Ministerial Formation,* January 1999.

Getui, Mary, "Women's Priesthood in Relation to Nature", in Musimbi Kanyoro and Nyambura Njoroge (eds), *Groaning in Faith: African Women in the Household of God*, Nairobi: Acton, 1996, pp. 31-39.

Gnanadason, Aruna, *No Longer Silent: The Church and Violence against Women*, Geneva: WCC, 1993.

Govinden, Devakarsham Betty, "'The Mother of African Freedom' – The Contribution of Charlotte Maxeke to the Struggle for Freedom in South Africa," in Isabel Apawo Phiri, Devakarsham Betty Govinden and Sarojini Nadar (eds), *Her-stories: Hidden Histories of Women of Faith in Africa*, Pietermaritzburg: Cluster, 2002, pp. 304-326.

Gutierrez, Gustavo, "The Meaning of the Term *Liberation*," in Deane William Fern, *Third World Liberation Theologies. A Reader,* New York: Orbis, 1986.

Haddad, Beverly, "*Gender* Violence and HIV/AIDS: A Deadly Silence in the Church," *Journal of Theology in Southern Africa*, 11.2003, pp. 93-106.

James, Rhodah Ada, "The Scope of Women's Positions in the Church," in Mercy Amba Oduyoye and Musimbi Kanyoro (eds), *Talitha Qumi. Proceedings of the Convocation of African Women Theologians 1989*, Accra-North: Sam-Woode, 2001, pp. 192-200.

Kabanda, Peggy Mulambya, "Single Women Parents in Africa," in Mercy Amba Oduyoye, and Musimbi Kanyoro (eds), *Talitha Qumi, Proceedings of the Convocation of African Women Theologians 1989*, Accra-North: Sam-Woode, 2001, pp. 183-191.

Kalu, Ogbu U., "Daughters of Ethiopia Constructing a Feminist Discourse in Ebony Strokes," in Isabel Apawo Phiri and Sarojini Nadar (eds), *Women, Religion and Health, Essays in Honour of Mercy Amba Ewudziwa Oduyoye*, Pietermaritzburg: Cluster, 2006.

Kanyoro, Musimbi and Nyambura Njoroge (eds), *Groaning in Faith: African Women in the Household of God*, Nairobi: Acton, 1996.

Kanyoro, Musimbi, "Beads and Strands: Threading More Beads in the Story of the Circle," in Isabel Apawo Phiri, Devakarsham Betty Govinden, and Sarojini Nadar (eds), *Her-stories: Hidden Histories of Women of Faith in Africa*, Pietermaritzburg: Cluster 2002, pp. 15-38.

Kanyoro, Musimbi, *Introductions in Feminist Theology: Feminist Cultural Hermeneutics. An African Perspective*, Sheffield Academic Press, 2000.

Kapuma, Getrude Aopesyaga, "'Troubled but not Destroyed': Women of Faith Reclaim their Rights," in Isabel Apawo Phiri, Devakarsham Betty Govinden and

Sarojini Nadar (eds), *Her-stories: Hidden Histories of Women of Faith in Africa*, Pietermaritzburg: Cluster, 2002, pp. 348-369.

Kok, Bregje de, *Christianity and African Traditional Religion: Two Realities of a Different Kind*, Zomba: Kachere, 2004.

Landman, Christina (ed), *Digging up our Foremothers. Stories of Women in Africa*, Pretoria: UNISA, 1996.

Landman, Christina, "A Land Flowing with Milk and Honey", in Musimbi Kanyoro and Nyambura Njoroge (eds), *Groaning in Faith: African Women in the Household of God*, Nairobi: Acton, 1996, pp. 99-111.

Longwe, Hany, *Christians by Grace – Baptists by Choice. A History of the Baptist Convention of Malawi*, Mzuzu: Mzuni Press, 2011.

Longwe, Molly, *Growing Up. A Chewa Girls' Initiation*, Zomba: Kachere, 2007 (available through African Books Collective, Oxford).

Manda, Christine, "A Testimony against Polygamy," in Mercy Amba Oduyoye and Musimbi Kanyoro (eds), *Talita Qumi. Proceedings of the Convocation of African Women Theologians 1989*, Accra-North: Sam-Woode, 2001, pp. 152-154.

Mijoga, Hilary, *Separate but Same Gospel. Preaching in African Instituted Churches in Southern Malawi*, Blantyre: CLAIM-Kachere, 2000.

Mlenga, Joyce, *Dual Religiosity in Northern Malawi. Ngonde Christians and African Traditional Religion*, Mzuzu: Mzuni Press, 2016.

Mlenga, Moses, *Polygamy in Northern Malawi. A Christian Reassessment*, Mzuzu: Mzuni Press, 2016.

Moosa, Najma, "The Flying Hadji," in Denise Ackermann et al (eds), *Claiming Our Footprints. South African Women Reflect on Context, Identity and Spirituality*, Matieland: EFSA Institute of Theological and Interdisciplinary Research, 2000, p. 98ff.

Mosala, Itumeleng J., *Biblical Hermeneutics and Black Theology in South Africa*, Grand Rapids: Eerdmans, 1989.

Mouton, Elna, "After the Locusts: Letters from a Landscape of Faith," in Denise Ackermann et al (eds), *Claiming Our Footprints. South African Women Reflect on Context, Identity and Spirituality*, Matieland: EFSA Institute of Theological and Interdisciplinary Research, 2000.

Mulambya, Peggy, "Single Women Parents in Africa," in Mercy Amba Oduyoye and Musimbi Kanyoro (eds), *Talitha Qumi. Proceedings of the Convocation of African Women Theologians 1989*, Accra-North: Sam-Woode, 2001, pp. 192-198.

Mwaura, Philomena Njeri, "Stigmatization and Discrimination of HIV/AIDS Women in Kenya: A Violation of Human Rights and its Theological Implications", Exchange, vol 37, 2008, pp. 35-51

Mwaura, Philomena Njeri, "The Anthropological Dimension of a Patient's Treatment: A Response to Prof. Bernard Ugeux", *International Review of Mission*, vol 95, pp. 136-142.

Mwaura, Philomena Njeri, "Women's Healing Roles in Traditional Gikuyu Society", in Musimbi Kanyoro and Nyambura Njoroge (eds), *Groaning in Faith: African Women in the Household of God*, Nairobi: Acton, 1996, pp. 253-269.

Nadar, Sarojini, "Emerging from Muddy Waters. For the Man in My Life - My Inspiration to Soar," in Denise Ackermann, Eliza Getman et al (eds), *Claiming Our Footprints. South African Women Reflect on Context, Identity and Spirituality*, Matieland: EFSA Institute of Theological and Interdisciplinary Research, 2000, pp. 15-31.

Ndyabahika, Grace, "Women's Place in Creation," in Musimbi Kanyoro and Nyambura Njoroge (eds), *Groaning in Faith: African Women in the Household of God*, Nairobi: Acton, 1996, pp. 23-30.

Njoroge, Nyambura and Irja Askola (eds), *There were also Women Looking from Afar*, Geneva: World Alliance of Reformed Churches, 1998.

Njoroge, Nyambura and Musa W. Dube (eds), *Talitha Cumi! Theologies of African Women,* Pietermaritzburg: Cluster 2001.

Njoroge, Nyambura and Irja Askola (eds), *There were also Women Looking from Afar*, Geneva: World Alliance of Reformed Churches, 1998.

Njoroge, Nyambura, *Kiama kia Ngo: An African Christian Feminist Ethic of Resistance and Transformation*, Legon Theological Studies: Legon 2000.

Oduyoye, Mercy Amba (ed), *Transforming Power: Women in the Household of God. Proceedings of the Pan-African Conference of the Circle of Concerned African Women Theologians*, Accra-North: Sam Woode, 1997.

Oduyoye, Mercy Amba and Elizabeth Amoah (eds), *People of Faith and the Challenge of HIV/AIDS*, Ibadan: Sefer, 2004.

Oduyoye, Mercy Amba and Musimbi Kanyoro (eds), *Proceedings of the Convocation of African Women Theologians 1989*, Accra-North: Sam-Woode, 2001.

Oduyoye, Mercy Amba and Musimbi Kanyoro (eds), *Talitha Qumi, Proceedings of the Convocation of African Women Theologians 1989*, Accra-North: Sam-Woode, 2001.

Oduyoye, Mercy Amba and Musimbi Kanyoro (eds), *The Will to Arise: Women, Tradition, and the Church in Africa*, Maryknoll: Orbis, 1992.

Oduyoye, Mercy Amba, "Women Theologians and the Early Church. An Examination of Historiography," in *Voices from the Third World Women, Colombo*: EATWOT, 1885, vol. viii 3, pp. 70-72.

Oduyoye, Mercy Amba, *And Women, where do they Come in?* Lagos: Methodist Church Nigeria Literature Bureau, 1977.

Oduyoye, Mercy Amba, *Daughters of Anowa. African Women and Patriarchy*, Maryknoll: Orbis, 1995.

Oduyoye, Mercy Amba, *Hearing and Knowing: Theological Reflections on Christianity in Africa*, New York: Orbis, 1986.

Oduyoye, Mercy Amba, *Introducing African Women's Theology*, Sheffield Academic Press, 2001.

Oduyoye, Mercy Amba, *Transforming Power: Women in the Household of God. Proceedings of Pan-African Conference of the Circle of Concerned African Women Theologians,* Accra-North: Sam Woode, 1997.

Ogundipe, Chief (Mrs) G.T., *The Ordination of Women,* Lagos: Methodist Church Nigeria Literature Bureau, 1977.

Paas, Steven, *From Galilee to the Atlantic. A History of the Church in the West,* Zomba: Kachere, 2004.

Parratt, John (ed), *A Reader in Christian Theology,* London: SPCK 1987.

Pemberton, Carrie, *Circle Thinking: African Women Theologians in Dialogue with the West,* Leiden: Brill, 2003.

Phiri, Isabel Apawo and Sarojini Nadar (eds), *African Women, Religion, and Health: Essays in Honour of Mercy Amba Ewudziwa Oduyoye,* Pietermaritzburg: Cluster 2006.

Phiri, Isabel Apawo and Sarojini Nadar (eds), *African Women's Voices and Visions,* Geneva: World Council of Churches, 2005.

Phiri, Isabel Apawo and Sarojini Nadar (eds), *On Being Church: African Women's Voices and Visions,* Geneva: World Council of Churches, 2005.

Phiri, Isabel Apawo, "A Convocation of African Women in Theology, Trinity College, Legon, Accra, Ghana 24-30th September, 1989," *Religion in Malawi,* no. 3, 1991, pp. 39-41.

Phiri, Isabel Apawo, "A Theological Analysis of the Voices of Teen Age Girls on Men's Role in the Fight against HIV/AIDS in KwaZulu-Natal, South Africa," in Steve de Gruchy et al, Special Issue, *The Agency of the Oppressed Discourse: Consciousness, Liberation and Survival in Theological Perspective.* 120, November 2004.

Phiri, Isabel Apawo, "African Women of Faith Speak out in an HIV/AIDS Era" in Isabel Apawo Phiri, Beverly Haddad and Madipoane Masenya (ng'wana Mphahlele) (eds), *African Women, HIV/AIDS and Faith Communities,* Pietermaritzburg: Cluster 2003, pp. 6ff.

Phiri, Isabel Apawo, "African Women's Theologies in the New Millennium," *Agenda* 61, 2004, p. 18.

Phiri, Isabel Apawo, "Department of Religious Studies 1973-1988," *Religion in Malawi,* no. 2, 1988.

Phiri, Isabel Apawo, "Healing from the Traumas of Crime in South Africa: Interaction of African Religion with Christianity as Perceived by African Female Traditional Healers" in *The Lutheran Federation,* 2005, p. 25.

Phiri, Isabel Apawo, "HIV/AIDS: An African Theological Response in Mission," *Ecumenical Review,* vol. 56, no. 4, 2004.

Phiri, Isabel Apawo, "Marching, Suspended and Stoned: Christian Women in Malawi 1995," in Kenneth R. Ross (ed), *God, People and Power in Malawi: Democratization in Theological Perspective,* Blantyre: CLAIM-Kachere, 1996, pp. 63-105.

Phiri, Isabel Apawo, "Stand up and be Counted. Identity, Spirituality and Theological Education in my Faith Journey," in Denise Ackermann et al (eds), *Claiming Our Footprints. South African Women Reflect on Context, Identity and Spirituality*, Matieland: EFSA Institute of Theological and Interdisciplinary Research, 2000.

Phiri, Isabel Apawo, "The Church as Healing Community: Voices and Visions from Chilobwe Healing Centre," in Isabel Apawo Phiri and Sarojini Nadar (eds), *On Being Church: African Women's Voices and Visions*, Geneva: World Council of Churches, 2005, pp. 13-27.

Phiri, Isabel Apawo, "Transformation in South African Universities: The Case of Female Academics in Leadership Positions in Theological Institutions," in Roswitha Gerloff (ed), *Mission is Crossing Frontiers*, Pietermaritzburg: Cluster, 2003.

Phiri, Isabel Apawo, "Women in Theological Education in Malawi," *Religion in Malawi*, no. 2, 1988, pp. 24-28.

Phiri, Isabel Apawo, "African Women's Theologies in the New Millennium," *Agenda* 61, 2004.

Phiri, Isabel Apawo, Betty Devakarsham and Sarojini Nadar (eds), *Her-stories: Hidden Histories of Women of Faith in Africa*, Pietermaritzburg: Cluster, 2002.

Phiri, Isabel Apawo, Beverly Haddad et al, *African Women, HIV/Aids and Faith Communities*, Pietermaritzburg: Cluster, 2003.

Phiri, Isabel Apawo, Beverly Haddad, Madipoane Masenya (ng'wana Mphahlele) (eds), *African Women, HIV/AIDS and Faith Communities*, Pietermaritzburg: Cluster, 2003.

Phiri, Isabel Apawo, Devakarsham Betty Govinden and Sarojini Nadar (eds), *Her-stories: Hidden Histories of Women of Faith in Africa*, Pietermaritzburg: Cluster, 2002.

Phiri, Isabel Apawo, *Women, Presbyterianism and Patriarchy. Religious Experiences of Chewa Women in Central Malawi*, Blantyre: CLAIM-Kachere, [2]2000(1997); Zomba: Kachere, [3]2007.

Report of the EATWOT Women's Commission Conference, St. Lucia Park, Harare, Zimbabwe, 21st – 25th June 1999, in Philomena N. Mwaura and Lilian D. Chirairo, *Theology in the Context of Globalization. African Women's Response*, Nairobi: EATWOT Women's Commission, 2005, pp. 96-106.

Ross, Kenneth R., "The Theology of Hope," in Kenneth R. Ross, *Gospel Ferment in Malawi: Theological Essays*, Gweru: Mambo-Kachere, 1995, pp. 65-80.

Ross, Kenneth R., "Theology and Religious Studies at the University of Malawi 1993-1998," *Religion in Malawi* no. 9, 1999, pp. 3-9.

Ruether, Rosemary Radford, *Sexism and God-Talk: Towards a Feminist Theology*, Boston: Beacon Press, 1999.

Russell, Letty M., *The Future of Partnership*, Philadelphia: Westminster, 1979.

Schalkwyk, Annalet van, "The Story of Anne Hope: A White Woman's Contribution towards South African Liberation," in Isabel Apawo Phiri, Devakarsham Betty

Govinden and Sarojini Nadar (eds), *Her-stories. Hidden Historiesof Women of Faith in Africa*, Pietermaritzburg: Cluster, 2002, pp. 279-304.

Schalkwyk, Annalet van, "Writing Southern African Women's Stories of Transformation – Some Methodological Aspects," *Journal of Constructive Theology*, no. 6 (2), 2000, pp. 21-37.

Shisanya, Constance Ambasa, "Professor Hannah Wangeci Kinoti: Your Seeds are Germinating in Kenya," in Isabel Apawo Phiri, Devakarsham Betty Govinden and Sarojini Nadar (eds), *Her–stories: Hidden Stories of Women of Faith in Africa*, Pietermaritzburg: Cluster, 2002, pp. 327-345.

van den Bosch, H.M., "African Theology: Is it Relevant for Global Christianity?" *NGTT*, 2009, pp. 530-537.

Walker, Alice, *In Search of Our Mothers' Gardens. Womanist Prose*, New York: Harcourt, Brace, Jovanovich, 1983, pp. xi-xii.

Wamue, Grace and Mary Getui (eds), *Violence against Women: Reflection by Kenyan Woman Theologians*, Nairobi: Acton, 1996.

Yinda, Hélène and Kä Mana, *Pour la Nouvelle Théologie des Femmes Africaines. Repenser la difference sexuelle, promouvoir les droits des femmes et libérer leurs energies créatives*, Yaoundé: Editions CLE-CIPRE, 2001.

Yinda, Hélène, *Cercle des Théologiennnes Africaines Engagées: Femmes Africaines. Le Pouvoir de Transformer le Monde*, Yaoundé: Editions Sherpa, 2002.

Unpublished

Adwoa, Nana, The Helper's Ministry. A Letter to my Grand Children, Circle meeting 17-21 January 2002.

Banda, Rachel NyaGondwe [Fiedler], "Liberation through Baptist Polity and Doctrine. A Reflection on the Lives of Women in the History of Women in the Baptist Convention of Malawi," MA, University of Malawi, 2001.

Chalimba, Jannie, Daughters of the King. Women in CCAP Blantyre Synod. MA, University of Malawi, 2011.

Fiedler, Rachel NyaGondwe, "The Circle of Concerned African Women Theologians (1989-2007): History and Theology," PhD, University of the Free State, 2011.

Gadama, Richard, The Bible Believers in Malawi: History, Teachings and Practices (1977-2011), MA, Mzuzu University, 2012.

Getman, Eliza Jane, "Giving Birth to God Our Mother: Nurturing a Theology of Birth as Creative Power," Malaka-le Theologies 2005.

Haddad, Beverly Gail, The Mothers' Union in South Africa. Untold Stories of Faith, Survival and Resistance, PhD, University of KwaZulu Natal, 2000.

Kalalo, Chimwemwe, "Women's Sexual and Reproductive Health in the Context of HIV/Aids: The Involvement of the Anglican Church in the Upper Shire Diocese in Southern Malawi," MA, University of Malawi, 2006.

Kanyoro, Musimbi, "Revisiting the History of the Circle," paper presented at a conference on Biographies of Women, Kempton Park, 2003.

Kawamba, Bright, The Blantyre Spiritual Awakening 1969 to 1986: An Antecedent of the Charismatic Movement in Malawi, MA, University of Malawi, 2013.

Khetwayo Banda, "Apostle (Dr) Stanley Ndovie's Contribution to Malawi's Socio-Religious Development," MA module, Department of Theology and Religious Studies, Mzuzu University, 2009.

Kinoti, Hannah Wangeci, "Aspects of Gikuyu Traditional Morality," PhD, University of Nairobi, 1983.

Kishindo, Monica, "A Survey of Likoma Island from Early Times to 1935," Final Year History Paper 1969/70, University of Malawi.

Labeodan, Helen Adekunbi, "Women Reproductive Health in Nigeria, A Theo-Philosophical Approach," Malaka-le Theologies 2005.

Longwe, Hany, "Democratization of the Christian Faith: The Influence of the Baptist Doctrine of 'Priesthood of All Believers' on the History of the Baptist Convention of Malawi (BACOMA)," PhD, University of Malawi, 2008.

Longwe, Molly, "From *Chinamwali* to *Chilangizo*: The Christianisation of Pre-Christian Chewa Initiation Rites in the Baptist Convention of Malawi," MTh, University of Natal, 2003.

Longwe, Molly, A Paradox in a Theology of Freedom and Equality: The Experiences of Pastors' Wives (Amayi Busa) in the Baptist Convention of Malawi (BACOMA), University of KwaZulu Natal, 2012.

Mlenga, Joyce, An Investigation of Dual Religiosity between Christianity and African Traditional Religion among the Ngonde in Karonga District in Northern Malawi, PhD, Mzuzu University, 2013.

Mlenga, Joyce, Women in Holy Ministry in the CCAP Synod of Livingstonia. A Study of Perceptions, PhD Module, Department of Theology and Religious Studies, Mzuzu University, 2008.

Mlenga, Moses, Polygamy and the Synod of Livingstonia in Northern Malawi: Biblical, Moral and Missiological Implications, PhD, Mzuzu University, 2013.

Moyo, Fulata, "Red Beads," Malaka-le Theologies: Women, Religion and Health. A Circle of Concerned African Women Theologians Pan-African Conference, Kempton Park, South Africa, July 10-15, 2005.

Moyo, Fulata, "Women, Sexuality Envisioned as Embodied Interconnected Spirituality and Sexual Education in Southern Malawi. A Quest for Women's Sexual Empowerment in the HIV/Aids Context – The Case of *Kukhonzera Chinkhoswe Chachikhristu* (KCC) among Mang'anja and Yao Christians of T/A Mwambo in Rural Zomba," PhD, University of KwaZulu Natal, 2009.

Mwase, Towera, The Marriage Instructions for Girls and Women in Mzuzu Churches, MA, Mzuzu University, 2012.

Mwaura, Philomena Njeri, "Perceptions of Women's Health and Rights in Neo-Pentecostal and Charismatic Churches in Kenya," Malaka-le Theologies, 2005.

Nadar, Sarojini, "Power, Ideology and Interpretation/s: Womanist and Literary Perspectives on the Book of Esther as Resources for Gender-Social Transformation," PhD, University of KwaZulu Natal, 2003, p. 2.

Nkhoma, Anthony, "Women in Search of Identity. The Case of Women's Ordination in Zambezi Evangelical Church," BA, University of Malawi, 2005.

Okeyere-Manu, Beatrice, "Sacrificing Health for Well Being: Sex Work as a Livelihood Option for the Poor Women in Pietermaritzburg," Malaka-le Theologies 2005.

Provisional Addis Ababa Circle Report, accessed 6.3.2006.

Public Seminar, Circle Meeting, Lydia Foundation Building, Zomba, 13.7.2006.

Schalkwyk, Annalet van, "Sister, we Bleed and we Sing: Women's Stories, Christian Mission and SHALOM in South Africa," PhD, UNISA, 1999.

Tribute to the Very Rev Charles K. Yamoah in a Brief Biography of the Very Rev Charles Kwa Yamoah BD (London) in Souvenir Programme for the Home Call of the Very Rev Charles Kwa Yamoah (B.D. London), January 23, 1987.

Umeagudosu, Margaret A., "'Act of God?' The Experience of Women Living with Vesico Vagina Fistula (VVF) among Women in Northern Nigeria," Malaka-le Theologies 2005.

Yila, Othniel Mintang, "The Place of Women in the Church Ministry as Shown in 1 Timothy 2:9-15," MA, Nairobi International School of Theology, 1998.

Oral Sources

Focus Group Discussion, 7.10.2006.

Focus Group Presentation, 2002 Circle Conference, Johannesburg, South Africa.

Focus Group, Isabel Phiri and Fulata Moyo, Malaka-le Theologies, 14.7.2005.

Focus Group, Rev Peggy Mulambya Kabonde and Lilian Siwila, Malaka-le Theologies, 14.7.2005.

Group interview through participatory investigation, 12 Baptist convention women in Jali, Zomba, June 2005.

Interview Bishop Patrick Kalilombe, Postgraduate Colloquium 2003, Department of Theology and Religious Studies, University of Malawi.

Interview Circle woman from Uganda, Kempton Park, 12.7.2005.

Interview Circle women in ministerial formation, Addis Ababa, 2002.

Interview Constance Ambasa Shisanya, Circle meeting, 13.7.2005.

Interview Denise Ackermann, Cape Town, May 2002.

Interview Isabel Apawo Phiri, Kempton Park, 14.7.2005.

Interview Joyce Boham, 16.9.2005.

Interview Mary Getui, The Institute of Religion and Culture, Ghana, 2005, 14.9.2005.

Interview Mary Mumo, Nairobi International School of Theology, 8.2005.

Interview member of Namibia Circle, Kempton Park, 14.7.2005.

Interview Mercy Amba Oduyoye, Institute of Women in Religion and Culture, 14.9.2005.

Interview Mercy Amba Oduyoye, Kempton Park, 13.10.2003.

Interview Mercy Amba Oduyoye, The Institute of Women in Religion and Culture, Accra, 14.9.2005.
Interview Miranda N. Pillay, Kempton Park, South Africa, 14.7.2005.
Interview Modupe Dube, Sept 2005.
Interview Musa Dube, 2005.
Interview Philomena Njeri Mwaura, Kempton Park, South Africa, 15.7.2005.
Interview Prof Elna Mouton, Stellenbosch University, International Office, 2002.
Interview Prof. Noel Q. King, Ndangopuma, Zomba, Nov 2002.
Interview Sr Annie Nasimiyu, 14.7.2005, Kempton Park.
Interview Sr Annie Nasimiyu, Circle Conference, Kempton Park, 13.7.2005.
Interview Sr Annie Nasimiyu, Kempton Park, 12.7.2005.
Interview Sr NN, 15.7.2005.
Interview Sr Teresa, Kempton Park, 12.7.2005.
Interview Ugandan man, Kampala, 28.4.2006.
Interview, Nyambura Njoroge, Addis Ababa, 2002.
Oral presentation, Addis Ababa, 4-9.8.2002.
Oral presentation, Mercy Amba Oduyoye and Brigalia Bam, Pan African Conference, Institute of Women in Religion and Culture, Accra, Trinity College, 12.9.2005.
Oral presentation, Rev Afo Blay, Pan African Conference, 12.9.2005.
Pastor's wife's talk, bridal shower, 1.10.2006.
Personal observation, Institute of Women in Religion and Culture Meeting, Ghana 12.-16.9.2005.

Correspondence and other Archival Sources

Acknowledgement Letter, Anne Harding Col Territorial President of Women's Ministry, to Mercy Amba Oduyoye, 9.9.2003.
Assessment Grade Reports 1993, Chancellor College, accessed 2001.
Assessment Grade Reports 1994, Chancellor College, accessed 2001.
Assessment Grade Reports 1995/96, Chancellor College, accessed 2001.
Assessment Grade Reports, 1967-1997, Chancellor College, accessed 2001.
Assessment Record, University of Malawi, Chancellor College, 1992, accessed 2001.
Circle Newsletter no. 6, April 2006, p. 2.
Circle Newsletter no. 9, 2006, p. 3.
Circle of Concerned African Women Theologians, Process of Creating Biennial Institutes of African Women in Religion and Culture, nd, no author, The Institute, Ghana.
Circular Letter, Mercy Amba Oduyoye to Persons Invited to the 2003 Institute of Women in Religion and Culture Meeting, 8.9.2003.
Circular Letter, Mercy Amba Oduyoye, 2003 Correspondence File, accessed 15.9.2005.
Conference Programme Document, 18-23 July, Nigeria/Lagos.

Conference Programme, The Circle of Concerned African Women Theologians Biennial Institutes Project, Session Zonal Conferences (West Africa), 18-23 July 1993 Lagos/Nigeria.

Graduates of the University of Malawi 1992-1993, accessed 2001.

International Arrivals, Institute Correspondence, 8.9.2003.

Joyce Boham, Circular Letter to Circle members, 6.11.2001.

Letter by John Pobee to Elizabeth Amoah, 10.9.1993.

Letter by Mercy Amba Oduyoye to Elizabeth Harding, 17.12.2002.

Letter by Mercy Amba Oduyoye to Margaret Umeagudosu and Rhodah Ada James, Geneva, 16.6.1993.

Letter by Mercy Amba Oduyoye to Rev Dr Dan Antwi, Principal, Trinity College, 12.8.1999.

Letter for Nyambura Njoroge, World Alliance of Reformed Churches, 19.11.1993.

Letter form Mercy Amba Oduyoye, WCC, 16.7. July 1993 to Monsieur le Pasteur Harry Henry.

Letter from Mercy Amba Oduyoye to Elizabeth Calvin, 17.9.2005.

Letter from Mercy Amba Oduyoye to Rachel Tetteh, Geneva, 3.6.1993.

Letter from Mercy Amba Oduyoye to Rev Janice Nessiboo, Women's Coordinator, PROCMURA, 14.7.1994.

Letter from Mercy Amba Oduyoye, the Director, Institute of Women in Religion and Culture, Trinity Theological College, addressed to all participants, 8.9.2003.

Letter from Musimbi Kanyoro to Friends, Circle, c/o World YWCA- 16, Ancienne Route Grand Saconnex, Geneva, Switzerland, 12.4.2001.

Letter from Musimbi Kanyoro to Mary Getui and Teresa Hinga, 21.9.1993.

Letter of Acknowledgement from Angela Dwamera Aboagye, Executive Director, The Ark Foundation, Ghana, 18.08.2003.

Letter of Invitation Mercy Amba Oduyoye, to all Participants, 8.9.2003.

Letter of Invitation to Elizabeth Calvin, 17.12.2002.

Letter of Invitation, Mrs Hannah Agyeman, National Women's Secretary, Apostolic Church, Ghana, 21.7.2003.

Letter to Prof Amoah from Mercy Amba Oduyoye, Correspondence File, accessed 15.9.2005.

Letter to Sisters by Mercy Amba Oduyoye, 24.3.1993.

Letter, Institute of Women in Religion and Culture, Ghana to Teresa Hinga, 20.12.2001.

Mouton, Elna, "'From Woundedness Towards Healing'. Rhetoric or Pastoral-Theological Vision?" 14th National Conference: Southern African Association for Pastoral Work, Cape Town, 12-14 May 2003.

Peggy Mulambya Kabonde, "Women and Health in Africa in the Face of HIV/Aids Based on Mt 8:14-17, Malaka-le Theologies 2005.

Phiri, Isabel Apawo, "1995: The Struggle of Women in the Church and the University of Malawi" Paper, no date, no publisher, accessed 2.3.2006.

Regional Circle Report 2005, Circle of Concerned African Women Theologians.
Report by Nyambura Njoroge, 13.4.1998.
Report Circle Study Commissions, Institute of Women in Religion and Culture, Trinity Theological College, Legon, Ghana, 20.-25.3.1998.
Report on the 1996 Institute of Women in Religion and Culture, no date, no author, accessed 14.9.2005.
Written Interview by Mercy Amba Oduyoye, Circle meeting, Kempton Park, Johannesburg 13.10.2003.

INDEX

AACC, 20f, 27, 165
Aba Imo State, 152
Abease, Ghana, 12
Abuja, 20, 58
Academia, 132
Accra, 7, 18, 20, 28, 30, 34, 57, 76, 90, 101f, 116, 118, 120, 126, 164f, 168f
Achebe, Chinua, 156
Ackermann, Denise, 71, 73f, 124, 127, 131, 134, 137, 168
Ada, Sr Mary Juliana, 154
Addis Ababa, 20, 41, 45, 47f, 63, 124, 128, 135, 146, 157f
Adekunbi, Helen Labedeodan, 58, 142
Affiduase, 16
African American, 34
African Baby, 10, 164
African Bible Translators' Course, 20
African Bible College in Lilongwe, 113
African context, 27, 87
African Feminism, 29, 31
African Feminist Theology, 10, 24, 133
African Instituted Churches, 112, 151
African Synod of 1994, 32
African Theology, 19, 22, 24, 26, 146
African Traditional Religions, 120-122, 169
African Women's Theologies, 10, 24, 56, 70
AIDS, 45, 48, 65, 68, 70, 77, 128, 136-138, 146, 156-162
Akan, 26f, 165
Akintan, Oluwatosin, 142
Akintunde, Dorcas Olubanke, 47, 57, 80, 135, 140, 142, 147
Akpan, Mrs A., 155
Akropong Trinity College, 17
Akwa, Grace, 127

Alangizi, 108
Alkali, Zaynab, 156
All Africa Conference of Churches, 20f, 27, 165
Amisi, Sylvia, 146
AMKA, 69, 123
Ammah, Dr Rabiatu, 57, 118, 128f
Amoah, Elizabeth, 33, 51, 57, 80, 118-120, 128f, 134, 138, 165
Amoah, Mercy Dakwaa, 13-15, 130
Androcentric, 90
Anglican, 62f, 65f, 73, 75, 111, 145, 160, 162, 168, 172
Anglophone, 42, 47, 55, 57, 80, 117, 124, 156, 170
Anneke Geesense-Ravestein, 127
Apartheid, 71, 73f, 80
Appel, Doris, 46
Appia, Evelyn, 46
Appropriation, 124, 145, 157
Arabic, 20
Asia, 23, 34
Asogwa, Cecelia, 149f
Assemblies of God, 92
Association of Asian Women Theologians, 46
Atere, Martina, 142
Atheism, 39
Axum, 41
Ayanga, Prof Hazel, 50, 63, 138, 147

Baëta, Prof Christian G., 19
Bam, Brigalia, 23-25, 29-31, 56, 70, 80f, 165, 168
Banda, Kamuzu, 100
Banda, Rachel, 97, 108, 113
Baptist Convention of Malawi, 97, 106, 108-113, 144, 152
Baptist Theological Seminary of Malawi, 97, 110, 113
Beijing Conference (1994), 33

188

Benin, 38, 58, 123
Bible, 14, 20, 23, 33, 62, 67, 73, 87, 94, 97, 101, 103, 106, 108, 110, 120-122, 127, 136f, 140-143, 146, 152f, 159-162
Bible Believers, 155
Bible studies, 127, 146, 160, 166
Bible translation, 33
Biblical, 107, 120, 122, 139, 142
Biblical Hermeneutics, 73
Biblical re-interpretation, 139
Biblical Studies, 147
Biennial Conferences, 169
Biennial Institutes, 117, 123, 125
Biographies of Women, 26, 74, 126, 144, 146
Birth, 10, 23, 29, 40, 51, 161, 164, 165f
Black Theology, 71, 73
Blantyre, 92, 97-99, 109, 113, 151f
Blantyre Awakening, 92
Blantyre Synod, 98f, 105, 151
Blay, Essie T., 13f
Bloemfontein, 92, 94
Bobbina, Essie F., 14
Body of Christ, 22
Boham, Joyce, 14, 47, 52f, 129, 156
Botswana, 76, 79f, 117, 139, 169
Bouka–Coula, Colette, 123
Bredt, Rev Sampa, 69
Brussels, 30
Bula, Omega, 68f, 127, 172
Burundi, 123

Calvary Family Church, 89
Cambridge University, 21
Cameroon, 33, 48, 123, 156, 166, 169
Cape Town, 7, 70-76, 85, 90, 131, 134, 168
Cape Town Chapter, 70-76, 168
Catholic University of Malawi, 31
Centre for Constructive Theology, 45, 72, 171

Centurion's daughter, 127
Chabloz, Diana, 46
Chalimba, Jannie, 113f
Chancellor College, 82-86, 89, 94-96, 98, 101-104, 114, 172
Chaomba, Mrs Mary, 88
Chaponda, Pastor Carol, 92f
Charismatic, 89, 92, 94, 96, 112, 115
Cherinda, Felicidade, 47, 128
Chigodi, 99
Chikuta, 166, 168, 171
Chile, 34, 165
Chilembwe, Mercy, 87f, 107
Chinangwa, Mrs, 97f
Chinkwita, Mary, 151
Chinkwita, Rev Emmanuel, 109
Chipande, Rev, 110
Chirwa, Akim, 108, 112
Chirwa, Martha, 97, 112f
Chiyanjano, 87f, 107
Christian Council of Nigeria, 27
Christian Council of Zambia, 69
Chunda, Bertha, 89
Church and society, 10f, 14f, 24, 30, 33, 71, 90, 97, 111, 114f, 139f, 152
Church of Central Africa Presbyterian (CCAP), 90
CIRA, 146
Circle theologies, 10f, 22-24, 29, 39, 85f, 89, 91, 145, 154f, 159
Cobbina, Essie J., 13
Collaboration, 26, 36f, 39, 47, 139
Coloured, 10, 74
Congo, 123, 146, 166, 169
Congregation, 32, 68, 75
Congregation of the Handmaids of the Holy Child Jesus, 31
Constant, Brigitte, 46
Constitution, 52f
Constitution of the Circle, 53
Contextual Theologies, 10, 17

189

Continental Conference, Nairobi (1996), 37f, 42, 44, 63
Continental Convocation (2002), 47, 52
Convocation (1989), 38, 41, 56, 60, 63, 66, 76, 90, 125, 127, 165, 167
Convocation (1996), 170
Convocation (2002), 173
Cuff, Sallie, 127
Cultural Hermeneutics, 141
Cultural Reinterpretation, 115, 140, 142f
Culture and religion, 10f, 21, 26

Dar es Salaam, 29, 34
Daughters of Anowa, 133, 134
Daystar University, Nairobi, 59, 62
Deaconess Ekundayo, 121
Dearth of African women theologies, 26, 167
Denise, Philippe, 159
Denmark, 68
Department of Religions and Culture, 60
Department of Religious Studies, 105
Diaspora, 10, 30, 37
Dickson, Kwesi A., 19, 128
Dogmatics, 21
Douala, 123
Doula, 169
Dube, Modupe, 10, 19-21, 40
Dube, Dr Musa, 49, 52, 76f, 79f, 101, 128, 137, 139, 147, 158, 170
Duker, Mrs Sophia, 12
Dumezweni, Bongiwe, 147
Durban Chapter, 72, 78, 171

East Africa, 6, 43, 59-61, 63-66, 78, 99, 124, 131, 168, 170, 172
East African Chapter, 59
East African Revival, 66, 172
Eastern Africa Zone, 117

EATWOT, 6, 24, 28-30, 33-36, 38-40, 46, 59-61, 64, 85, 99-100, 133f, 155, 165, 168
EBCOM, 87f, 97f, 106f
Economic exploitation, 21
Ecumenical, 164
Ecumenical Association of Third World Theologians (EATWOT), 99
Ecumenical surroundings, 10, 19
Ecumenical Theological Education, 37, 85
Edet, Sr Rosemary, 31, 57, 118-120, 139, 142f, 145, 154, 165
EDICESA, 6, 117, 121, 169
Edinburgh, 75
Editorial Work, 173
Education and Renewal, 29
Egerton University, 30, 165
Ekeya, Sr Betty, 30, 32, 55, 165
Equality, 14, 25, 152
Ereme, Grace, 33, 127
Ethical Resources, 128
Ethiopia, 41, 48, 128, 135, 157
Ethiopian Evangelical Church Fellowship, 41
Ethiopian Evangelical Church Mekane Yesu, 41
Eucharistic Heart of Jesus Generalate, 119
Europe, 21, 38f
Evangelical, 62f, 65-67, 70, 83, 87f, 96f, 106, 111f, 145, 147, 160
Evangelical Bible College of Malawi, (EBCOM) 87f, 97f, 106f
Evangelicalism factor, 65, 66
Evangelism, 20
Extended family, 11
Ezekiel, 17

Family, 10, 11, 13-15, 42, 64, 71, 91, 92f
FEMEC, 123

Feminist, 10, 19, 22-24, 26, 29f, 39, 84, 86, 88-90, 98, 100f, 114, 133, 143
Feminist Cultural Hermeneutics, 141
Feminist Theologies, 10, 23, 29, 85
Fiedler, Rachel NyaGondwe 49, 86, 98, 144
First World Feminist Movements, 24
First World Feminist Theologies, 30
First World Theologies, 29, 35
Folayan, Ruth, 97
Francophone, 30, 42, 47, 50, 55, 117, 123f, 131, 140, 169f
Francophone Africa Zone, 123
Frank, Mrs Monica, 107
Funding, 43f, 53, 54, 85, 127, 157
Funerals, 17f, 39, 87

Gambia, 38
Ganusah, Ms Rebecca, 120
Gender and Human Justice, 133
Gender inequalities, 10, 15, 25, 33, 45, 62, 67, 70, 97f, 116, 134, 139f, 160, 161
Gender of God, 39
Geneva, 21, 29, 42, 43, 45-49, 51f, 84, 165-167
Getman, Eliza, 73-75
Getui, Dr Mary, 30, 37, 44, 61, 63f, 80, 122, 124f, 138, 168-170
Ghana, 7, 10, 12-19, 28, 30, 33f, 36, 47, 51f, 54, 56f, 60, 78-81, 101f, 116, 118f, 126-130, 164-166, 168f, 173
Girls' initiation, 87
Global South, 33
Gnanadason, Aruna, 46
Gomez, Eva, 123, 170
Govinden, Dr Devakarsham Betty, 7, 75, 128, 138, 146, 170
Grant, Jacquelyn, 34
Grass roots, 45, 130
Gruchy, Prof John Walter de, 85

Gujarati, 71
Harrison, Nancy, 156

Institute of Women in Religion and Culture, 52, 57, 101, 126-130
International Planning Committee, 10, 23, 29, 31, 33, 39, 55, 80, 85, 89, 116, 118, 123, 140, 165
International Planning Meeting, 39, 43, 76, 119
IPC, 6, 10, 22f, 26, 29-32, 44, 55-57, 66, 80f, 89, 100, 117, 124, 142, 165-170
Irish, 32
Irruption within an irruption, 29, 35
Ivory Coast, 123, 169
Iwuchukwu, Rebecca, 118, 120
Jacobson, Wilma, 75
Jairus, 127
James, Rhodah Ada, 118,
Jesus, 15, 17, 31, 68, 119, 127, 143, 145, 160
Jewish, 71f
Johannesburg, 54, 68, 74, 126, 131, 133, 146
Johnson, Isabel, 27
Kabonde, Peggy Mulambya, 68, 70
Kafwamba, Mabel, 69
Kafwimbi, Mrs, 70
Kagundi, Mrs E., 99
Kahungu, Rev Sr Justine, 37, 123
Kaiya, Rev Fletcher, 109
Kalako, Rev Liddah, 112
Kalilombe, Bishop Patrick, 34, 35, 95, 100
Kampala, 32, 66f, 168
Kanyoro, Dr Musimbi, 7, 33, 37, 41-51, 59, 78-80, 101, 122, 125, 128, 131, 136, 139, 141-143, 156f, 165, 169f
Kapuma, Rev Getrude, 86, 98f, 114
Kasenda, Miss Grace, 107
Katahweire, Mabel, 66, 128, 172

Kathindi, Ms, 131
Katoppo, Marianne, 34
Kehinde Edewor, 142
Kempton Park, 13, 21, 25, 28, 133
Kenya, 7, 30, 37f, 43, 56, 58-64, 78-81, 101, 117, 121f, 134, 146f, 153, 155, 158, 165f, 168f
Kenyatta University, 32, 59f, 62f, 80, 90, 168, 170
Kgosana, Rev Phina Olga, 117, 169
Khota, Alice, 87, 106f
King, Prof Noel Q., 18, 61
Kingdom of God, 120
Kinoti, Prof Hannah Wangeci, 60f, 63, 127
Kivengere, Bishop Festo, 66, 172
Koomson, Rev T. Wallace, 18
Kotzé, Hantie, 73
Kumasi, 16, 18
Kumpoola, Mrs Deborah, 106f
Kwadaso Women's Training Centre, 15f
KwaZulu Natal Chapter, 72, 78, 101, 171

Labeodan, Prof Helen, 50
Lagos, 118-120, 169, 179
Lancaster, 84
Landman, Prof Christina, 127f, 138
Lasebikan, Esther, 142
Latin America, 23, 34
Leadership, 13-15, 19, 41-45, 50, 52-54, 59f, 67, 76, 78-80, 97f, 108, 111f, 119, 121, 123, 125, 131, 135, 145, 150f, 154, 157
Legon, 18, 21, 33, 61, 90, 102, 118, 126, 165f
Lenka-Bula, Puleng, 127
Lesotho, 166, 171
Levirate marriages, 141
Liberation, 10, 12, 14, 21f, 24, 30f, 33, 35, 38, 71, 80, 84, 86-90, 97, 99f, 106, 111f, 114, 133, 137, 145, 150, 155
Liberation theology, 61, 84-86
Lilongwe, 110
Limuru, 44, 59, 61, 62, 80, 101, 147, 168
Limuru Theological College, 168
Literalistic interpretation, 160f
Literature, 65, 98, 132f, 155, 171
Little Sisters of St Francis, 168
Living Waters Church, 89, 93
Livingstonia, 90, 99, 151
Local chapters, 54, 56-61, 65, 68f, 72, 76f, 80-82, 86, 98f, 116, 118, 123, 125, 130f
Longwe, Dr Molly, 97, 108, 110, 112
Lubumbashi, 30, 37
Lufani, Mrs Agnes, 108
Lumen Vitae, 30
Lusophone Africa, 42, 47, 55, 123, 170
Lutheran, 33, 65, 71, 77, 79, 165, 171f
Lutheran World Federation, 33, 79, 165
LWF, 33, 79
Lydia Foundation, 98

Madagascar, 123
Madise, Nyovani, 82f, 172
Makapola, Miss Jennie L.C., 107
Makina, Mrs Mellia, 108
Makupola, Mrs D., 87
Malawi, 27, 42, 45, 48-50, 56, 64, 69f, 78-80, 82-90, 92, 95-97, 99-103, 105f, 112-114, 117, 122, 125, 144, 146, 151, 153, 155, 166, 168, 169-172, 174
Male domination, 143
Manda, Christiane, 90
Mandela, Winnie, 156
Manzini, 117, 169
Maponda, Prof Anastasie, 50

Maputo, 47
Marginalization, 22, 65, 149, 155
Mariology, 145
Marriage, 15, 75, 91, 160
Masayiti, Bridget, 70
Masculinity, 159f
Masenya, Madipoane, 138, 147
Matembo, Juliet, 68f, 172
Matrilineal, 11
Matupi, Grace, 108
Mbewe, Rose Morleene, 89, 91
Mbuy-Beya, Sr Bernadette, 30f, 56, 124, 128
Mbwiti, Justine Kahungu, 127
Menstrual blood, 142
Mentoring, 19, 32, 54, 76, 79-81, 86, 89, 96, 98, 117, 124, 135-137
Methodist, 12, 15-19, 57, 121, 133, 165, 168f
Methodist Church of Ghana, 15f, 165
Methodist Girls Middle School in Kumasi, 18
Methodologies, 84, 97, 101, 146
Mexico, 34
Mgeni, Mrs Mercy, 113
Mindolo Ecumenical Foundation, 69
Miss White, 16
Mixed Parenting, 19
Mkamanga, Simon, 109
Mkwasho, Mrs Katherine, 111
Mkwezalamba, Mrs, 107
Mndende, Nokuzola, 140
Mombo, Esther, 61f, 80, 168
Monographs, 54, 135-137, 145f, 154
Moosa, Najma, 71
Mother Kenna, 32
Mother of the Circle, 7f, 10, 24, 36, 39, 50, 129, 164
Mouton, Prof Elna, 73f
Moyo, Fulata, 41f, 47-49, 69, 76, 80, 83-86, 96-98, 113, 146
Moyo, Fulata Lusungu, 172
Mujerista Theology, 35

Mukono, 66
Mulambya Kabonde, Peggy, 172
Mumo, Mary, 62
Munthali, Mrs E.C., 99
Murigande, Richard, 46
Muslim, 38f, 71f, 118, 120, 130, 140
Mwale, Mrs M., 99
Mwaura, Philomena Njeri, 30, 61, 134, 155
Mwiche, Mary, 70
Mzimba, 48
Mzuzu University, 49f, 84, 101f, 105, 133

Nadar, Sarojini, 7, 47, 72, 75f, 138, 140, 147
Nairobi Evangelical Graduate School of Theology (NEGST), 62
Nairobi International School of Theology (NIST), 62
Nalwamba, Kuzipa, 69
Namibia, 45, 72, 77f, 96f, 117, 122, 131, 166, 169, 171
Namibia Chapter, 72, 77f
Nankhuni, Flora, 82, 83, 95, 172
Nasaka, Olivia, 75
Nasimiyu-Wasike, Sr Annie, 31f, 59, 61, 63f, 66, 127, 146, 168
Ncozana, Rev Dr Silas, 113
Ndossi, Emeline, 143
Ndovi, Stanley, 93
Ndyabahika, Rev Grace, 117, 169
New Delhi, 34
New Testament, 77, 133, 139, 151
Ngo, Mbenda, 127
Ngoni, 48
Nigeria, 31, 57, 165f, 168f
Nigerian, 10, 19f, 27-29, 31, 36, 47, 56-58, 78-81, 118-120, 142f, 145-147, 149, 151-155, 157
Njoroge, Nyambura, 37f, 43f, 49, 59, 62, 65, 80, 122, 124f, 128, 131, 133, 136, 143, 145, 170

Nkhoma Synod, 82, 85, 99, 151
Norway, 68
Nsukka, 58
Nwachukwu, Daisy, 127
Nyabaika, Grace, 66, 172
Nyanchama, Mary Getui, 61, 122, 124f
Nyika, Margaret, 108
Nyirongo, Rev Jane, 70

Oaxtepec, 34, 36
Obi, Daisy, 27f
Obianga, Dr Rose Zoë, 32, 37, 123, 165
Oduyoye, Mercy Amba, 7-29, 33, 36-46, 48, 50f, 53-55, 58f, 64, 66f, 70, 76, 78, 80f, 85, 116, 118-120, 126f, 129, 131, 133-136, 140, 142, 156, 164-167, 169f, 173
Oduyoye, Modupe, 10, 13, 19f, 138, 165
Ofori-Owusu, Rev Dora, 118f, 169
Oguntoyinbo-Atere, 127
Ohala, USA, 20
Oke, Ruth Oluwakemi, 58, 142
Okon, Bassey A., 155, 156
Okunola, Oluwafeni Abosede, 142
Okure, Sr Teresa, 31, 128, 152, 165, 172
Old Testament, 62
Omoigui, Mery Itohan, 142
On Being Church, 126, 138
Ordination, 19, 31, 62f, 67, 75, 87f, 97-99, 109f, 113, 133, 144f, 150-153
Orebiyi, Olutundun A., 142
Ortega, Ofelia, 46
Owusu-Ansah, Rev Sylvia, 50

Pacific School of Religion, 22
Pan African Conference, 23, 128
Parvey, Constance, 28
Pastors' wives, 16, 89, 91, 97, 108, 130, 144
Patriarchy, 21, 67, 91f, 97, 111, 114f, 154, 158
Patrilineality, 11
Paul, 152f
Peace, 119, 156f
Pemberton, Carrie, 20, 31, 34
Pentecostal, 70, 112, 115
Phiri, Prof Isabel Apawo, 7, 41f, 45-48, 50f, 69, 70, 72-80, 82-86, 90, 94- 99, 101f, 105, 113, 124f, 128f, 131, 134, 137f, 144, 146, 151, 158-162, 168, 170-172
Pietermaritzburg, 7, 45, 47, 72, 75f, 79f, 84, 101, 111, 134, 162, 171
Pietermaritzburg Chapter, 72, 75f
Pobee, John, 28, 37f, 46, 118, 169
Politics, 14, 22, 25, 70, 77, 118f, 153-155, 157
Port Harcourt, 27
Postclassical, 64
Postgraduate, 19, 21, 32, 42, 65, 90
Power balance, 106
Presbyterian, 19, 48, 74, 82f, 97, 113, 127, 152, 168
Presbyterian Church of East Africa (PCEA), 113
Presbyterian Church of Nigeria, 152
Presbyterian Church of USA, 127
Princess Moremi, 154
PROCMURA, 37
Professor, 14, 19, 22, 47, 60, 72, 74
Programme for Theological Education (PTE), 28, 43
Prophet, 17
Publishing, 20, 28, 32, 51, 57, 60, 64f, 69, 73-76, 86, 89f, 95f, 98, 101, 114, 123, 129, 131f, 135, 142, 159

Racism, 21, 156
Rape, 83, 95

Rebecca, 118, 120
Reformed, 73f, 137
Regional Conferences, 28
Reisenberger, Azila, 74
Religion and Culture, 25, 31, 39, 60, 116, 126, 129, 140
Religious Studies, 18, 27, 29, 31, 75, 82, 101-103
Re-reading, 90, 139, 145
Research, 24, 30, 32, 39, 47, 51, 58, 60f, 64f, 68, 77f, 81-83, 86, 89f, 92, 95-98, 114, 116-118, 126, 129, 132, 137, 139f, 144, 146f, 151, 157, 167
Roman Catholic, 31f, 66, 99f, 152, 165
Ross, Prof Kenneth, 102
Rotational leadership, 47, 53
Ruether, Rosemary Radford, 24
Russel, Letty M., 22, 24, 128
Ruth, 97, 142
Rwanda, 123

Salvation Army, 67, 129
Samaritan woman, 143
Sarah, 122
Schüssler-Fiorenza, Elisabeth, 24
Second Convocation (1996), 37, 41
Second Vatican Council, 32
Semu, Linda, 82f, 95, 172
Senegal, 123
Sermon, 17, 144
Setting aside/ordaining Women's Coordinators, 88
Seventh-day Adventist Church, 64
Sexism, 21, 156
Sexual harassment, 82f, 95
Shishanga, Constance Ambasa, 60, 146
Sierra Leone, 28, 38, 166
Simpson, Miss, 111
Sisters, 12, 30-32, 55f, 100, 118
Siwila, Lilian, 47, 69, 76, 81, 134, 147

Small Christian Communities, 100
South Africa, 13, 30, 46, 49, 52, 56, 70-74, 78, 80, 82, 96, 98f, 117, 122, 125f, 131, 137, 145, 147, 153, 158f, 166, 168f, 173f
South African Christian Council, 30, 70, 165, 168
Southern Africa, 70, 78, 96, 117, 121, 124, 158f
Southern African Zones, 45, 124
Sri Lanka, 34
St Paul's Theological Seminary in Limuru, Kenya, 59, 61, 101
Stellenbosch University, 74
Stephens, Rev Dr Jacobs A., 18
Stigma, 157
Strasbourg, 20
Student Christian Federation, 19, 20
Student Christian Federation of Ghana, 19
Student Christian Movement in Nigeria, 20
Study Commissions, 48, 54, 125f, 139, 167, 170, 173
Swahili, 58
Swai, Lal, 46
Swaziland, 117, 122, 166, 169
Sweden, 68
Switzerland, 42, 80, 122, 165f

Taboo, 95, 120, 122
Talitha Qumi, 68f, 127, 132, 135f, 166, 168
Talitha Qumi Centre, 127
Tamez, Elsa, 128
Tanzania, 34, 38, 58, 63, 65, 78f, 81, 117, 122, 134, 166, 168f, 171f
Tappa, Rev Louise Ngo, 123
Temu, William, 46
Tetteh, Rachel, 57, 118-120, 165, 168f
Theological Education, 29, 44, 85, 105, 145

Theological Faculties, 74
Theological Institutions, 25, 38, 77, 97, 133, 143
Theology from the Underside of History, 34
Theology of sacredness of life, 161
Third Convocation (2002), 41
Third World, 21, 30, 39, 61
Third World Theologies, 29f, 33, 99
Thomson, Janet, 46
Tinkasiimire, Teresa, 140, 146
Tobler, Judy, 74
Togo, 38, 123
Tonga, 69
Torres, Fr Sergio, 34, 165
Trinity Theological College, 17, 36, 126f
Trinity Theological Seminary, 12, 57, 127
Tsabede, Joyce, 131
Turkson of Asamankese, J.E., 12
Tusuubira, Mary (Barongo), 63, 67, 128
Two-winged theology, 39

Ucheaga, Dorothy, 146
Uganda, 38, 58, 63, 65-68, 75, 78f, 117, 122, 146, 166, 168f, 171f
Uka, E.M., 153
UMCA, 111
Umeagudosu, Dr Margaret, 58, 118, 120, 145, 152f, 169
UN Decade for Women, 24
UNESCO, 21
United Bible Societies, 33
United Church of Canada, 69
United Church of Zambia, 68-70, 172
United Church of Zambia Theological College, 68, 69
United States of America, 14, 166
University of Botswana, 77
University of Calabar, 31, 165

University of Cape Town, 70, 75, 82, 85
University of Durban-Westville, 72
University of East Africa, 42
University of Ghana, 14, 18, 33, 118, 165
University of KwaZulu Natal, 45, 47, 98, 147
University of Malawi, 82, 84, 85 (see also Chancellor College)
University of Nairobi, 42
University of Western Cape, 74, 134
University of Westville, 171
Ursuline Sisters, 30
USA, 30, 42, 55, 119, 122
Vatican, 21, 32, 100
Vatican II, 32, 100
Vernacular, 130
Vienna World Conference on Human Rights (1993), 33
Violence against Women, 63-65, 83, 121, 158
Vuadi, Vibila, 128, 143, 146

WCC, 6, 21, 23f, 28f, 37-40, 42-46, 49, 64, 77, 85, 99, 101, 121, 123, 137, 139, 147, 158, 165f
WeGeHe, 12
Wennappuwa, 34
Wesleyan deaconess, 12
Wesleyan Girls High School, 12
Wesleyan kindergarten, 12
West African Student and Youth Christian Leadership Conference, 20
Western Africa Zone, 118
Wilson, Myra, 97
Womanist Theology, 35
Women Development Education Centre, 149
Women in the Commonwealth of God, 119
Women of colour, 73

Women pastors, 92, 97, 110, 144, 151
Women's Commission, 30, 33, 36, 61
Women's Desk, 27, 33, 42, 84
Women's experiences, 106, 122
Women's fellowship, 15f
Women's leadership, 97, 111
Women's liberation, 10, 22, 24, 33, 38, 87, 111f, 133, 137, 150
Women's ministry, 13, 145
Women's Training Centre, 15
World Christian Students Federation, 19f, 40, 165
World Council of Churches, 8, 19, 21-23, 40, 42f, 51, 84f, 95, 99, 133, 158f, 165
Writing, 7f, 20, 23f, 39, 45, 61, 64f, 68, 73, 75, 77f, 81f, 86, 90, 92, 96-98, 111, 116f, 119, 122, 129, 133f, 137, 150, 158, 162, 164-172

Yale Divinity School, 22, 128, 146
Yamoah, Charles, 12, 16, 18
Yamoah, Essie Ewusiwa, 14
Yamoah, Johnny B., 14
Yamoah, Joseph A., 13
Yamoah, Kojo Ewudzi, 13
Yamoah, Martha, 14
Yamoah, Mercy Dakwaa, 11-16
Yaoundé, 48, 156
Yinda, Hélène, 47, 123, 127f, 140, 169, 170
Yoruba, 142, 154
Yoswa School, 99
YWCA, 43, 45, 47

Zaire, 30, 56, 123, 166
Zambezi Evangelical Church, 87f, 106
Zambia, 68-70, 78-81, 84, 117, 122, 134, 147, 166, 168f, 171f
ZAWO, 87
ZEC, 87f, 106
Zimbabwe, 38, 52, 78-81, 83f, 91, 117, 122, 140, 166, 169, 171
Zomba Action Group, 95
Zomba Theological College, 97, 99, 112, 113
Zonal, 36, 58, 63, 116-118, 121-125, 129, 131, 157
Zonal Institutes, 123f, 131
Zonal meetings, 48, 60, 116-118, 124f, 125, 129, 169, 171

www.ingramcontent.com/pod-product-compliance
Lightning Source LLC
Chambersburg PA
CBHW051613230426
43668CB00013B/2094